Supranational Governance of Europe's Area of Freedom, Security and Justice

This book examines the evolution towards increased supranational governance in the EU's Area of Freedom, Security and Justice (AFSJ). At the end of 2009, a successor programme to the Tampere and Hague Programmes was developed under the Swedish Presidency. Called the 'Stockholm Programme', it was adopted at a special EU Council Summit on 10–11 December 2009. The new agenda covers the period 2010–2014 and emphasises six areas of priority. In the context of these priorities, as well as the innovations introduced by the Lisbon Treaty, this edited book analyses policy change in the AFSJ, especially as it has been affected by the rise of supranational governance in this domain. From police cooperation and crime fighting to border management and counter-terrorism, much has changed, and the EU has taken yet another step forward in the direction of supranational governance. However, the various contributions also highlight that there are still problems and challenges remaining for the AFSJ. Collectively, this book considers how consequential the Lisbon Treaty has been for the AFSJ, as well as how successful the EU has been in achieving its stated goals as expressed in the Stockholm Programme. Thus, this book makes a significant contribution to the scholarly investigation of the AFSJ, and also to the study of European integration in general.

This book was published as a special issue of the *Cambridge Review of International Affairs*.

Christian Kaunert is Professor of International Politics, Jean Monnet Chair in EU Justice and Home Affairs Policy, as well as Director of the European Institute for Security and Justice at the University of Dundee, Scotland, UK. He is Co-Director of the EUSA special interest section on the AFSJ.

John D Occhipinti is Professor in Politics, Director of European Studies, and Departmental Chair at Canisius College, Buffalo, USA. He is Co-Director of the EUSA special interest section on the AFSJ.

Sarah Léonard is Senior Lecturer in Politics, Jean Monnet Coordinator of the PhD Summer School on the EU's Area of Freedom, Security and Justice, as well as Deputy Director of the European Institute for Security and Justice at the University of Dundee, Scotland, UK.

Supranational Governance of Europe's Area of Freedom, Security and Justice

Edited by
Christian Kaunert, John D Occhipinti and Sarah Léonard

Routledge
Taylor & Francis Group

LONDON AND NEW YORK

First published 2015
by Routledge
2 Park Square, Milton Park, Abingdon, Oxon, OX14 4RN, UK

and by Routledge
711 Third Avenue, New York, NY 10017, USA

Routledge is an imprint of the Taylor & Francis Group, an informa business

British Library Cataloguing in Publication Data
A catalogue record for this book is available from the British Library

ISBN 13: 978-1-138-81240-6

Typeset in Palatino
by RefineCatch Limited, Bungay, Suffolk

Publisher's Note
The publisher accepts responsibility for any inconsistencies that may have
arisen during the conversion of this book from journal articles to book chapters,
namely the possible inclusion of journal terminology.

Disclaimer
Every effort has been made to contact copyright holders for their permission to
reprint material in this book. The publishers would be grateful to hear from any
copyright holder who is not here acknowledged and will undertake to rectify
any errors or omissions in future editions of this book.

Contents

Citation Information

The chapters in this book were originally published in the *Cambridge Review of International Affairs*, volume 27, no. 1 (March 2014). When citing this material, please use the original page numbering for each article, as follows:

Chapter 1
Introduction: supranational governance in the Area of Freedom, Security and Justice after the Stockholm Programme
Christian Kaunert, John D Occhipinti and Sarah Léonard
Cambridge Review of International Affairs, volume 27, no. 1 (March 2014) pp. 39–47

Chapter 2
Police, policy and politics in Brussels: scenarios for the shift from sovereignty to solidarity
Monica den Boer
Cambridge Review of International Affairs, volume 27, no. 1 (March 2014) pp. 48–65

Chapter 3
EU cooperation on terrorism prevention and violent radicalization: frustrated ambitions or new forms of EU security governance?
Raphael Bossong
Cambridge Review of International Affairs, volume 27, no. 1 (March 2014) pp. 66–82

Chapter 4
Whither the withering democratic deficit? The impact of the Lisbon Treaty on the Area of Freedom, Security and Justice
John D Occhipinti
Cambridge Review of International Affairs, volume 27, no. 1 (March 2014) pp. 83–105

Chapter 5
Tacit procedural politics: institutional change and member states' strategies in police and judicial cooperation in criminal matters
Marat Markert
Cambridge Review of International Affairs, volume 27, no. 1 (March 2014) pp. 106–126

Chapter 6

Tempering the EU? NGO advocacy in the Area of Freedom, Security, and Justice
Emek M Uçarer
Cambridge Review of International Affairs, volume 27, no. 1 (March 2014)
pp. 127–146

Chapter 7

The EU's growing external role in the AFSJ domain: factors, framework and forms of action
Jörg Monar
Cambridge Review of International Affairs, volume 27, no. 1 (March 2014)
pp. 147–166

Chapter 8

Exporting EU integrated border management beyond EU borders: modernization and institutional transformation in exchange for more mobility?
Raül Hernández i Sagrera
Cambridge Review of International Affairs, volume 27, no. 1 (March 2014)
pp. 167–183

Please direct any queries you may have about the citations to
clsuk.permissions@cengage.com

Introduction: supranational governance in the Area of Freedom, Security and Justice after the Stockholm Programme

Christian Kaunert
University of Dundee

John D Occhipinti
Canisius College

Sarah Léonard
University of Dundee

Following several months of uncertainty in the wake of the rejection of the treaty establishing a constitution for Europe, the Lisbon Treaty eventually entered into force in December 2009. Although it fell short of establishing a constitution for the European Union (EU), it introduced several noteworthy changes, notably for EU internal security policies, also known as the 'Area of Freedom, Security and Justice' (AFSJ). This special section considers how various dimensions of the AFSJ have been affected by the Lisbon Treaty and the gradual reinforcement of supranational governance that it has generated in this key policy area.

Over the past decade, the AFSJ has experienced tremendous development, making it one of the most dynamics areas of European integration. The AFSJ is a broad and heterogeneous policy domain, which includes asylum, immigration and border policies, counter-terrorism, justice and police cooperation, as well as the external dimension of these activities. Given the crucial importance of current internal security threats, such as terrorism, and the sensitivities surrounding policy responses to them, it is necessary to take stock of how far the EU has progressed toward its goals of an AFSJ and how this has been influenced by the most recent treaty changes. To accomplish this goal, this special section brings together some of the most distinguished scholars in the field and several younger scholars conducting cutting-edge research on the AFSJ.

The rapid development of the AFSJ in recent years has led to an expansion of the scholarly literature on this topic, including legal analyses (Walker 2004; Peers 2006; 2012). Most scholars have argued that EU policy developments have been mainly driven by security concerns and that, as a result, freedom, justice and

Research for this article was supported by two Marie Curie Career Integration Grants within the Seventh European Community Framework Programme, which have been granted to Christian Kaunert and Sarah Léonard.

human rights have been relatively neglected, if not damaged (Monar et al 2003; Baldaccini et al 2007; Balzacq and Carrera 2006; Huysmans 2006; Guild and Geyer 2008; van Munster 2009; Bigo et al 2010). Other works have focused on examining the policy developments in EU internal security using security studies frameworks and concepts, such as 'homeland security' (Kaunert et al 2012) and 'comprehensive security' (Kaunert and Zwolski 2013). Recently, some literature has also emerged on the external dimension of the EU's internal security policies. It has particularly emphasized how the EU has sought, and managed in some cases, to exercise some level of influence on the internal security policies of third states, in particular in its neighbourhood (Balzacq 2009; Wolff et al 2009; Wolff 2009; 2012; Trauner 2011).

The literature on the AFSJ in general has also been complemented by more specialized works that have focused on one specific internal security policy. In that respect, the EU counter-terrorism policy has arguably been the focus of most debates (Zimmermann 2006; Spence 2007; Eckes 2009; Brown 2010; Bures 2006; 2011; Argomaniz 2011; Kaunert and Léonard 2011; Léonard and Kaunert 2012; Kaunert et al 2012; Bossong 2008; 2012; MacKenzie et al 2013), whilst the EU asylum and migration policy (Baldaccini et al 2007; Geddes 2008; Léonard 2009; Boswell and Geddes 2011), EU cooperation on criminal justice matters (Fletcher and Lööf 2008; Eckes and Konstadinides 2011) and EU police and judicial cooperation (Anderson and Apap 2002; Occhipinti 2003; Guild and Geyer 2008) have also received some attention. In contrast, institutional issues have overall been less studied, apart from some early works focusing on the legal intricacies of the then 'third pillar' (for example, Bieber and Monar 1995), Kaunert's works (2005; 2007; 2010a; 2010b; 2010c; Kaunert and Della Giovanna 2010) on the role of the European Commission and the Secretariat of the Council in the AFSJ, as well as the emerging literature on the European Parliament's (EP's) role (Ripoll Servent 2010; 2011; Ripoll Servent and MacKenzie 2011).

Thus, little attention has generally been given to the institutional arrangements governing European internal security. The EU has now acquired an impressive legal and institutional infrastructure to manage its external borders and combat transnational organized crime and terrorism. This is the result of an incremental process that began in earnest with the entry into force of the Maastricht Treaty in 1993, which made 'Justice and Home Affairs' (JHA) a formal policy area of the EU.

However, the nature of decision-making on JHA was highly intergovernmental during its earliest years. Even as the Maastricht Treaty bestowed new legislative powers on the EP in many areas pertaining to the single market, the EP remained largely excluded from decision-making on JHA. Moreover, the legal basis of the EU's 'third pillar' on JHA, as it was then known, also prevented the European Commission from playing a meaningful role in policy development. The European Court of Justice (ECJ) was also sidelined in this policy domain. In addition, member states were still protective of their national sovereignty on internal security and retained the right to veto legislation on JHA. With only few exceptions, this intergovernmental setting contributed to slow progress on JHA during the 1990s.

Over time and through a series of reforms to its treaties, the EU's policy environment for internal security gradually changed. With each reform, the role of the supranational Commission, EP and ECJ gradually increased, whilst the areas of law-making subject to national vetoes in the Council decreased. The Lisbon

Treaty can be seen as the latest step in this process, which has gradually brought about a degree of supranational governance in the EU internal security policy domain.

Along the way, the EU has established ambitious, multi-year policy programmes for creating and implementing new legislation, mechanisms and institutions across the whole AFSJ. This began in 1999, when the Amsterdam Treaty entered into force, establishing the broad objective of creating the AFSJ. In order to achieve this objective, the EU heads of state and government convened a special meeting of the European Council in October 1999 and agreed upon the so-called 'Tampere Programme', which set out the agenda for developing the AFSJ in the following five years. Progress would be helped by a series of crises and shocks that drew attention to the challenge of managing internal security in the EU. This included the death of 58 human-trafficking victims in a shipping container in 2000, the terrorist attacks on the United States (US) of 11 September 2001, gains made by far-right political parties in some member states on the issue of irregular immigration in 2002 and the terrorist attacks on Madrid in March 2004. During this time, progress on the realization of the AFSJ was also promoted by the expectation that several states would soon join the EU, which would complicate decision-making on new legislation and magnify many of the existing security challenges. Indeed, during the period of 1999–2004 there was much progress in the AFSJ on many fronts, ranging from the adoption of the European Arrest Warrant, the harmonization of substantive criminal law for some crimes, the creation of Eurojust (a liaison network of criminal prosecutors), CEPOL (European Police College), the post of counter-terrorism coordinator, and Frontex (the external border management agency), as well as the development of enhanced security relationships with third countries, such as the US.

In November 2004, the EU approved the next multi-year agenda for the AFSJ, known as 'the Hague Programme', which set priorities until 2009. In many regards, this simply followed on from the Tampere agenda. It was mainly directed at completing ongoing initiatives and making the most of newly created institutions. However, it was also shaped by new perceptions of security threats and priorities, such as terrorism and many aspects of border security. At the same time, the new agenda was also conceived amid optimism for European integration with regard to the growing membership of the EU and initial progress on the treaty establishing a constitution for Europe. By the end of 2005, the EU's policy agenda was also influenced by the terrorist attacks in London on 7 July 2005 and the development of its first comprehensive Counter-Terrorism Strategy.

Subsequently, the AFSJ remained the most dynamic policy of the EU, but the pace of new legislation somewhat slowed compared with the immediate post-9/11 period under the Tampere agenda. One reason for this was the rejection of the treaty establishing a constitution for Europe, the ensuing malaise concerning European integration and the endurance of national vetoes. By the summer of 2007, the plans for a constitution were scaled back and incorporated into what would become the Lisbon Treaty. Although this new treaty would be finalized and signed on 13 December 2007, it would not enter into force before 1 December 2009.

Moreover, this new treaty would lack several of the bold innovations for the AFSJ that had been proposed by the Constitutional Convention that had drafted the treaty establishing a constitution for Europe. For example, the vision of a true 'bill of rights' for an EU constitution had been replaced by the less impressive

Charter of Fundamental Rights attached to the new treaty via a protocol. The vision of an EU public prosecutor with extensive powers was scaled back to an option to create a prosecutorial component within Eurojust that would be limited to the protection of the EU's finances. Instead of the complete elimination of national vetoes for the harmonization of criminal law, the interests of member states were to remain protected by emergency brakes that could block new legislation. In addition, the delay caused by the rejection of the treaty establishing a constitution for Europe afforded the United Kingdom (UK) the opportunity to change its position and eventually win the option of opting out of many aspects of the AFSJ, of which it is now considering the exercise. In addition, the delayed ratification of the Lisbon Treaty coincided with the onset of a financial and economic crisis in the Eurozone in 2008. This crisis has not only been a distraction; it has actually cast a shadow of doubt over the future progress of European integration, including the further development of the AFSJ.

Nevertheless, progress on the AFSJ continued on many fronts under the Hague Programme. Again, progress was recorded with regard to many aspects of the AFSJ, including the adoption of some common minimum standards for asylum systems, the decision to create a Visa Information System (VIS) to support the Schengen zone, the adoption of a variety of measures regarding data retention and information-sharing for law enforcement, the negotiation of key agreements with third countries, notably on the sharing of passenger name record (PNR) data with the US, as well as the incorporation of the EU's AFSJ objectives in its neighbourhood policy.

Despite mixed results in some areas and implementation delays in others, the Commission analyzed the achievements of the Tampere and the Hague Programmes in a positive light, particularly with regard to the principles of freedom, security and justice and the balance among these across a wide range of new measures. Yet, that is precisely what has been criticized by a number of scholars, some non-governmental organizations (NGOs) and some members of the EP (MEPs). They have notably claimed that various measures in the AFSJ have threatened the right to privacy of European citizens, as well as the human rights of irregular migrants and refugees trying to enter the EU.

At the end of 2009, a successor programme to the Tampere and Hague Programmes was developed under the Swedish presidency. Called the 'Stockholm Programme', it was adopted at a special EU Council Summit on 10–11 December 2009. The new agenda covers the period 2010–2014 and emphasizes six areas of priority. The first of these is the promotion of citizenship and fundamental rights, particularly those identified in the Charter of Fundamental Rights, including notably the protection of personal data and human rights. Secondly, the priority concerning 'a Europe of law and justice' promotes greater access to justice for citizens through training of and cooperation amongst professionals, as well as the elimination of any barriers to the recognition of legal decisions in other member states. Thirdly, regarding 'a Europe that protects', the Stockholm Programme prioritizes the goals of the EU Internal Security Strategy, particularly strengthening cooperation in law enforcement, border management, civil protection, disaster management and judicial cooperation in criminal matters. This priority area also highlights the Lisbon Treaty's innovative solidarity provision (Article 222 of the Treaty on the Functioning of the European Union [TFEU]) that commits member states to act jointly if one of them is the victim of a terrorist attack or a natural or man-made disaster. The fourth priority area concerns 'access to Europe in a globalized world'. It refers to the need to strengthen the EU's integrated border management system and visa policies to provide security, whilst ensuring access for legitimate travellers and those in need of international protection. Fifthly, the Stockholm Programme highlights the importance of 'A Europe of responsibility, solidarity and partnership in migration and asylum matters'. This emphasizes effective policies based on solidarity and responsibility, including the need to develop a common asylum system and 'prevent, control and combat illegal immigration'. The sixth and final priority area is 'the role of Europe in a globalized world', which calls for increased and coherent integration of the AFSJ into the EU's external policies.

In the context of these priorities established by the Stockholm Programme, as well as the innovations introduced by the Lisbon Treaty, this special section analyzes policy change in the AFSJ, especially as it has been affected by the rise of supranational governance in this domain. Each of the contributions included here deals with a different dimension of this issue. Collectively, this special edition considers how consequential the Lisbon Treaty has been for the AFSJ, as well as how successful the EU has been in achieving its stated goals as expressed in the Stockholm Programme.

Monica den Boer's article examines the impact of the Lisbon Treaty on police cooperation. While the EU's latest treaty makes some gains in this area, den Boer argues that further steps are still needed to establish a more coherent and consistent system of European police cooperation, as well as improved parliamentary involvement, independent oversight and a Europe-wide cultivation of police professionalism. To achieve this, the European Commission will have to maximize its competences under the Lisbon Treaty, but this may be insufficient to overcome the attachment of member states to national sovereignty in the policing domain.

Similarly, Raphael Bossong is rather critical of the EU's plans to prevent radicalization that can lead to terrorism. His article highlights the way in which the Stockholm Programme has renewed this ambition, which has emphasized the role of sub-national levels of government and support for the horizontal exchange of experience, best practice and information. Bossong concludes that the proposed network of local and professional actors could indeed make a contribution to the identification and prevention of radicalism, but that it should not be expected to provide a major breakthrough for EU counter-terrorism.

John Occhipinti is somewhat less pessimistic in his evaluation of the effect of the Lisbon Treaty on the EU's so-called 'democratic deficit'. He concludes that the Lisbon Treaty has addressed the democratic deficit from the perspective of 'throughput'-based legitimacy, given the stronger roles for the EP, the ECJ and national parliaments. These same changes have also improved output-based legitimacy regarding accountability. However, legitimacy measured in terms of efficient outcomes could actually be harmed by the politicization of some aspect of the AFSJ. Moreover, little has been done to address input-based legitimacy, because the Lisbon Treaty cannot be expected to foster a proper debate on the goals of the Stockholm Programme or its successor among national politicians and citizens.

Marat Markert takes a different approach in his article. Instead of evaluating the effect of the Lisbon Treaty on a particular aspect of the AFSJ, he examines the policy environment that it has modified in order to study a broader theoretical question related to institutional change and European integration: despite increasing institutional constraints, why have national governments been successful in deliberately countering pro-integrationist legislative proposals by the European Commission? Focusing on criminal justice and police cooperation and taking into account developments since 1999, Markert's article explains the interplay between increasing institutional constraints on the policy discretion of actors at the EU level and their policy preferences. He reaches the conclusion that member states deploy strategies of legislative pre-emption which allow them to overcome both preference heterogeneity in the Council and structural impasses that are usually assumed to benefit supranational actors, particularly the European Commission.

Emek M Uçarer also takes up an issue that has been examined by EU scholars outside the realm of the AFSJ, namely the role and impact of NGOs on policy-making. Key issues in her study include when and why NGOs pick a particular level of governance at which to operate. Uçarer argues that the EU–NGO interface is affected by the institutional realities of the EU, the opportunity structures that those have created for lobbying, and the capacities of NGOs to exploit these opportunity structures. Her contribution focuses on immigration, asylum and judicial cooperation in criminal matters and explains NGO strategies in the EU policy environment as it has been shaped by the Lisbon Treaty and the Stockholm agenda.

Jörg Monar's article considers the internal factors and external pressures that have influenced the development of the external dimension of the AFSJ. On the basis of his analysis in terms of strategy formulation, cooperation with third countries, capacity-building and cooperation with and within international organizations, Monar brings to light a few major shortcoming of the external dimension of the AFSJ. While recognizing many past achievements and areas of likely growth in the future, Monar argues that the coherence and effectiveness of the external side of the AFSJ has been diminished by the diversity of the fields covered in this area and the complex post-Lisbon decision-making structures, such as provisions for opt-outs.

Raül Hernández also considers an external aspect of the AFSJ, focusing his analysis on the EU's promotion of its Integrated Border Management (IBM) model in the context of the Lisbon Treaty and the Stockholm Programme. Hernández's article analyses the roles of Frontex and the EU mission at the Ukrainian–Moldovan border (EUBAM) in exporting IBM to Russia and the Eastern Partnership countries. He notably shows that the development of IBM in Eastern Europe has taken place because it is a condition for the progress of cooperation in other areas, such as visa liberalization or the establishment of mobility partnerships. Thus, Hernández's article also raises questions of how effectively IBM can be exported by Frontex, as well as how the EU can carry out the goals of IBM in the southern Mediterranean region, where it lacks the kind of leverage that it enjoys over Eastern Europe.

Collectively, the articles gathered in this special section demonstrate that the Lisbon Treaty and the Stockholm Programme have had a profound impact on the AFSJ. From police cooperation and crime-fighting to border management and counter-terrorism, much has changed, and the EU has taken yet another step forward in the direction of supranational governance. However, the various contributions also highlight that problems and challenges still remain for the AFSJ. This special section makes a significant contribution to the scholarly investigation of the AFSJ, but also to the study of European integration in general, including the topics of institutional dynamics, democracy, the influence of NGOs, and the EU's role as an actor on the world stage. We hope that both specialists focusing on the AFSJ and scholars from other fields will the find the articles included here valuable for their theoretical and empirical studies.

Notes on contributors

Christian Kaunert is Professor of International Politics and Jean Monnet Chair in EU Justice and Home Affairs at the University of Dundee, United Kingdom. He also holds a Marie Curie Career Integration Grant (2012–2016) funded by the Seventh European Community Framework Programme.

John D Occhipinti is Professor of Political Science and director of the European Studies programme at Canisius College, Buffalo, United States.

Sarah Léonard is Senior Lecturer in Politics at the University of Dundee, United Kingdom. She holds a Marie Curie Career Integration Grant (2013–2017) funded by the Seventh European Community Framework Programme.

References

Anderson, M and J Apap (eds) (2002) *Police and justice co-operation and the new European borders* (The Hague: Kluwer)

Argomaniz, J (2011) *The EU and counter-terrorism: politics, polity and policies after 9/11* (London: Routledge)

Baldaccini, A, E Guild and H Guild (eds) (2007) *Whose freedom, security and justice? EC Immigration and asylum law and policy* (Oxford: Hart)

Balzacq, T (ed) (2009) *The external dimension of EU justice and home affairs: governance, neighbours, security* (Basingstoke, UK: Palgrave Macmillan)

Balzacq, T and S Carrera (eds) (2006) *Security versus freedom? A challenge for Europe's future* (Aldershot, UK: Ashgate)

Bieber, R and J Monar (eds) (1995) *Justice and home affairs in the European Union: the development of the third pillar* (Brussels: European Interuniversity Press)

Bigo, D, S Carrera, E Guild and Walker, RBJ (eds) (2010) *Europe's 21st century challenge: delivering liberty* (Farnham, UK: Ashgate)

Bossong, R (2008) 'The action plan on combating terrorism: a flawed instrument of EU security governance', *Journal of Common Market Studies*, 46:1, 27–48

Bossong, R (2012) *The evolution of EU counter-terrorism: European security policy after 9/11* (London: Routledge)

Boswell, C and A Geddes (2011) *Migration and mobility in the European Union* (Basingstoke, UK: Palgrave Macmillan)

Brown, D (2010) *The European Union, counter terrorism and police cooperation, 1992–2007* (Manchester: Manchester University Press)

Bures, O (2006) 'EU counter-terrorism policy: a "paper tiger"?', *Terrorism & Political Violence*, 18:1, 57–78

Bures, O (2011) *EU counterterrorism policy: a paper tiger?* (Farnham, UK: Ashgate)

Eckes, C (2009) *EU counter-terrorist policies and fundamental rights: the case of individual sanctions* (Oxford: Oxford University Press)

Eckes, C and T Konstadinides (eds) (2011) *Crime within the Area of Freedom, Security and Justice: a European public order* (Cambridge, UK: Cambridge University Press)

Fletcher, M, R Lööf and withB Gilmore (2008) *EU criminal law and justice* (Cheltenham, UK: Edward Elgar)

Geddes, A (2008) *Immigration and European integration: beyond Fortress Europe?* (Manchester: Manchester University Press)

Guild, E and F Geyer (eds) (2008) *Security versus justice? Police and judicial cooperation in the European Union* (Aldershot, UK: Ashgate)

Huysmans, J (2006) *The politics of insecurity: fear, migration and asylum in the European Union* (London: Routledge)

Kaunert, C (2005) 'The Area of Freedom, Security and Justice: the construction of a "European public order"', *European Security*, 14:4, 459–483

Kaunert, C (2007) '"Without the power of purse or sword": the European Arrest Warrant and the role of the Commission', *Journal of European Integration*, 29:4, 387–404

Kaunert, C (2010a) 'The external dimension of EU counterterrorism relations: competences, interests, and institutions', *Terrorism & Political Violence*, 22:1, 41–61

Kaunert, C (2010b) 'Europol and EU counterterrorism: international security actorness in the external dimension', *Studies in Conflict & Terrorism*, 33:7, 652–671

Kaunert, C (2010c) *European internal security: towards supranational governance in the Area of Freedom, Security and Justice?* (Manchester: Manchester University Press)

Kaunert, C and M Della Giovanna (2010) 'Post-9/11 EU counter-terrorist financing cooperation: differentiating supranational policy entrepreneurship by the Commission and the Council Secretariat', *European Security*, 19:2, 275–295

Kaunert, C and S Léonard (2011) 'EU counterterrorism and the European neighbourhood policy: an appraisal of the southern dimension', *Terrorism & Political Violence*, 23:2, 286–309

Kaunert, C, S Léonard and A MacKenzie (2012) 'The social construction of an EU interest in counter-terrorism: US influence and internal struggles in the cases of SWIFT and PNR', *European Security*, 21:4, 474–496

Kaunert, C, S Léonard and P Pawlak (eds) (2012) *European homeland security: a European strategy in the making?* (London: Routledge)

Kaunert, C and K Zwolski (2013) *The EU as a global security actor: a comprehensive analysis across CFSP and JHA* (Basingstoke, UK: Palgrave Macmillan)

Léonard, S (2009) 'The creation of FRONTEX and the politics of institutionalisation in the European Union external borders policy', *Journal of Contemporary European Research*, 5:3, 371–388

Léonard, S and C Kaunert (2012) '"Between a rock and a hard place?" The European Union's financial sanctions against suspected terrorists, multilateralism and human rights', *Cooperation and Conflict*, 47:4, 473–494

MacKenzie, A, C Kaunert and S Léonard (2013) 'EU counterterrorism and the southern Mediterranean countries after the Arab Spring: new potential for cooperation?', *Democracy and Security*, 9:1–2, 137–156

Monar, J, W Rees and V Mitsilegas (2003) *The European Union and internal security: guardian of the people?* (Basingstoke, UK: Palgrave Macmillan)

Occhipinti, JD (2003) *The politics of EU police cooperation: towards a European FBI?* (Boulder, Colorado: Lynne Rienner)

Peers, S (2006) *EU justice and home affairs law*, 2nd edn (Oxford: Oxford University Press)

Peers, S (2012) *EU justice and home affairs law*, 3rd edn (Oxford: Oxford University Press)

Ripoll Servent, A (2010) 'Point of no return? The European Parliament after Lisbon and Stockholm', *European Security*, 19:2, 191–207

Ripoll Servent, A (2011) 'Co-decision in the European Parliament: comparing rationalist and constructivist explanations of the "returns" directive', *Journal of Contemporary European Research*, 7:1, 3–22

Ripoll Servent, A and A MacKenzie (2011) 'Is the EP still a data protection champion? The case of SWIFT', *Perspectives on European Politics and Society*, 12:4, 390–406

Spence, D (ed) (2007) *The European Union and terrorism* (London: John Harper)

Trauner, F (2011) *The Europeanisation of the Western Balkans: EU justice and home affairs in Croatia and Macedonia* (Manchester: Manchester University Press)

Van Munster, R (2009) *Securitizing immigration: the politics of risk in the EU* (Basingstoke, UK: Palgrave Macmillan)

Walker, N (2004) *Europe's Area of Freedom, Security and Justice* (Oxford: Oxford University Press)

Wolff, S (2009) 'The Mediterranean dimension of EU counter-terrorism', *Journal of European Integration*, 31:1, 137–156

Wolff, S (2012) *The Mediterranean dimension of the European Union's internal security* (Basingstoke, UK: Palgrave Macmillan)

Wolff, S, N Wichmann and G Wichmann (eds) (2009) *The external dimension of justice and home affairs: a different security agenda for the European Union?* (London: Routledge)

Zimmermann, D (2006) 'The European Union and post-9/11 counterterrorism: a reappraisal', *Studies in Conflict & Terrorism*, 29:1, 123–145

Police, policy and politics in Brussels: scenarios for the shift from sovereignty to solidarity

Monica den Boer
VU University

Abstract *This article analyses the evolution of European Union (EU) police cooperation on the basis of structural processes in the form of agencification, regulation and standardization, as well as substantive processes in the form of information-sharing and multi-disciplinary cooperation. The Lisbon Treaty holds some key conditions for further integration. The level of integration of police cooperation in the EU is measured by analysing institutional power, the regulatory framework and transnational professionalism. Despite a positive score on each of these levels, member states remain caught between national sovereignty and solidarity. As a consequence, they face an implementation gap and have not embedded European police cooperation in their domestic systems. Building on the pro-integrative moves that have been introduced by virtue of the Lisbon Treaty, improved governance and deeper integration can be achieved by means of more active parliamentary involvement, independent police oversight (both at European and at the national level), the mainstreaming of cooperation mechanisms and a systematic Europe-wide cultivation of police professionalism. Within the realm of internal security cooperation in the EU, a concerted effort is required which demands close consultation between relevant institutional actors and the professional actors in the member states.*

Introduction

Police cooperation has become a core policy field in the integration process of the European Union (EU). The Lisbon Treaty has consolidated its status and introduced major improvements to decision-making procedures as well as to levels of democratic and judicial control. Before the entry into force of the Lisbon Treaty, progress was characterized by incremental steps in the form of agencification, regulation, standardization, information-sharing and multi-disciplinary cooperation. Intergovernmental decision-making was the dominant mode, which meant that the integration process of the member states was uneven. When applying indicators of levels of EU integration[1] (Stone Sweet and Sandholtz 1997, 10), police cooperation meets certain levels of institutionalization, such as EU

The author wishes to express her gratitude to the anonymous reviewers. She is solely responsible for errors or omissions.

[1] 'Integration' is defined as the process by which the horizontal and vertical linkages between social, economic and political actors evolve, moving from the one end of the continuum—intergovernmental politics—to the other—supranational politics (Stone Sweet and Sandholtz 1997, 10).

institutional capacity, regulatory capacity and transnational professionalism. However, despite the relatively positive scores on these dimensions of integration, it remains a policy field far removed from supranational politics.

The reason for this halfway position is that certain deep-seated issues have not been solved in a sustainable manner. These issues include, inter alia, the complex relationship between national and international actors, accountability deficits, technological challenges and the move towards preventive security governance. Despite the increasingly binding character of the relevant instruments in the field of EU policing, there is an implementation gap, which indicates a lack of deep integration between the domestic police systems of the EU member states. Caught between a ritualistic defence of national sovereignty and the need for more cooperation in the form of sharing and pooling, the member states have not deeply embedded their police organizations in the EU. This reflects a relatively slow adjustment of the member states, marked by a predominantly reactive stance of governments as well as a continued emphasis on national sovereignty.

Reflecting on the incremental growth of police cooperation in the EU, this article seeks to identify structural shortcomings through a historical reconstruction of integrative moves realized in this field. The identification of five sub-processes—agencification, regulation, standardization, information-sharing and multi-disciplinary cooperation—aids our understanding of how sustainable governance of this dynamic and sensitive field of policy-making can be achieved. In doing so, we must take account of several trends in the transnational discourse on security and policing which will continue to influence EU and domestic agenda-setting. Although the Lisbon Treaty paves the path towards supranational integration in the field of EU police cooperation, additional movements may be required for a sustained swing towards that goal.

Historical reconstruction: the evolution of police cooperation in the EU

Police cooperation[2] is one of the early fields of justice and home affairs (JHA) cooperation in the EU, and it can also be said that it has been one of the fastest-growing areas, given the sizeable number of instruments that have been adopted (Block 2011b; Vermeulen 2011) and the 'plethora of initiatives' in the field of policing, police cooperation and internal security (Bruggeman and den Boer 2011, 135). However, EU police cooperation remains embedded in a complex discourse on transnational policing, which has been characterized as a disorderly terrain contextualized by fragmented governance and authority 'resulting in a sense of randomness and weak political accountability' (Sheptycki 2007, 33). In order to provide a basis for the later discussion, this section discusses the evolution of police cooperation with a focus on agency competences,[3] regulatory instruments, standardization, information-sharing and multi-disciplinary cooperation.

---

[2] This article does not take into account the responsibility of the EU for civil police (training) missions or police reform programmes.

[3] Throughout this article, I employ the term 'agencification', which refers to the formal establishment of specialist agencies within the institutional realm of the EU. In the field of JHA cooperation, one may think particularly of Europol, Eurojust and Frontex.

Tracing police cooperation through the treaties

While the Maastricht Treaty provided the first formal basis for police cooperation in the EU,[4] the concept of police cooperation already existed as a field of common activity in the context of the Trevi intergovernmental network created in 1975 (Fijnaut 1993, 13) and as an element of Schengen cooperation (den Boer 1995). The Maastricht Treaty created the first basis for an EU agency on police cooperation in Article K.1.9 of the intergovernmental pillar on justice and home affairs (Fijnaut 1993, 15).[5] In the face of resistance to a federalized European police (Occhipinti 2003, 72), a succinct proposal to create a European Drugs Unit (EDU) was adopted, with an agreement about its remit: it would (initially) be a unit for strategic analysis and the coordination of criminal investigation into drug-trafficking and related money-laundering offences. (Europol, the police coordination and assistance agency, was formally created by virtue of the 1995 Europol Convention.[6]) The main improvement introduced by the superseding Maastricht Treaty was, according to Elsen (2007, 15), that coherent action was brought about involving all the European actors. Nevertheless, the Maastricht Treaty was criticized for a number of reasons. These included the intricate hierarchical working structure, the lack of meaningful competences for EU institutions, the significant margin of discretion for the member states, and the lowest common denominator decision-making process of the unanimity rule (Gruszczak 2009; Guyomarch 1995; Skinner 2002; Weyembergh 2000).

The ensuing Amsterdam Treaty had a more significant impact (Elsen 2007, 15). Ushered in by a pro-European wind and adopted in 1997 with the prospective enlargement of the EU, it was possible to obtain political endorsement for the creation of an Area of Freedom, Security and Justice (AFSJ). Moreover, the conclusion of the Amsterdam Treaty allowed for the integration of the Schengen *acquis* into the EU by means of a protocol (Kaunert 2010, 55; Philippart and Edwards 1999), bringing some matters under Community competence. In the field of police cooperation, the Treaty of Amsterdam created a basis for pragmatic police cooperation and more powers for Europol, especially with regard to transnational organized crime (Fijnaut 2004), which was facilitated by the introduction of new legislative instruments that would guarantee some flexibility for the member states alongside a more binding implementation path.

The Nice Treaty of 2001[7] simplified the mechanism of enhanced cooperation[8] as a formula for working together, which also had resonance in the field of law enforcement.

---

[4] Treaty on European Union, *Official Journal* C 191, 29 July 1992.

[5] See declaration on police cooperation: <http://eur-lex.europa.eu/en/treaties/dat/11992M/htm/11992M.html#0108000052>, accessed 30 November 2011.

[6] Council Act of 26 July 1995 (Convention on the Establishment of a European Police Office); Europol became operational on 1 July 1999.

[7] Treaty of Nice amending the Treaty on European Union, the treaties establishing the European Communities and Certain Related Acts, Official Journal C 80/1, 2001, <http://eur-lex.europa.eu/en/treaties/dat/12001C/pdf/12001C_EN.pdf>, accessed 30 November 2011.

[8] The mechanism by which at least nine member states may cooperate within an EU structure without the others.

In a significant move for police cooperation, the Lisbon Treaty, which entered into force on 1 December 2009, introduced the co-decision procedure, qualified majority voting in the Council and Community legislative instruments with direct effect and a stronger role for the Court of Justice (Bruggeman and den Boer 2011). However, in the field of operational police cooperation, the unanimity procedure was preserved for the Council with a consultative role for the European Parliament. Also, the Court of Justice would not have jurisdiction to review the validity or proportionality of police operations carried out in a member state (Art 240c). Internal security remains the sole responsibility of the member states (Art 4 [2] TEU). The Lisbon Treaty brings Europol within the Community system (De Moor and Vermeulen 2010a):[9] its structure, functioning and tasks were to be laid down in a future regulation in accordance with the ordinary legislative procedure.

Main trends in European police cooperation

Police cooperation throughout Europe is diverse and situated at various crossing-cutting levels of governance. Similarly, the evolution of European police cooperation through the treaties interacts with surrounding policy developments, such as external security, environmental security and crisis management, and security sector reform initiatives undertaken in other contexts and regions. The evolution of police cooperation can be characterized by general processes such as agencification, regulation and standardization, as well as by substantial developments in the form of cross-border information-sharing and multi-disciplinary cooperation. Below, we discuss each of these developments separately.

Agencification. The 'deepening' of the field of European police cooperation by a process of agencification was set in motion before the 'big-bang' enlargement of the EU with ten new member states in 2004 (Ekelund 2010; Groenleer 2009; Lord 2011). In 1999, it was easier to gain agreement on institutionalization issues between a much smaller group of member states. The Tampere Programme of 2000[10] provided the main basis for agencification in EU police cooperation (Busuioc and Groenleer 2011, 5). It bolstered the powers of the then embryonic Europol (De Moor and Vermeulen 2010b), created Eurojust and set down the groundwork for Joint Investigation Teams (JITs) as well as a European Police Academy (CEPOL).

Upon Tampere's enactment, Europol soon went through a rapid transformation, becoming responsible for the coordinated investigation of a wide range of crimes.[11] Europol concluded a number of agreements with third countries and relevant international organizations, and it developed a series of products, including the annual Organized Crime Threat Assessment (OCTA), the European Crime Intelligence Model (ECIM) and the Trends and Situation Report on Terrorism (Te-SAT). Also, its supporting capacity in JITs could be seen as a precursor to an executive European Police Office (De Moor 2009). However,

---

[9] Europol had already become an EU agency by virtue of the Council Decision.

[10] Presidency Conclusions, Tampere European Council, 15 and 16 October 1999.

[11] Europol's mandate was extended to include money-laundering in general by the Council Act of 30 November 2000. After this, all aspects of international organized crime set out in the annex to the Europol Convention by the Council Decision of 6 December 2001 were added to the Europol mandate. Further amendments followed in 2003 to reinforce the operational support that Europol provides to the national police authorities.

Europol still faces challenges, such as the tendency of local or regional police organizations to use different channels for international criminal investigations ('forum shopping') and insufficient intelligence transfer to Europol (den Boer 2002a). Europol has been cautious in exercising its new powers (Busuioc and Groenleer 2011, 10), such as the right of initiative (the authority to ask member states to conduct criminal investigations) and of participation in JITs, because policing remains a primary responsibility of member states.

Eurojust, the judicial counterpart to Europol, was the first JHA agency to be financed from the European Community budget. Eurojust assists national judges and prosecutors in ongoing criminal investigation cases by facilitating international mutual legal assistance and extradition requests. Like Europol, Eurojust can also play a supportive and coordinative role in a JIT. The creation of the agency reflects 'an increased integration in the field of police and judicial cooperation' (Busuioc and Groenleer 2011, 9). The Lisbon Treaty provides for the possibility to develop Eurojust into a European Public Prosecution Office, albeit with limited competence. Such a move will be subject to the unanimity procedure in the Council (Vlastnik 2008).

The path was also cleared for the establishment of JITs, which, as well as having a potential ad hoc character, may also be established as more permanent forms of police cooperation. Thus far, however, the member states have not made extensive use of this instrument (Block 2011a): the more sensitive the criminal investigation, the more difficult it is for member states to generate sufficient and sustainable trust to participate in a team where intelligence is shared and operationalized. Most JITs that have been established are of a bilateral and/or parallel nature (Block 2011b, 143–163). With a supporting budget from the EU, the Council Secretariat seeks to stimulate member states to initiate JITs; there are now regular meetings at the Eurojust secretariat. The Council Act of 28 November 2002 provides for Europol's participation in JITs.

CEPOL went on to be formally created through a Council Decision of 22 December 2000[12] and became operational on 1 January 2001. The Council Decision was amended and later replaced by a Council Decision of 20 September 2005 integrating CEPOL into the EU framework, implying that CEPOL would be funded from the EU budget and that EU rules on budgeting and staff, privileges and immunities would apply.[13] Though it has legal personality and its permanent secretariat is based in Bramshill (United Kingdom), CEPOL functions as a network between national police academies to train high-ranking officials, harmonize training programmes and disseminate best practices and police research findings.

In addition to all this, the Tampere Programme also provided for the establishment of a forum for policy influence by practitioners through the creation of the European Police Chiefs Task Force (EPCTF). The forum was never institutionalized, however. It was intended to focus on the planning of joint operations and the transfer of policy advice to the Council and to meet within the Europol framework with regard to its operational tasks, and within the Council framework as regards its strategic tasks (Peers 2011, 927).

---

[12] OJ L 336/1; see CEPOL website: <www.cepol.europa.eu>.
[13] OJ L 256/63, Council Decision 2005/681/JHA.

Regulation.   Since police cooperation became an official EU policy, around 200 Council documents have been adopted.[14] The EU member states are expected to implement all instruments, including those which are non-binding. However, the high number of instruments may have resulted in an implementation overload. Regulation that has facilitated European police cooperation includes the JITs and the Mutual Assistance Convention.[15] The latter instrument provides, inter alia, for the possibility to exchange information autonomously and for controlled delivery of illegal goods. Though originally negotiated outside the EU, the Schengen Convention and the Prüm Treaty have also provided a significant regulatory impulse for police cooperation.[16] Police cooperation is performed in the context of several bilateral,[17] multilateral[18] and regional frameworks,[19] including police–customs cooperation centres and the Cross-Channel Intelligence Conference, which is set up on the basis of a Memorandum of Understanding (see, for example, Bruinsma et al 2010; Kleiven 2012; Felsen 2012). Enhanced cooperation can have a tangible effect on (operational) practices of police. Its scope has recently been widened from criminal investigation to counter-terrorism and public order policing. The intersection of 'top-down' and 'bottom-up' vertical practices of police cooperation culminates in a 'horizontalization' of cooperation practices (den Boer 2010; Joutsen 2006; Guille 2010; Vermeulen 2011). This dynamic, where an intergovernmental agreement is lifted into the legislative and institutional core of the EU,[20] has also been severely criticized, as this process can produce policy inconsistencies and a democratic deficit (Balzacq et al 2006).

The Stockholm Programme[21] announced new regulatory ambitions, including a Commission communication on the status of cooperation between the European

---

[14] See appendix B in Block (2011b) for a sample of 137 EU Council instruments on police and judicial cooperation adopted between 1995 and 2004.

[15] Council Act of 29 May 2000 establishing in accordance with Article 34 of the Treaty on European Union the Convention on Mutual Assistance in Criminal Matters between the Member States of the European Union; OJ C 197 of 12 July 2005. The Convention entered into force on 23 August 2005 and replaced the Framework Decision on Joint Investigation Teams of 2002/465/JAI of the Council on 13 June 2002.

[16] Prüm Convention, 27 May 2005, <http://register.consilium.europa.eu/pdf/en/05/st10/st10900.en05.pdf>.

[17] See for instance the Treaty of Enschede, formally entitled 'Treaty between the Kingdom of the Netherlands and the Federal Republic of Germany Concerning Cross-Border Cooperation by Police and in Criminal Law Matters', Treaty Number 010856, entry into force 1 September 2006, Enschede (consolidated text in Dutch can be found at <http://wetten.overheid.nl/BWBV0001813/geldigheidsdatum_09-09-2010>).

[18] For instance, the Senningen Treaty, 8 June 2004, referred to in English as the 'Benelux Treaty on Cross-Border Police Intervention'; see Council of the European Union, Brussels, 20 October 2008, 14509/08.

[19] Such as EPICC (Euregional Police Information and Co-ordination Centre in Heerlen).

[20] This happened with the Schengen Convention as well as the Prüm Treaty; the latter was lifted into the Treaty on European Union in 2008: PJ 8 August, 2008, L 201.

[21] European Commission, Communication from the Commission to the European Parliament, the Council, the Economic and Social Committee and the Committee of the Regions, 'Delivering an Area of Freedom, Security and Justice for Europe's citizens', Brussels, 20 April 2010, COM (2010), 171 final; Council of the European Union, 'The Stockholm Programme—an open and secure Europe serving and protecting the citizens', Brussels, 2 December 2009, <http://www.se2009.eu/polopoly_fs/1.26419!menu/standard/file/Klar_Stockholmsprogram.pdf>.

Security and Defence Policy (ESDP) mission and Europol (2011), a proposal for a regulation on Europol (2013), a proposal on information exchange between Europol, Eurojust and Frontex (2011) and a communication on the improvement of police and customs cooperation in the EU. The Stockholm Programme also produced 'reflections on undercover officers, on Police and Customs Cooperation Centres, on an EU Approach to Intelligence led policing, and on common practices to improve operational police cooperation: assessment of state of play and possible recommendations'.

Therefore, such a wide variety of regulation practices have been enacted that, despite the fact that there is a manual for police officers involved in cross-border policing practices,[22] it may be difficult to see the wood for the trees.

Standardization. The itinerary of cooperation avenues has also included efforts to achieve standardization (Verpoest and Vander Beken 2005). The EU has facilitated and encouraged various projects that aim at achieving more synergy between the different strategies and policy cycles of the EU. A European Crime Intelligence Model (ECIM) was established in order to standardize the assessment of intelligence and the use of intelligence for coordinating investigations into organized crime (Brady 2008). Policy development in the AFSJ was pegged to the European Serious and Organized Crime Threat Assessment (SOCTA), which provides a picture of the criminal threats impacting on the EU (Vander Beken and Verfaillie 2008). SOCTA is developed by the relevant EU agencies under the leadership of Europol.[23] Policy-making and decision-making are based on a limited number of priorities, both regional and pan-European, which are identified by the European Council. For each of these priorities, the European Commission develops a Multi-Annual Strategic Plan (MASP) with the member states and experts from relevant agencies. The implementation and monitoring of annual Operational Action Plans (OAP) is performed in accordance with strategic goals determined in the MASP and validated by the Standing Committee on Operational Cooperation and Internal Security (COSI).[24] At the end of the policy cycle, a thorough evaluation is conducted by the European Commission. The scope of the policy cycle 2011–2013 has been limited to organized and serious international crime. If in the future new policy cycles have to be created (for example, for counter-terrorism or disaster management), these policy cycles will have to align with this methodology, requiring political authorities to determine the same priorities simultaneously.[25]

Information-sharing. Technology has considerable importance to police forces, particularly in the field of information and communication. As most international policing is primarily focused on information exchange, much effort has been spent building international databases as well as agreements making information more accessible for law enforcement. Examples of these information systems are the

---

[22] Council of the European Union, 'Manual on cross-border operations', Brussels, 14 December 2009.

[23] 'The Internal Security Strategy in action: five steps towards a more secure Europe', Brussels, 22 November 2010, COM (2010) 673 final.

[24] EU internal security cooperation is supervised by COSI, which was formally established on the basis of Article 71 TFEU as part of the Lisbon Treaty; see Curtin (2011, 11); Zonneveld and Toussaint (2011).

[25] As confirmed by the JHA Council on 2–3 December 2010.

Schengen Information System (SIS) and the Europol Information System (EIS). Related systems include the Visa Information System (VIS), the Customs Information System (CIS) and Eurodac (the EU system for fingerprints of asylum-seekers) (den Boer and Van Buuren 2012).

The Stockholm Programme advocated interoperability between the different EU databases. The Directive on Retention of Telecommunication Data, adopted in 2006,[26] enables law enforcement organizations to request communication data. Long before that, the cross-border interception of telecommunication had been endorsed by virtue of a resolution[27] as well as the Mutual Legal Assistance Convention.[28] Several new arrangements are in place, including the previously mentioned Europol–United States (US) agreements, the Terrorist Finance Tracking Programme (TFTP)[29] and the Passenger Name Record (PNR)[30] (Aldrich 2004; Balzacq 2008; Curtin 2011; Mitsilegas 2003; Occhipinti this issue). Though there has been an attempt to formalize horizontal information-sharing through the so-called principle of availability,[31] some member states do not have a culture of devolving discretionary power to exchange information with individual police officers.

Multi-disciplinary cooperation. The EU aims at multi-disciplinary cooperation against crime and terrorism and encourages cooperation between police organizations, customs organizations, immigration and naturalization services, border control authorities, special investigation agencies and intelligence services.[32] Various programmes have stimulated multi-agency cooperation, for instance the European Crime Prevention Network.[33] In addition, the EU strongly endorses public–private cooperation,[34] particularly with regard to investigations

---

[26] Directive 2006/24/EC. It was evaluated by the European Commission in 2011, and it was observed that its transposition into the domestic legal systems of the member states had been 'uneven' and that 'remaining differences between the legislations of the member states create difficulties for telecommunication service providers' (Press release, Brussels, 18 April 2011, <http://europa.eu/rapid/pressReleasesAction.do?reference = IP/11/484& type = HTML>, accessed 21 May 2012).

[27] Council Resolution of 17 January 1995 on the Lawful Interception of Telecommunications (OJ C329 04.11.96).

[28] See note 14.

[29] Agreement between the European Union and the United States of America on the Processing and Transfer of Financial Messaging Data from the European Union to the United States for the Purposes of the Terrorist Finance Tracking Programme, OJ 27.7.2010 L 195/5, <http://ec.europa.eu/home-affairs/policies/terrorism/terrorism_tftp_en.htm>, accessed 21 May 2012.

[30] On 19 April 2012, the European Parliament gave its consent to a new EU–US agreement for data exchange on passengers by carriers operating flights between the EU and the US (Council of the European Union, press release, Luxembourg, 26 April 2012).

[31] The principle of availability applies via the Prüm Treaty and the Swedish Framework Decision (Council Framework Decision 2006/960/JHA of 18 December 2006, OJ 29 December 2006, L 386). On the occasion of a revision of the treaty, this principle may be inserted.

[32] Act 'The prevention and control of organised crime: a strategy for the beginning of the new millennium', OJ C 124 of 3.5.2000, which also involved the creation of the Multi-Disciplinary Group on Organized Crime.

[33] Council Decision 2009/902/JHA of 30 November 2009 setting up a European Crime Prevention Network (EUCPN) and repealing Decision 2001/427/JHA.

[34] <http://ec.europa.eu/home-affairs/policies/crime/crime_prevention_en.htm>.

into money-laundering, illegal profits and financing terrorism. Europol acts as the European nucleus for inter-agency cooperation. Most employees are from police agencies, but Europol is open to liaison officers from related domestic agencies.

On a more fundamental level, the AFSJ itself embraces different policy sectors within internal security. EU Security Strategies of 2003 and 2008 (Mosca Moschini 2008), as well as the Internal Security Strategy (2010)[35] endorse inter-sectoral efforts to achieve a more comprehensive answer to common threats. Mixed areas of interest relevant for policing are the prevention of terrorism and radicalization, the management of border controls, as well as civil–military cooperation. Policing is also an essential element of Security Sector Reform (SSR), the European Neighbourhood Policy Instrument (ENPI) and the EU dialogues (see Monar this issue).

The integrative step from sovereignty to solidarity

On the basis of the above historical tracing, it can be argued that police cooperation has gradually been transferred to the institutional core of the EU, and that this has been accompanied by a gradual increase of institutional powers regarding policing. More broadly, as Busuioc and Groenleer (2011, 27) argue, the former JHA agencies have now been brought to the institutional core of the EU and, as a result, we are witnessing a 'normalization of accountability arrangements'.

When considering the role of parliamentary oversight, it may be observed that the European Parliament has left behind a long and frustrating trail of limited power. The Council has managed to bypass the European Parliament a number of times, for example, when the Europol Convention was under negotiation (den Boer 2002b, 283). The Maastricht Treaty granted the European Parliament the right to be consulted. With the Treaty of Lisbon, the European Parliament gained co-legislative power.[36] The potential of this power was demonstrated when the European Parliament withheld approval of the new TFTP/Swift agreement (see, for example, Curtin 2011; den Boer and Van Buuren 2012), demanding amendments, only after which it gave its consent in July 2010 (Bigo et al 2011; De Hert and Papakonstantinou 2010). With regard to Europol and Eurojust, the European Parliament, together with the Council, is the budgetary authority. The Europol Council Decision[37] provides for hearings before the European Parliament. On the whole, 'democratic accountability is further on the rise' (Busuioc and Groenleer 2011, 22), now the director of Europol and the president of Eurojust can appear at hearings before the Committee on Civil Liberties, Justice and Home Affairs (LIBE). Also, the agencies will be subjected to evaluations that are to be forwarded to the European Parliament. In the future, it is expected that the European Parliament will widen its monitoring and sanctioning powers with regard to JHA agencies.

---

[35] 'The Internal Security Strategy in action: five steps towards a more secure Europe', Brussels, 22 November 2010, COM (2010) 673 final.

[36] Article 88(2) TFEU, which provides that the European Parliament and the Council shall determine Europol's structure, operation, field of action and tasks by means of regulations adopted in accordance with the ordinary legislative procedure. There are likely provisions for Eurojust.

[37] Council Decision of 6 April 2009 establishing the European Police Office (Europol); OJ L 121/37, 15.5.2009.

The European Commission has gradually gained more power in the field, and now enjoys a shared right of initiative, and can exercise administrative responsibilities in the sphere of facilitation, coordination and evaluation. By setting the budget, the European Commission can 'significantly influence' Eurojust's activities (Busuioc and Groenleer 2011, 13). Article 263 of the Treaty on the Functioning of the European Union (TFEU) grants the Court of Justice of the European Union (CJEU) full jurisdiction over the agencies' acts, including those of Europol, Eurojust and CEPOL (Busuioc and Groenleer 2011, 24). Transitional provisions are provided for in Article 10 of Protocol No 36, which specifies in Article 10 that the Court may exercise its full powers five years after the entry into force of the treaty.

Similar to other policy fields in the EU, four levels of policy identity are at play. There is currently little convergence between the member states as to how they have sought to embed international police cooperation in their national law enforcement strategies and capacities (den Boer and Doelle 2002). There are perhaps 'pockets' or 'islands' or even 'hemispheres' of convergence to the extent that some countries in the EU engage in similar models of policing (community policing, intelligence-led policing) and adopt similar structures of policing (such as developments towards a national integrated police in Scotland and the Netherlands, similar to Belgium, Sweden and Denmark). Subsidiarity is implicitly embedded in cooperation practices, such as in anti-drug-trafficking (Dorn 1993). However, in practice, legislative instruments tend to be implemented differently; member states determine the actor who is responsible for the implementation process and each state has a duty to report the progress that has been made in the implementation of a relevant instrument.

European police cooperation has not had a profoundly transformative effect on policing in member states. Except for greater standardization and decentralization of procedures as a consequence of the European Arrest Warrant, there is hardly any automaticity in integrating the European dimension in police information and computing technology (ICT), information exchange and standard procedures. 'Europe' is not yet part and parcel of police protocols or resource management, let alone recruitment (Alain 2001; Tupman and Tupman 1999). Offering sustainable commitment at the EU level is a process of fits, kicks and starts (Wallace 1994). The 'policing field' sees European police cooperation with a certain scepticism, as they think that European policing is mostly 'toys for the boys' or business for the police senior management. Police organizations themselves often remain focused upon their own internal processes, being involved in demanding restructuring exercises such as managing severe budget cuts and public dissatisfaction. Moreover, as Deflem (2000) maintains, the closer a police organization is to the politico-administrative centre, the more difficult it is for it to exercise professional autonomy and to develop cooperative practices across the national border. However, there are so-called 'enabling states' (Cope et al 1997), in which police cooperation practices have been able to thrive. One would expect budget cuts to open the door for more pooling and sharing between the national police forces—indeed, this is what defence organizations in the EU have done when faced with significant budget cuts.[38] Also, the transnationalization of crime

---

[38] See, for example, Vogel (2012).

and public order threats surely provides an incentive for police organizations to intensify mutual cooperation (Solomon 1995). So why do police organizations not follow suit?

Measuring the depth of integration in EU police cooperation

As the prime locus of democratic control on state services with a monopoly of violence still resides in the member states, organizing governance at the EU level may be one step too far. Yet, this is what is currently happening to Europol. In view of the cross-cutting trends that may have an impact upon European policing, it will be useful to think more about the levels that influence the (lack of deep) integration of European police cooperation in the EU member states. In this reflective analysis, we focus on three levels, namely, that of institutional power that is aggregated at the supranational level, the level of European regulation and the level of transnational professionalism. These are the constituent elements of a theory on European integration (Stone Sweet and Sandholtz 1997, 301), which can help us to grasp the depth of integration in the field of EU police cooperation.

Institutional level

The EU institutions have gradually gained more power in the field of EU police cooperation. Thus, they can be regarded as supranational organizations that have developed sufficient autonomous capacity to pursue an integrative agenda (Stone Sweet and Sandholtz 1997, 301). Thus far, the European Commission has enjoyed a shared right of initiative. The European Commission can propose legislative acts in the field of JHA cooperation, but an initiative can also come from a quarter of the member states. Article 76 TFEU provides that this also applies to police cooperation in criminal matters. In another role, the European Commission may need to maximize its competences as facilitator, coordinator, evaluator and exchequer of integrated international policing. The European Parliament's powers in this regard have also been increased, and it may develop a more assertive role in view of the EU 'quietly' emerging as a significant security actor in its own right as it gathers and processes information autonomously and it shares it both internally as well as externally (Curtin 2011, 9).

Currently, there is no single supranational actor able to coordinate or oversee the whole field of action. To a certain extent, COSI can coordinate operational police and internal security work between the member states. However, as it is a relatively new actor composed of high-level officials from member states' interior ministries and observers from EU agencies, its performance is not easily assessed at this stage. COSI itself is not subject to control, which fails to meet a criterion for deeper integration. Another actor with potential to coordinate is the EU Counter-Terrorism Unit, but its mandate is currently too limited (Deflem 2006). As most cooperative police ventures do not primarily focus on counter-terrorism, the reach of the Counter-Terrorism Coordinator in the European and domestic arenas of policing may be limited.

EU institutions are jointly responsible for a system of oversight on EU police cooperation. When considering the European Parliament, the question comes to mind of whether the current budgetary and co-legislative powers could be complemented by other powers, including the right to initiate a parliamentary inquiry, possibly in close cooperation with the national parliaments. The impression is that, with the exception of some parliamentary bodies such as the House of Lords,[39] national parliaments have hitherto demonstrated marginal interest in European police cooperation, despite the fact that these practices have a significant impact on civil liberties (Curtin 2011). In any case, parliamentary oversight has been rather differentiated, and this also applies to specific systems of police oversight (den Boer and Fernhout 2009). There is currently no provision for independent police oversight at the European level. The Lisbon Treaty gives national parliaments ample room for subsidiarity and national parliamentary scrutiny, but there is no permanent joint parliamentary committee on internal security issues in the EU.

As a collective security actor, the EU's primary role has been to coordinate, facilitate, (co-)finance and stimulate the member states to engage in a durable form of police cooperation. In the field of information-sharing between domestic law enforcement agencies, the EU has enabled the creation of databases and intelligence-sharing between national law enforcement organizations, and therefore carries responsibility for how these data systems are managed and used. National intelligence agencies and EU actors 'receive, produce and disseminate classified information' and they 'collect, analyse and disseminate information … to policy makers and other executive bodies' (Curtin 2011, 10). The Lisbon Treaty does not explain how and to what extent other institutional actors should have a mandate in the field of European police cooperation. While the EU has sufficient institutional power to pursue an integrative agenda, there is not yet an integrated vision of how the combined powers of the European Court of Auditors, the European Ombudsman, the European Data Protection Supervisor and the EU Fundamental Rights Agency fit into the wider picture. Currently, there is no strategic vision of how the competences of various institutions interrelate and whether police cooperation will be widened.

Regulatory level

The field of EU police cooperation has become the target of a regulatory complex. Numerous EU instruments exert normative expectations on political and professional actors of member states. The quality of regulation may become an issue to the extent that it should be consistent not only with EU legislation, but also with the domestic criminal justice systems of member states as well as with relevant legislation from the Council of Europe and the United Nations. As non-operational police cooperation will be subject to an ordinary legislative procedure as a consequence of the Lisbon Treaty, legislative process becomes more balanced and transparent.

The Hague Programme of 2004 set out priorities for the following five years, which included achieving more legislative coherence, while the aforementioned Stockholm Programme introduced the impact assessment of draft legislation. Sunset clauses and/or the demand for regular reviews have hardly been used to

---

[39] See, for example, House of Lords, *Europol's role in fighting crime*, Select Committee on the European Union, Session 2002–2003, 5th Report; House of Lords, *Europol: co-ordinating the fight against serious and organised crime*, Select Committee on the European Union, Session 2007–2008, 29th Report.

date. The adoption of binding instruments leaves actors in member states no possibility for lenience or escape. Despite arguments that the binding character of instruments has not generated tangible implementation effects in ordinary police practice (Block 2011b), European Community legislation will affect the implementation path, particularly when police matters become justiciable by the Court of Justice. Given the vast number of regulatory incentives, police organizations in the EU member states will no doubt be subjected to the gradual Europeanization of their models, practices and instruments (Monar 2001).

Professional level

Despite the fact that police organizations are often characterized as classic closed-rank bureaucracies, police officers themselves have turned more entrepreneurial and are increasingly exposed to European training and networking. National police systems differ widely in terms of history and accountability mechanisms. The EU has provided a space for systematic and Europe-wide cultivation of transnational police professionalism. In the field of internal security and police reform, the EU acts as an external security actor in the context of numerous programmes (Bowling and Sheptycki 2012; Kleinig 1990; Lavenex 2004; Manners 2008; Mounier 2009; Sheptycki 2007; Wolff et al 2009). A fundamental prerequisite for a more consistent and comprehensive system of European police cooperation is the creation of integrative power and priority inside relevant domestic professional organizations. With binding EU legislation, police organizations in member states experience international cooperation and a relative decrease of institutional discretion, Europol is playing a strategically supportive role in the development of an international police culture and overcoming the obstacles of cooperation between legally, culturally and professionally differentiated police organizations (Deflem 2006).

Concluding notes

European police cooperation is institutionally anchored and spans numerous legislative instruments. When following this thread through the treaties, one may increasingly identify elements of supra-nationalism and inter-state sovereignty, in the sense that the EU institutions have gradually gained more power (Börzel 2005; Vollaard 2009, 412). The Lisbon Treaty formalized scrutiny power of the national parliaments of member states and holds potential for more legislative coherence and improved governance, particularly regarding decision-making and the simplification of regulatory instruments.

Police cooperation is a sensitive field, occupying the space between sovereignty and solidarity. The recent changes in decision-making procedures on police cooperation are somewhat cosmetic, particularly because only national security safeguards apply to them. Significant challenges persist for implementation as well as 'deep integration' of European police cooperation in domestic law enforcement organizations. There is an absence of an integrated vision about the proper governance and legitimacy of police cooperation (Recasens 2000). Similarly, there has been little public debate about European police cooperation, particularly concerning the current imbalance between intrusive data-gathering and privacy protection (González et al 2011). More discussion is required to reform the governance and deep integration of EU police cooperation.

Member states may have to pay a high price for deep integration, such as the pooling and sharing of material and human resources, and they may wish to see the relative gains first. As long as member states are not pushed or forced to invest in deeper integration, genuine reciprocity in policy investment cannot be achieved, leaving ample space for institutionalized distrust between the member states. Hence, and very much in line with the current discourse about economic governance in the EU, the European Commission continues to act as broker, facilitator, coordinator, evaluator and exchequer of integrated EU policing. In addition, deep integration of European police cooperation can be encouraged by increased parliamentary involvement, independent police oversight (at European and national levels), the incorporation of EU cooperation mechanisms into regular working procedures, and a systematic and EU-wide cultivation of police professionalism.

The conditions for deeper integration of police cooperation in domestic law enforcement systems can be met by investing more effort in good governance. Quick wins can be made by guaranteeing sustainable codification and permanent exchange of good practices. EU institutions may exploit their extended powers by insisting on open and transparent decision-making, on good quality of legislation (for example, through impact assessments and by demanding the insertion of sunset clauses), on regular and independent review of legislative instruments and formally adopted policies, and by working together with national authorities to coordinate the governance of police cooperation in the EU. In the long run, European policing as a field of professional activity requires fundamental reframing. Securing a well-knit tapestry of agency competences, regulatory instruments and oversight mechanisms in the European arena of policing is a first and necessary step in this direction.

Notes on contributor

Monica den Boer holds a position at the Police Academy of the Netherlands and is a member of the Committee on European Integration of the Advisory Council on International Affairs. She obtained a PhD in 1990 from the European University Institute and has worked at Edinburgh University, the Netherlands Study Centre for Crime and Law Enforcement, the European Institute of Public Administration, Tilburg University and the European Institute of Law Enforcement Co-operation. Between March 2004 and January 2012 she was professor of comparative public administration at the VU University Amsterdam on behalf of the Police Academy of the Netherlands. In 2009, she was a member of the Dutch Iraq Investigation Committee, and in 2009–2010 she participated in the Defence Future Survey Group. She has published widely on European internal security co-operation and engages in teaching, coaching and supervision.

References

Alain, Marc (2001) '"The trapeze artists and the ground crew." Police cooperation and intelligence exchange mechanisms in Europe and North America: a comparative empirical study', *Policing & Society*, 11:1, 1–27

Aldrich, Richard (2004) 'Transatlantic intelligence and security cooperation', *International Affairs*, 80:4, 731–753

Balzacq, Thierry (2008) 'The policy tools of securitization: information exchange, EU foreign and interior policies', *Journal of Common Market Studies*, 46:1, 75–100

Balzacq, Thierry, Didier Bigo, Sergo Carrera and Elspeth Guild (2006) 'Security and the two-level game: the Treaty of Prüm, the EU and the management of threats', CEPS Working Document, No 234, Centre for European Policy Studies, Brussels

Bigo, Didier, Sergio Carrera, Gloria González Fuster, Elspeth Guild, Paul De Hert, Julien Jeandesboz and Papa Konstantinou (2011) 'Towards a new legal framework for data protection and privacy: challenges, principles and the role of the European Parliament', Policy Department C, Brussels, <http://www.europarl.europa.eu/activities/committees/studies/>

Block, Ludo (2011a) 'EU Joint Investigation Teams: political ambitions and police practices' in Saskia Hufnagel, Clive Harfield and Simon Bronitt (eds) *Cross-border law enforcement and regional law enforcement cooperation—European, Australian and Asia–Pacific perspectives* (London: Routledge), 87–107

Block, Ludo (2011b) *From politics to policing. The rationality gap in EU Council policy-making* (The Hague: Eleven/Boom Juridische Uitgevers)

Börzel, Tanja A (2005) 'Mind the gap! European integration between level and scope', *Journal of European Public Policy*, 12:2, 217–236

Bowling, Ben and James Sheptycki (2012) *Global policing* (London: Sage)

Brady, Hugo (2008) 'Europol and the European criminal intelligence model: a non-state response to organized crime', *Policing*, 2:1, 103–109

Bruggeman, Willy and Monica den Boer (2011) 'Policing and internal security in the post-Lisbon era: new challenges ahead' in Sarah Wolff, Flora Goudappel and Jaap de Zwaan (eds) *Freedom, security and justice after Lisbon and Stockholm* (The Hague: TMC Asser Press), 135–153

Bruinsma, M, M Jacobs, M Jans, H Moors, ACM Spapens and CJCF Fijnaut (2010) *Grensoverschrijdend politiewerk in de Euregio Rijn-Maas-Noord* (Antwerp: Intersentia)

Busuioc, Madalina and Martin LP Groenleer (2011) 'Beyond design—the evolution of Europol and Eurojust', Amsterdam Law School Research Paper No 2011-09; Amsterdam Centre for European Law and Governance Research Paper No 2011-03, <http://ssrn.com/abstract=1869994>, accessed 22 June 2011

Cope, Stephen, Frank Leishman and Peter Starie (1997) 'Globalization, new public management and the enabling state: futures of police management', *International Journal of Public Sector Management*, 10:6, 444–460

Curtin, Deirdre (2011), 'Top secret Europe', inaugural lecture delivered upon appointment to the Chair of Professor of European Law at the University of Amsterdam, 20 October, University of Amsterdam, <http://www.jur.uva.nl/acelg-news/news.cfm/79CDFCB7-D34E-43C5-82E327BAC76BF3F4>, accessed 6 December 2011

Deflem, Mathieu (2000) 'Bureaucratization and social control: historical foundations of international police cooperation', *Law & Society Review*, 34:3, 739–778

Deflem, Mathieu (2006) 'Europol and the policing of international terrorism: counter-terrorism in a global perspective', *Justice Quarterly*, 23:3, 336–359

De Hert, Paul and Vagelis Papakonstantinou (2010) 'The EU PNR framework decision proposal: towards completion of the PNR processing scene in Europe', *Computer Law & Security Review*, 26:4, 368–376

De Moor, Alexandra (2009) 'The role of Europol in Joint Investigation Teams. A foretaste of an executive European police office' in Marc Cools, Sofie De Kimpe, Brice De Ruyver, Marleen Easton, Lieven Pauwels, Paul Ponsaers, Gudrun Vande Walle, Tom Vander Beken, Freya Vander Laenen, Gert Vermeulen (eds) *Gofs Research Paper Series—Vol. 2 Readings on Criminal Justice, Criminal Law & Policing* (Antwerp: Maklu), 329–358

De Moor, Alexandra and Gert Vermeulen (2010a) 'The Europol Council Decision: transforming Europol into an agency of the European Union', *Common Market Law Review*, 47:4, 1089–1121

De Moor, Alexandra and Gert Vermeulen (2010b) 'Shaping the competence of Europol. An FBI perspective' in Marc Cools, Brice De Ruyver, Marleen Easton, Lieven Pauwels, Paul Ponsaers, Gudrun Vande Walle, Tom Vander Beken, Freya Vander Laenen, Gert

Vermeulen and Gerwinde Vynckier (eds) *EU and international crime control* (Antwerp: Maklu), 63–94

den Boer, Monica (1995) 'Police cooperation in the TEU: tiger in a Trojan horse?', *Common Market Law Review*, 32:2, 555–578

den Boer, Monica (2002a) 'Intelligence exchange and the control of organised crime: from Europeanisation via centralisation to dehydration?' in Joanna Apap and Malcolm Anderson (eds) *Police and justice cooperation and the new European borders* (The Hague: Kluwer Law International), 151–161

den Boer, Monica (2002b) 'Towards an accountability regime for an emerging European policing governance', *Policing and Society*, 12:4, 275–289

den Boer, Monica (2010) 'The governance of police cooperation in Europe: the twist between networks and bureaucracies' in F Lemieux (ed) *International police cooperation. Emerging issues, theory and practice* (Collumpton, United Kingdom: Willan), 42–61

den Boer, Monica and Patrick Doelle (2002) 'Converge or not to converge ... that's the question: a comparative analysis of Europeanisation trends in criminal justice organisations' in Monica den Boer (ed) *Controlling organised crime: organisational changes within the law enforcement and prosecution services in the EU member states* (Maastricht: European Institute of Public Administration), 1–69

den Boer, Monica and Roel Fernhout (2009), 'Police oversight mechanisms in Europe: towards a comparative overview of ombudsmen and their competencies', report for Asia Europe Foundation, Amsterdam/Singapore, <http://www.asef.org/index.php?download_publication=cHVibGljYXRpb25zL2RvY3VtZW50cy8x>

den Boer, Monica and Jelle Van Buuren (2012) 'Security clouds: towards an ethical governance of surveillance in Europe', *Journal of Cultural Economy*, 5:1, 85–103

Dorn, Nicholas (1993) 'Subsidiarity, police cooperation and drug enforcement. Some structures of policy-making in Europe', *European Journal on Criminal Policy and Research*, 1:2, 30–47

Ekelund, Helena (2010) 'The agencification of Europe: explaining the establishment of European Community agencies', (PhD thesis, University of Nottingham), <http://etheses.nottingham.ac.uk/1269/>, accessed 6 December 2011

Elsen, Charles (2007) 'From Maastricht to The Hague: the politics of judicial and police cooperation', *ERA Forum*, 8, 13–26

Felsen, Oliver (2012) 'European police cooperation: the example of the German–French Centre for Police and Customs Cooperation Kehl (GZ Kehl)' in Saskia Hufnagel, Clive Harfield and Simon Bronitt (eds) *Cross-border law enforcement and regional law enforcement cooperation—European, Australian and Asia–Pacific perspectives* (London: Routledge), 73–86

Fijnaut, Cyrille (1993) 'The internationalization of police cooperation in Western Europe' in C Fijnaut (ed) *The internationalization of police cooperation in Western Europe* (Dordrecht: Kluwer), 9–13

Fijnaut, Cyrille (2004) 'Police cooperation in the area of freedom, security and justice' in N Walker (ed) *Europe's area of freedom, security and justice* (Oxford: Oxford University Press), 242–282

González, Claudia, Paul De Hert and Serge Gutwirth (2011) 'Privacy and data protection in the EU security continuum', INEX/CEPS, Brussels, June, No 12, <http://www.ceps.be/book/privacy-and-data-protection-eu-security-continuum>

Groenleer, Martijn (2009) *The autonomy of European Union agencies. A comparative study of institutional development* (Delft, the Netherlands: Eburon Academic Publishers)

Gruszczak, Artur (2009) 'Governing internal security in the European Union', *Central European Journal of International and Security Studies*, 3:2, 86–103

Guille, L (2010) 'Police and judicial cooperation in Europe: bilateral versus multilateral cooperation' in F Lemieux (ed) *International police cooperation. Emerging issues, theory and practice* (Collumpton, United Kingdom: Willan), 25–41

Guyomarch, Alain (1995) 'Problems and prospects for European police cooperation after Maastricht', *Policing & Society*, 5:3, 249–261

Joutsen, Matti (2006) 'The European Union and cooperation in criminal matters: the search for balance', No 25, HEUNI, European Institute for Crime Prevention and Control,

Helsinki, affiliated with the United Nations, <http://www.heuni.fi/uploads/gg29d0zcr1rpk_1.pdf>, accessed 30 November 2011

Kaunert, Christian (2010) *European internal security. Towards supranational governance in the area of freedom, security and justice* (Manchester: Manchester University Press)

Kleinig, John (1990) 'Teaching and learning police ethics: competing and complementary approaches', *Journal of Criminal Justice*, 18:1, 1–18

Kleiven, Maren Eline (2012) 'Nordic police cooperation in Saskia Hufnagel' in Saskia Hufnagel, Clive Harfield and Simon Bronitt (eds) *Cross-border law enforcement and regional law enforcement cooperation—European, Australian and Asia–Pacific perspectives* (London: Routledge), 63–71

Lavenex, Sandra (2004) 'EU external governance in "wider Europe"', *Journal of European Public Policy*, 11:4, 680–700

Lord, Christopher (2011) 'The European Parliament and the legitimation of agencification', *Journal of European Public Policy*, 18:6, 909–925

Manners, Ian (2008) 'The normative ethics of the European Union', *International Affairs*, 84:1, 45–60

Mitsilegas, Valsamis (2003) 'The new EU–USA cooperation on extradition, mutual legal assistance and the exchange of police data', *European Foreign Affairs Review*, 8:4, 515–536

Monar, Jörg (2001) 'The dynamics of justice and home affairs: laboratories, driving factors and costs', *Journal of Common Market Studies*, 39:4, 747–764

Mosca Moschini, Rolando (2008) 'The comprehensive security concept of the European Union', in Hans Guenter Brauch, Urusla Oswald Spring, Czeslaw Mesjasz, John Grin, Pal Dunay, Navnita Chadha Behera, Bechir Chourou, Patricia Kameri-Mbote, PH Liotta (eds) *Globalization and environmental challenges: reconceptualizing security in the 21st century*, Vol. 3 Hexagon Series on Human and Environmental Security and Peace (New York: Springer), 651–657

Mounier, Gregory (2009) 'Europol: a new player in the EU external policy field?', *Perspectives on European Policy and Society*, 10:4, 582–602

Occhipinti, John D (2003) *The politics of EU police cooperation: toward a European FBI?* (Boulder, Colorado: Lynne Rienner)

Peers, Steve (2011) *EU Justice and Home Affairs Law*, 3rd edn (Oxford: Oxford University Press)

Philippart, Eric and Geoffrey Edwards (1999) 'The provisions on closer cooperation in the Treaty of Amsterdam', *Journal of Common Market Studies*, 37:1, 87–108

Recasens, Amadeu (2000) 'The control of police powers', *European Journal on Criminal Policy and Research*, 8:3, 247–269

Sheptycki, James (2007) 'The constabulary ethic and the transnational condition' in A Goldsmith and J Sheptycki (eds) *Crafting transnational policing. Police capacity building and global policing reform* (Oxford: Hart), 31–63

Skinner, Stephen (2002) 'The third pillar treaty provisions on police cooperation: has the EU bitten off more than it can chew?', *Columbia Journal of European Law*, 8:2, 203–220

Solomon, Joel S (1995) 'Forming a more secure union: the growing problem of organized crime in Europe as a challenge to national sovereignty', *Dickinson Journal of International Law*, 13, 623–648

Stone Sweet, Alec and Wayne Sandholtz (1997) 'European integration and supranational governance', *Journal of European Public Policy*, 4:3, 297–317

Tupman, Bill and Alison Tupman (1999) *Policing in Europe. Uniform in diversity* (Exeter: Intellect)

Vander Beken, Tom and Kristof Verfaillie (2008) 'Proactive policing and the assessment of organised crime', *Policing*, 31:4, 534–552

Vermeulen, Gert (2011) 'Justitiële en politiële samenwerking in strafzaken in de Europese Unie. Bilan en toekomstopties' in B de Ruyver, P Ponsaers, G Vermeulen and T Vander Beken (eds) *Strafrechtshandhaving in België en Nederland* (Antwerp: Maklu), 101–124

Verpoest, Karen and Tom Vander Beken (2005) 'The European Union methodology for reporting on organised crime', Report for 6th Framework Programme 'Assessing organised crime: testing the feasibility of a common European approach in a case study of the cigarette black market in the EU', <http://biblio.ugent.be/input/download?func=downloadFile&fileOId=897823>, accessed 7 December 2011

Vlastnik, Jirí (2008) 'Eurojust—a cornerstone of the federal criminal justice system in the EU?' in Elspeth Guild and Florian Geyer (eds) *Security versus justice? Police and judicial cooperation in the European Union* (Aldershot, United Kingdom: Ashgate), 35–50

Vogel, Toby (2012) 'EU seeks greater defence cooperation', *European Voice*, 22 March, <http://www.europeanvoice.com/article/2012/march/eu-seeks-greater-defence-co-operation-/73967.aspx>, accessed 10 July 2013

Vollaard, Johannes Paul (2009) 'Political territoriality in the European Union: the changing boundaries of security and healthcare', (doctoral thesis, Leiden University), <https://openaccess.leidenuniv.nl/handle/1887/13883>, accessed 7 December 2011

Wallace, William (1994) 'Rescue or retreat? The nation state in Western Europe, 1945–93', *Political Studies*, 42:s1, 52–76

Weyembergh, Anne (2000), 'Building a European legal area: what has been achieved and what has still to be done?', lecture in the Cicero Foundation Great Debate seminar 'Justice and Home Affairs—How to implement the Amsterdam Treaty?', Paris, 13–14 April, <http://www.cicerofoundation.org/lectures/p4weyembergh.html>, accessed 30 November 2011

Wolff, Sarah, Nicole Wichmann and Gregory Mounier (2009) 'The external dimension of justice and home affairs: a different security agenda for the EU?', *Journal of European Integration*, 31:1, 9–23

Zonneveld, Michelle and Mascia Toussaint (2011) *Mapping COSI. Een oriënterende studie naar het permanente comité operationele samenwerking op het gebied van binnenlandse veiligheid* (Brussels: OCMC European Affairs)

EU cooperation on terrorism prevention and violent radicalization: frustrated ambitions or new forms of EU security governance?

Raphael Bossong
Europe University Viadrina

Abstract *This article questions the effectiveness of EU efforts to prevent terrorism and violent radicalization as well as the future prospects of such efforts. Driven by the pressure of attacks, member states have agreed on a comprehensive strategy to prevent radicalization and recruitment into terrorism, but simultaneously the strategy traces the limits of EU authority in member states in this regard. Meanwhile, the European Commission has focused on indirect measures, such as research support, for counter radicalization. However, over time, both flexible cooperation among a subset of member states and new EU initiatives have generated only few or biased policy outputs. The Stockholm Programme renewed the ambition to prevent terrorism at an early stage and underlined the EU's role in evaluation and knowledge exchange. This article questions the resulting proposal to create a network of local or subnational actors for best practice exchange. The article argues that preventive counterterrorism relies on contentious scientific evidence and that authoritative evaluations remain tied to national policy-making. Finally, the EU Commission cannot mobilize sufficient resources to ensure that 'frontline' organizations, such as police services, implement new practices. Taken together, this limits the potential for depoliticizing multilevel governance approaches to terrorism prevention. The conclusions of this article raise further research questions on the use of knowledge and complex governance patterns in EU internal security.*

Introduction

By early 2012, officials in the United States proclaimed that the threat posed by Al-Qaeda had declined substantially (Schmitt 2012). However, the increasingly loose or virtual nature of transnational terrorist networks (Sageman 2008) still presented a persisting challenge to national security services (Jenkins 2012). Apart from diverse Al-Qaeda affiliated groups around the world, so-called 'lone wolf' actors living within Western societies, who endorse a wide variety of ideological convictions, (re)emerged as the main terrorist threat. In 2011 and 2012 this was tragically evidenced by the devastating attacks by Anders Breivik in Norway and by a series of killings by a self-proclaimed French Jihadist (Council 2012).

Such unpredictable attacks underline the need to reduce the probability of terrorist violence at an early stage and at a structural level. A preventive approach involves countering 'violent radicalization' or the 'conditions that are conducive to the emergence of terrorism' (Coolsaet 2011). Addressing social problems and ideational developments that may be associated with these concepts may also have broader benefits, such as improved social cohesion. In addition, preventive counterterrorism policies may avoid the inherent dilemma of defensive and repressive security strategies, which can become excessively costly, and which still leave potential terrorists able to choose among a vast range targets (Enders and Sandler 2006; Mueller 2010).

The actual practice of preventive counterterrorism is more contentious. There is no consensus on which set of political, social or psychological factors are related to terrorist violence, and the link between extremist thought and violence is highly context specific or simply spurious (Githens-Mazer and Lambert 2010). Preventive counterterrorism policies may miss their intended objective and instead lead to a problematic criminalization of radical ideas, stigmatize communities or taint social policy with questionable security objectives (Pantazis and Pemberton 2009).

In this context, the EU's ambition to contribute to the prevention of terrorism (Council 2005a) also needs to be scrutinized. The EU's fight against terrorism as a whole has been criticized for its lack of coherence and questionable implementation record (Argomaniz 2011; Bureš 2011). Extended empirical, theoretical and legal critiques have mostly been developed with regard to the EU's activities in the area of criminal justice cooperation and information sharing for the purposes of prosecuting terrorist suspects. In contrast, preventive counter-terrorism has mainly been analysed from a national angle (Richards 2011) or from the wider perspective of terrorism research (Coolsaet 2011).

The dearth of studies that focus on the EU's role in the prevention of terrorism (Dittrich 2007; Coolsaet 2010) is significant for two reasons. First, the EU does not have a remit for involvement in member states' national integration or education policies that could influence 'conditions conducive to the emergence of terrorism'. These limitations are made more complex by the fact that several member states do not consider terrorism as a salient threat at the national level (Meyer 2009; Bureš 2011). Nevertheless, initiatives for preventive counterterrorism have been prominently mentioned in The Hague and the Stockholm Programme for the development of the European Area of Freedom Security and Justice (AFSJ). In particular, the EU claims to improve national policy by research support and the exchange of 'best practices'. The first part of this article therefore presents a historical overview of the emergence and evolution of EU counterterrorism prevention policy.

Recent initiatives of the Stockholm Programme to upgrade the EU's terrorism prevention policy have not yet attracted the attention of security analysts and EU scholars. This revolves around the creation of a network of local or subnational actors for best practice exchange, the so-called Radicalization Awareness Network (RAN). As the network is taking shape at the time of writing, this second part of this article reviews a number of systematic challenges to a coherent EU terrorism prevention policy and critically assesses the prospects of the RAN network. The conclusions raise further research questions on related complex governance patterns in EU internal security.

The emergence of EU strategy to combat radicalization and recruitment into terrorism

The events of 9/11 led to a massive expansion of counterterrorism policies at the domestic and international levels. In the US, terrorists were categorically labelled as 'evil' (Jackson 2005), which blocked more thorough investigations into the causes of the attacks. In Europe, the initial reflex was to point to the Palestinian conflict, repression in the Middle East and underdevelopment in other parts of the world (Council 2002). Yet the US War on Terror and the resulting intra-European divisions quickly put an end to hopes for a more robust common foreign policy in relation to these protracted conflicts.

Meanwhile, security agencies in Europe states became increasingly worried about new internal threats. In 2002 Dutch security authorities conducted their first systematic investigation into Islamic extremist recruitment after two Dutch nationals died in a failed attack in Kashmir, and the assassination of the nationalist populist politician Pim Fortuyn increased worries about domestic political polarization (den Boer 2007). Other member states faced similar terrorist threats by their own citizens, as exemplified by the British 'shoe-bomber' Richard Reid. Nevertheless, the new concern with 'home-grown terrorism' did not directly lead to policy-making activity in Brussels. Although the EU had committed to an extensive programme for counterterrorism cooperation after 9/11, it had made little headway into the highly sensitive area of intelligence exchange, which at the time was seen as the most important aspect of terrorism prevention.

This situation changed following terrorist attacks on a Madrid train station in March 2004. The terrorists had chosen commuter trains for their attack and had been overlooked by security forces, who had been focused on higher-profile targets. The Madrid attacks thus underlined the fundamental dilemma faced by counterterrorist organizations: that terrorists can escape detection by choosing unprotected and ordinary civilian targets (Enders and Sandler 2006). These considerations provide a compelling justification for more proactive counter-terrorism policies, which also aim at wider social environments and structures that support terrorist organizations and campaigns. The European Council (EC) clearly recognized this need for a new type of counterterrorism, as seen by its determination to 'address the factors which contribute to support for and recruitment into terrorism' as well as to maintain more traditional policies (EC 2004, 16).

This set a new political direction for EU counterterrorism policy. However, it was far from clear how to proceed in practice. A first round of expert discussions revolved around the question whether 'bottom-up' process of radicalization or 'top-down' recruitment by Al-Qaeda best explained the Madrid attacks (Coelsaet 2010, 867). The incoming Dutch Presidency during the second half of 2004 was critical in forcing a move from such general deliberations to more concrete policy proposals. This was supported by the European Commission, which published an ambitious communication on EU antiterrorism policy in the autumn of 2004 (Commission 2004). This communication listed a wide range of issue areas that could substantiate the new objective of terrorism prevention, such as the need for increased cooperation with civil society, community policing, public–private partnerships and EU support for security research. Most importantly, the Commission coined the term 'violent radicalization', although it also emphasized that radical thought would not be equated with terrorism.

In November 2004 the murder of Dutch film-maker Theo van Gogh underlined the threat posed by extremists individuals rather than organized groups (Peters 2011). This tragic event ensured that the need combat 'violent radicalization' would also become inscribed into the next long-term programme of the EU's Area of Freedom, Security and Justice. The Hague programme, negotiated under the

Dutch EU Presidency, argued that the 'prevention and suppression of terrorism' will be a 'key element in the near future' and that 'a long-term strategy to address the factors which contribute to radicalization and recruitment for terrorist activities' should be developed in the course of a year (EC 2005, 8–9).

Discussions and preparations for this strategy coincided with another serious terrorist attack in London in July 2005. As the attacks on the London public transport system were perpetrated by UK nationals, the response of the UK government focused on improving domestic security measures. Nevertheless, the government also used its incumbent EU presidency to upload the existing UK national counterterrorism strategy to the EU level, listing prevention as one of four fundamental objectives (Council 2005a). This reframing of the EU's fight against terrorism did not immediately lead to new policy proposals, but provided an important reinforcement for negations over the strategy to combat radicalization and recruitment into terrorism. In addition, the European Commission maintained its political support and published a second communication on radicalization, which sought to set out a compromise to reconcile EU cooperation with national prerogatives in sensitive security areas. On the one hand, the Commission deferred to the leadership of member states and acknowledged that terrorism prevention is 'a very complex question with no simple answers and which requires a cautious, modest and well-thought approach' (2005, 2). On the other hand, the Commission argued that 'the EU with its span of policies in various areas that could be used to address violent radicalization, is well placed to gather and spread ... the relevant expertise that is being acquired by the Member States' (3). Thus, existing EU programmes for academic exchanges or labour market integration were cited as a contribution to terrorism prevention, and the Commission committed an additional € 7 million to synthesize research on different aspects of radicalization.

In this way, a string of successful as well as failed terrorist plots between 2002 and 2005 propelled policy-makers to focus on terrorism prevention. The timely advocacy of The Netherlands and UK during their respective EU presidencies, as well as the supportive and mediating role of the European Commission, helped to entrench the issue in the formal policy-making processes. As a result, the strategy against radicalization and recruitment thus passed without much controversy by the end of 2005 (Council 2005b).

The prolonged discussion and negotiation process was also reflected in the contents of the strategy, which touched on a wide range of perspectives. The strategy both endorsed the established focus on disrupting recruitment by Al Qaeda and called for new initiatives to address more dispersed patterns of violent radicalization. Similarly, the document stressed the need to counter misleading extremist messages and underlined the EU's ambition to address the structural grievances of injustice and lack of opportunities. Finally, it aimed for a 'non-emotive lexicon' to discuss terrorism and elaborated on the distinction between radical ideas and the willingness to perpetrate violent acts.

Yet this breadth also resulted in an absence of priorities and realistic objectives. Although the strategy touched on a wide range of possible causes and drivers of terrorism, it did not directly engage with the critical question, namely which kind of ideological, structural or social factors would be most relevant or amenable to policy intervention. This created a large gap between rhetorical objectives of comprehensive action and capacities for effective action. Additionally, towards the end of the very same strategy paper, member states decided to underline their sovereignty concerns:

> [t]he challenge of combating radicalisation and terrorist recruitment lies primarily with the Member States, at a national, regional and local level. They set the social, education and economic policies that can foster … inclusion within mainstream society. It is they who determine foreign, defence and security polices and the manner in which these are publicly communicated. The challenge of radicalism and means to counter it vary greatly in each Member states. (Council 2005b, 6)

Translating concepts into practice

Although the action plan to implement the strategy against radicalization and recruitment remains classified (Council 2005c), resulting difficulties soon became evident. For instance, in 2006 the EU Terrorism Working Groups and EU Situation Centre were asked to make further recommendations to flesh out the action plan (Council 2006a). The document proposed measures to disrupt terrorist recruitment (for example, by focusing on travel patterns or 'hot spots', such as prisons), leaving the problem of early or structural prevention open to debate. In addition, although the EU agreed on a media communication strategy as a means to counter extremist messages (such as by providing support to nonextremist Muslim media sources), it constituted little more than an internal guideline for EU officials to avoid contentious terminology (Council 2006b, 2007a).

In the meantime, the European Commission worked on demonstrating the EU's potential contribution via research policies and knowledge exchange mechanisms. It set up a high-level expert group on radicalization to generate policy advice and extended the budget line for crime prevention to terrorism prevention (Commission 2006; Council 2007b). As a first step, this budget line was used to commission three research studies that investigated the role of social dynamics among migrants and youth, ideology and online networks in processes of radicalization (Change Institute 2008; Dyre and Belaala 2008; Neumann and Brook 2007). Wider research activities on terrorism and violent radicalization were stimulated by a growing number of related calls in the multiannual Framework Programmes for European research funding.[1] Thus, the first review of the implementation of the Strategy on radicalization and recruitment argued optimistically that the EU had 'focused minds on how we can tackle the problem collectively' (Council 2006c, 2).

Barely a year later, the newly appointed EU Counterterrorism Coordinator Gilles de Kerchove[2] admitted to the lack of concrete results and continued political ambiguity:

> EU policy in the field of radicalisation and recruitment, particularly in the area of integration, is the result of a compromise between Member States whose traditions and policies sometimes divergence. In consequence, the wording of some of the

---

[1] Some projects under the sixth framework programme began to investigate the issue of radicalization; the following seventh round would include specific calls for European research funding.

[2] Mr de Kerchove had previously played a leading role in the formulation of the EU's counterterrorism policy from within the Council Secretariat.

recommendations in the Strategy and the classified Action Plan attached to it is vague and difficult to translate into operational action ... fresh ideas for implementation ... need to be developed. (Council 2007c, 8)

Subsequent attempts to address these deficits branched out into two different directions: first, towards more fragmented operational cooperation among a subset of member states; second, towards increased EU regulation to disrupt recruitment. Backed with a new resolution by the Council of Ministers that was triggered by new terrorist plots (Council 2008a), the EU Counterterrorism coordinator aimed to improve exchanges among national security actors (Council 2008b). A handful of member states were designated as 'lead countries' for different aspects of terrorism prevention, such as community policing, countering propaganda or relations with civil society. Although this broadened the range of initiatives that were discussed at the EU level, these initiatives mostly built on preestablished national programmes. Germany, for example, would lead on the question of monitoring online communications, as it had already set up a related pilot programme two years earlier (Council 2006c).

That this pragmatic approach deemphasized the need for common EU action was underlined by the simultaneous formation of the so-called Policy Planners Network on countering polarization and radicalization.[3] Again, the UK and The Netherlands provided the initial impulse to set up a more informal group of eight member states that were particularly interested in this issue area.[4] Discussions of this policy network have not been made public, but they clearly run in parallel to the EU's efforts. For instance, a UK think-tank that provides support to the Policy Planners' Network also fed into EU conferences on radicalization (Institute for Strategic Dialogue 2010) and attracted a grant from the European Commission for collecting related information sources.[5] Such connections demonstrated that interested national actors used the EU as a discussion platform and financial resource, but did not rely on the EU for informal and horizontal cooperation.

The concluding report from the Commission-sponsored expert group on radicalization was not published (Expert Group on Violent Radicalization 2008). Nonpublication or a lack of dissemination can be explained both by recourse to political factors and the inherent difficulties of the issue area. In 2008, the change of Commissioner for Justice and Home Affairs from Franco Frattini to Jacques Barrot led to a lack of continuity in political support. In addition, the Expert Group highlighted the fragmented state of research, arguing that the concept of radicalization remained problematic. Although the latter argument constituted an important warning, it also meant that the report of the expert group did not lend support to concrete policy proposals, making it vulnerable to dismissal as an academic exercise.

Similar considerations applied to the three studies on radicalization dynamics (Change Institute 2008; Dyre and Belaala 2008; Neumann and Brook 2007) that had been commissioned in 2006. At the risk of oversimplification, the studies argued that the socioeconomic situation of Muslim minorities was likely to be important than purely ideological factors. They also argued that, although radical

---

[3] <http://www.strategicdialogue.org/islam-diversity-social-cohesion/ppn/>.
[4] <http://www.strategicdialogue.org/policy-planners-network/>.
[5] <https://www.counterextremism.org/resources > .

online material was significant, it remained secondary to personal interactions in Mosques or recruitment 'hot spots' such as prisons. However, although some of these speculations could be identified in national pilot projects (see below), the lack of EU authority in related policy fields meant that the studies could not be followed by new Commission initiatives in the area of education, social integration or penal institutions.

Instead, the Commission aimed to increase the EU's visible contribution by a means of legislative proposals. It proposed to amend the existing EU framework decision on combating terrorism[6] to criminalize 'preparatory' acts of terrorism in all EU member states. 'Preparatory' included travel to training camps and material support to terrorist groups, as well as public statements that could be construed as 'incitement' of terrorism. Problematically, the expansion of repressive legal instruments for the disruption of recruitment and propaganda was not balanced by new initiatives for early prevention, that is, measures to reduce the likelihood that certain groups or individuals would turn to radical propaganda (Mellinger 2010, Ronen 2010).

Further attempts to buttress the EU's 'added value'

Over the following months it became increasingly evident that the lead country approach generated only limited results that could be applied across multiple EU member states. Germany, Austria and France jointly drafted and disseminated a handbook on radicalization processes in prisons, and Spain and France produced guidance on the public training of Imams (Council 2009a). Although these handbooks remain classified, so that making assessment of their substantive impact or usefulness remains speculative, officials[7] have argued that their use remains entirely voluntary and that the peculiarities of each national security or education systems limit cooperation or standardization. Other national lead projects, such as on community relations, were even more informal in nature and some failed to attract collaboration from more than one member state.

Only the German lead project on monitoring extremist websites constituted a significant exception to the paucity of standardization. In this case the technological possibilities of transnational information- and burden-sharing were easy to define and resonated with EUROPOL's improving capacities for the aggregation and analysis of data on Islamist terrorism via its electronic information systems (the so-called Analytical Work Files). Over the following years, EUROPOL went on to assume a growing role in online communications surveillance and analysis with regard to terrorism and terrorist propaganda (Bureš 2011).

These limited and narrowly focused outcomes were critically reviewed in Brussels, leading to a revision of the EU's action plan to combat radicalization and recruitment into terrorism (Council 2009b). As the then Swedish Presidency failed in its attempt to make this document public, it is impossible to make more precise statements about the scope of these revisions. But it is clear that the main impulse

---

[6] In 2002, this EU framework decision had provided a common definition of terrorism and required member states to approximate the related criminal law provisions.

[7] Interviews in national interior ministries, November 2010.

for a new direction in EU preventive counterterrorism came from a different direction. The next multiannual programme for the EU's Area of Freedom, Security and Justice, which was concluded during the Swedish Presidency, reinstated the ambition for an effective and wide-ranging prevention policy. Specifically, the Stockholm Programme called for more efforts to combat discrimination, achieve early detection of radicalization and to evaluate existing policy instruments at both European and national levels (EC 2010, 52).

The following EU presidencies took up the call, but could not achieve a breakthrough. In the first half of 2010, Spain proposed a standardized format for exchanging information on 'radicalization episodes'. This proposal was regarded as overly complicated or formalistic by other member states,[8] and was only adopted as a nonbinding recommendation (Council 2010a). The subsequent Belgian presidency promoted the involvement of civil society to counter radicalization at an early stage. But due to highly divergent state-society relations in Europe, this initiative equally did not move beyond another Council recommendation of largely symbolic value (Council 2010b). A related Belgian pilot project of 'community policing' generated a small handbook that patrolling police officers could use to recognize symbols of radical ideologies. However, it has been claimed that the project was initiated for political reasons to produce a tangible policy output on terrorism prevention during the Belgian EU presidency.[9]

Meanwhile, the European Commission reverted to knowledge generation and exchange activities, which corresponded with the emphasis on evaluation and best practice exchange within the Stockholm programme. It reinstated the expert group on radicalization on a more permanent basis. To ensure greater visibility beyond expert seminars, the network now features a website that aims to provide authoritative definitions for terrorist-related concepts.[10]

The Commission also committed €5 million per year to support a horizontal network among subnational authorities, the so-called Radicalisation Awareness Network (RAN), designed to increase best practice exchanges in the area of terrorism prevention. This proposal had already been highlighted in the Stockholm programme (EC 2010, 52) and could be seen as a fitting answer to the reservations set out in the EU strategy on combating violent radicalization. Specifically, horizontal and voluntary exchanges among lower-level national actors could sidestep national sovereignty concerns and draw on a wealth of operational project experience across Europe. Such transnational networks among experts or subnational authorities have been a common factor in EU integration processes (Hooghe and Marks 2001).

In particular, in 2001 the EU formed a professional network on crime prevention, which was given a new political basis during the negotiation period on the Stockholm programme (Council 2009c). In addition, between 2005 and 2007 the Commission funded a pilot project on counterterrorism cooperation between cities, which built on an existing Council of Europe Forum for Urban Security.[11] These precedents help to explain the decision to create the RAN network, which is discussed in more detail further below.

---

[8] Interview with counterterrorism official, April 2011.

[9] Personal conversation with the author at conference workshop.

[10] <http://www.ec-ener.eu/home>.

[11] <http://www.efus.eu/>.

The prospects of EU best practice exchange on counterterrorism

EU counterradicalization policy, therefore, started with an 'upload' of national concepts from The Netherlands and the UK; subsequent policy diffusion from the EU level to other member states has been highly limited. Competing political interests—due to different threat profiles or different preferences over the desirable extent of political integration—partly explain this trajectory (Bossong 2008; Kaunert 2007). Driven by short-term considerations and terrorist shocks, member states have symbolically agreed to face pressing security issue together. However, when it comes to substantive cooperation, divergent national interests have frustrated progress. This tendency is only countered by EU institutions acting as policy entrepreneurs in order to increase their standing in a new area of European integration. Occasionally they have succeeded when favourable political circumstances and timing, such as a pro-European presidency and the scheduled adoption of a long-term policy programme, have worked in their favour. By and large, however, member states are careful to maintain their national sovereignty, which results in endemic gaps between 'comprehensive' EU strategies or action plans and national implementation.

The remainder of this contribution seeks to develop another perspective. The previous section mentioned that both EU member states and EU institutions sponsored research and experimented with different cooperation formats to minimize such political conflicts over the limits of EU integration. Was this only a second rate strategy, or could the EU's efforts for knowledge generation and best practice exchange eventually generate substantial results? The most recent proposal to create the Radicalisation Awareness Network provides a useful focus to address this question. In the following, three related critical issues are reviewed: first, the inherent complexity, uncertainty and contentious nature of terrorism prevention; second, the political context of evaluating counterterrorism measures; and third, the challenges of implementing new knowledge in 'frontline' organizations.

The problem of knowledge about preventive policies

The case of the 'expert group on radicalization', which was first sponsored and then discontinued by the European Commission, illustrates that epistemic communities and scientific knowledge are subject to significant constraints in contentious policy areas (Boswell 2008; Monaghan 2010).[12] Moreover, the group could not claim to present an authoritative consensus. In a recent review of the academic literature, Daalgard-Nielsen (2010) argues that radicalization research remains divided into three different schools, which accentuate social and political modernization, internal group dynamics or individual dislocating experiences respectively.

These three schools cut across analyses that emphasize processes within European societies, or that focus on international or external developments, the latter even if terrorist attacks may nonetheless be carried out in Europe. The

---

[12] For a contrasting argument that defends the epistemic community approach in European security policy, see Cross (2011).

analysis of 'root causes' of terrorism also intersects with a continuing debate on whether terrorism should be regarded as an individually or socially rational activity (van Um 2009; Wilner and Dubouloz 2011; Pisoiu 2012). That is, should terrorist activities not only be accounted for by recourse to powerful social or individual factors and experiences, but also be considered as a risky, but rational choice, which occasionally generates high benefits to the perpetrators?

Further divides can be made out between academic studies on international jihadists (Sageman 2008) and 'home-grown' terrorists in Europe. This does not only apply to the persistent or possibly even growing threat from nationalist or left-wing extremists that have long historical roots in various European member states (Egene 2004). Even within the supposedly transnational milieu of Islamic radicals, one can make out clear differences in socialization and background in Europe (Bakker 2011).

These persistent and complex debates continue to stimulate high quality research, but do not lead to authoritative policy recommendations for preventive counterterrorism or counterradicalization policies. At a high level of abstraction, the growing body of economic research on terrorism has supported the usefulness of counterterrorism approaches that employ both positive and negative incentives (Frey and Luechinger 2003; Brzoska et al 2011). One can also point to increasingly integrated models that attempt to specify which set of structural conditions rationality assumptions and group processes are most relevant in relation to different terrorist organizations or individual perpetrators (King and Taylor 2011).[13] However, at the time of writing this research is simply too recent and includes too many contextual variables to be considered as a solid basis for expert or epistemic community-driven policy-making.

This state of the art could be seen to increase the appeal of the proposed network for radicalization awareness. In particular, a 'community of practice' for counterterrorism officials could diffuse more embedded and less formalized forms of knowledge (Freeman 2007). A practice-centred approach could also generate common professional norms such as appropriate behaviour for dealing with 'radical' groups whilst avoiding stigmatizing practices that backfire over the long term. A practice-oriented network could finally support one of the few shared points of the academic literature on radicalization, namely the need to differentiate from case to case and to emphasize the role of social context over abstract arguments, such as a 'clash of cultures'. This is because policy interventions at the subnational or local level are likely to target contextual conditions, such as education structures, social services or job opportunities, whereas a confrontation of ideological world-views or the criminalization of radical propaganda typically requires senior policy-makers or public leaders.

However, due to its very informality and openness, a community of practice cannot reliably address the question of which type of policy intervention or programme deserves to be labelled as 'good' or 'best' practice. In the case of preventive counterterrorism policy, this problem is especially acute. The successful execution of an attack does not necessarily say much about the failure

---

[13] For instance, attacks by lone wolves are more likely to be related to specific dislocating experiences, whereas terrorist campaigns are more determined by endogenous group dynamics.

of a particular preventive policy, as it may still decrease the overall number of attacks or may only work in concert with a wide set of contextual factors (van Dongen 2009). And if no attacks take place, it is even more difficult to establish causal effects. Such counterfactual arguments remain inherently contentious, as the absence of or decrease in terrorist attacks could be attributed to a multitude of factors other than deliberate political intervention (Cronin 2009). This explains why studies that focus on the effectiveness of counterterrorism policies are limited in number and have yet to generate a coherent framework for evaluation (Pisoiu and van Um 2011).

Political pressures on counterterrorism policy

From a political perspective, it remains unclear how to assess counterterrorism projects across European countries and across different level of government. At the time of writing, significant evaluations in counterterrorism remain dependent on national policy-making structures. In December 2011, the European Parliament drew on its expanded role in EU security policy under the Lisbon Treaty and called for a comprehensive evaluation of the fight against terrorism. The European Parliament resolution outlined a wide range of actors and issues that would have to be covered in such an exercise. Yet such an evaluation process critically hinges on the active participation of national parliaments, which have also been given an increased power of review under article 70.

By 2013 little progress could be made out. Parliamentary control mechanisms on security policy showed no tendency of convergence across European member states and remained subject to domestic political considerations. In a nutshell, member states remain divided by diverse legal and institutional provisions, which conditioned the acceptability of different counterterrorism policies (Foley 2009), as well as by divergent security perceptions and interests (such as with regard to different kind of terrorism or the relative weight of terrorism *vis-à-vis* other threats) (Meyer 2009).

At the time of writing, the UK is the only EU member state to have subjected its preventive counterterrorism measures to an authoritative review by Lord Carlile of Berriew (2011). This review contained no reference to the European level, instead discussing domestic relations between security actors and various social or ethnic groups. It also should be noted that the review sidelined many of the contentious scientific or empirical questions outlined above by drawing on the political and legal authority of the House of Lords. As a result, some controversial aspects in UK counterterrorism policy, such as financial support for former radicals and linkages between social integration policies and counterterrorism, were cut back.

The national political framework for evaluating counterterrorism policies needs to be kept in mind when assessing the prospects of the EU network on radicalization awareness. As discussed above, horizontal expert networks can serve as a channel to bypass or influence national interests that block formal EU policy-making. The ideal of this kind of expert-driven multilevel governance (Hooghe and Marks 2001) should lead to a transnational policy community that may generate new professional norms and policy approaches.

However, even if EU cooperation on internal security has long passed the stage of 'high' or intergovernmental politics, there are limits to a more horizontal and depoliticized approach. The sensitivity of preventive counterterrorism programmes requires authoritative and accountable political decisions that cannot be taken by lower-level authorities or operational security actors in isolation. This is most readily evident with regard to the question whether public authorities should engage with nonviolent radicals to prevent terrorism, which divides security experts both within and across European member states (Vidino 2009). Moreover, decisions on this issue are also conditioned by the wide variety of extremist groups as well as competing security interests across EU member states. In short, although the network might collect a wide range of possible policy interventions, it cannot decide whether certain security practices should be discontinued or receive prioritized funding with any authority.

The use of knowledge in implementing organizations

This leads to a final political challenge that arises from the gap between international knowledge diffusion and operational practice. The contrast between hierarchical policy-making and the autonomy of 'street-level' bureaucrats is a persistent concern of public administration and implementation studies (Brodkin 2011). For instance, the political ideal of 'evidence-based policing' contrasts with the entrenched organizational routines, prejudices and political interests of police authorities (Lum et al 2011). This equally applies to other institutions with extensive operational responsibility and experience, such as educational establishments or social service providers. Such bureaucratic obstacles, or cultural resistance, are another argument for supporting horizontal networks, which provide room for bottom-up experience and may increase voluntary involvement by 'frontline actors' (Freeman 2007).

However, it is insufficient to aim for participatory networks, flat hierarchies and an open exchange of ideas. Significant organizational learning and policy reform on the basis of new knowledge and experience also require dedicated resources for knowledge codification, dissemination and training (Benner and Rotmann 2008; Contandriopoulos et al 2010). Furthermore, informal networks between security practitioners raise the problem of accountability (den Boer et al 2008). Beyond high-level political control and review activities by senior political actors (see above), transparency should be facilitated by regular reporting and identifiable management structures. Effective governance networks need to strike a balance between proximity and accessibility to implementing actors, and shared or centralized capacities for information processing and management.

The EU's official evaluation of the European Crime Prevention Network determined that the network lacked administrative support structures to maintain a constant level of activity and to collect and disseminate good practices (Council 2009c). However, Bullock and Eckblom (2010) have argued that problems run deeper. Although the network actually produced a database of preventive crime programmes in various European member states, this information needs to be of more consistent quality to influence practice. In other words, aside from the general debates on counterterrorism effectiveness and 'roots' of terrorism outlined above, administrators and policy-makers need to develop a more coherent system for quality control, reporting and benchmarking on existing preventive projects. This is required to move from single case studies or anecdotal evidence about 'what works' to transferable and scalable interventions and policy instruments.

The European Commission promised to support the proposed radicalization awareness network with €5 million per year. This should be sufficient for a permanent secretariat and basic structures for information management (websites, databases, conference reports). However, this sum does not seem to allow for the development of more rigorous data collection and analysis procedures across the EU. Perhaps some of these tasks may be undertaken by parallel research funding. However, if this is the case then links to the RAN network need to be specified more clearly.

Most importantly, the budget line is insufficient to ensure a timely and widespread dissemination of experiences and practices across the whole of the EU. In a different context the European Commission supported a UK institute that focuses on the relation between counterterrorism prevention and training of local staff.[14] This latter example illustrates the kind of investments that might be needed across European member states. Unless the EU Commission changes funding priorities from research on radicalization to training, or significantly boosts overall investment levels, the proposed network is more likely to deepen strategy subgroups, such as the Policy Planners' Network on Radicalization, whereas most member states and local authorities in Europe will likely remain indifferent.

This outcome could be viewed as justifiable, in so far as terrorist threat levels remain highly divergent across member states. However, such an outcome can also be viewed as suboptimal, as policy improvements are less likely to be adopted by nonleading actors, and terrorist organizations could still tactically relocate to areas where they face little countervailing pressures from preventive policies. Recent research on the growth of transnational municipal networks in other areas of European integration which highlights the tradeoff between network inclusiveness and scope of network outputs, could also be used to test this prediction in a more systematic manner (Kern and Bulkeley 2009).

Conclusions

This article has analysed the evolution and 'added value' of the EU's preventive counterterrorism policy, which has become linked to the wider development of the Area of Freedom, Security and Justice. The repeated shock of terrorist attacks by EU nationals and the advocacy of rotating EU presidencies and the European Commission, has led to a dynamic expansion of the EU's counterterrorism agenda. However, the EU's strategy to combat radicalization and recruitment into terrorism has also underlined the limits to further integration. As a result, policy-makers have experimented with flexible integration; the Commission has generally emphasized research support and knowledge exchange. EU-sponsored research has highlighted the diversity and complexity of the terrorist challenge, but concrete policies and pilot projects have largely accentuated repression policies over early prevention. In light of these limited outcomes and persistent

---

[14] < www.recora.eu/ >.

divergence among member states' involvement in terrorism prevention, the Stockholm Programme emphasized lower levels of government and support for the horizontal exchange of experiences among experts.

The second part of this article explored the prospects of the proposed network for radicalization awareness. Three main obstacles were discussed. First, the scientific and methodological challenges to define 'good' or 'best' preventive counterterrorism practices; second, political pressures that either work against more evidence-based counterterrorism policy or that favour authoritative political decisions at the national level; and third, the resource requirements for transmitting new knowledge and practice to inert or resistant street-level organizations. Therefore, the proposed network of local and professional actors could make a step forward, but should not be expected to provide a breakthrough for EU cooperation on terrorism prevention. A few interested actors are likely to utilize the additional opportunities and resources of the network to continue the transnational exchange of experiences in this issue area. This could, for instance, apply to the existing 'policy planner network' on radicalization that unites eight member states. Yet, due to the lack of scientific and political consensus on policy priorities in the fight against terrorism, significant and widespread changes and standardization across all EU member states should not be expected.

Notes on contributor

Raphael Bossong is lecturer in European Studies at the European University Viadrina, Frankfurt, and researcher at the Institute for Peace Research and Security Policy, Hamburg. He holds a BA in Social and Political Sciences from the University of Cambridge, and a MA and PhD in International Relations from the London School of Economics and Political Sciences. His research, which has appeared in leading international peer-reviewed journals, focuses on the intersection between EU crisis management, internal and external security policy, and public administration. He recently published a monographic study on the historical evolution of EU security and counterterrorism policy since 9/11.

References

Argomaniz, Javier (2011) *The EU and counter-terrorism: politics, polity and policies after 9/11* (Abingdon: Routledge)

Bakker, Edwin (2011) 'Jihadi terrorist in Europe and global Salafi jihadis' in Rik Coolsaet (ed) *Jihadi terrorism and the radicalization challenge in Europe* (Aldershot: Ashgate), 131–145

Benner, Thorsten and Phillip Rotmann (2008) 'Learning to learn? UN peacebuilding and the challenges of building a learning organization', *Journal of Intervention and Statebuilding*, 2:1, 43–62

Bossong, Raphael (2008) 'The action plan on combating terrorism: a flawed instrument of EU security governance', *Journal of Common Market Studies*, 46:1, 27–48

Boswell, Christina (2008) 'The political functions of expert knowledge, knowledge and legitimation in European Union immigration policy', *Journal of European Public Policy*, 15:4, 471–488

Brodkin, Evelyn (2011) 'Putting street-level organizations first: new directions for social policy and management research', *Journal of Public Administration Research and Theory*, 21:2, 199–201

Brzoska, Michael, Eric van Um and Raphael Bossong (2011) 'Security economics in the European context – implications of the EUSECON project', EUSECON Working Paper (58)

Bullock, Karen and Peter Ekblom (2010) 'Richness, retrievability and reliability—issues in a working knowledge base for good practice in crime prevention', *European Journal on Criminal Policy and Research*, 16:1, 29–47

Bureš, Oldrich (2011) *EU counterterrorism policy: a paper tiger?* (Farnham: Ashgate)

Change Institute (2008) *Studies into violent radicalisation: Lot 2. The beliefs ideologies and narratives: a study carried out for the European Commission* (London: Change Institute)

Commission of the European Communities (2004) 'Communication from the Commission to the Council and the European Parliament Prevention, preparedness and response to terrorist attack', COM(2004) 698 final

Commission of the European Communities (2005) 'Communication from the Commission to the Council and the European Parliament concerning terrorist recruitment, addressing the factors contributing to violent radicalisation', COM(2005) 313 final

Commission of the European Communities (2006) 'Commission decision of 19 April 2006 setting up a group of experts to provide policy advice to the Commission on fighting violent radicalisation (2006/299/EC)', *Official Journal*, L:111, 9–11

Commission of the European Communities (2010) 'The EU internal security strategy in action: five steps towards a more secure Europe', COM(2010)673

Contandriopoulos, Damien, Marc Lemire, Jean-Louis Denis and Emile Tremblay (2010) 'Knowledge exchange processes in organizations and policy arenas: a narrative systematic review of the literature', *Milbank Quarterly*, 88:4, 444–483

Coolsaet, Rik (2010) 'EU counterterrorism strategy: value added or chimera?', *International Affairs*, 86:4, 857–873

Coolsaet, Rik (2011) 'Counterterrorism and counter-radicalisation in Europe: how much unity in diversity?' in Rik Coolsaet (ed) *Jihadi terrorism and the radicalisation challenge in Europe*, second edition (Aldershot: Ashgate), 227–246

Council of the European Union (2002) 'Council conclusions on EU external action against terrorism', 11037/1/02

Council of the European Union (2005a) 'The European Union counter-terrorism strategy', 14469/3/05

Council of the European Union (2005b) 'The European Union Strategy for combating radicalisation and recruitment to terrorism', 14347/05

Council of the European Union (2005c) 'The European Union action plan for combating radicalisation and recruitment to terrorism', 14348/05

Council of the European Union (2006a) 'Policy recommendations on counter-terrorism', 8205/06

Council of the European Union (2006b) 'Media communication strategy', 10862/2/06

Council of the European Union (2006c) 'Implementation report of the radicalisation and recruitment strategy and action plan', 15386/06

Council of the European Union (2007a) 'Revised media communication strategy', 5469/3/07

Council of the European Union (2007b) 'Decision 2007/125/JHA of 12 February 2007 establishing for the period 2007 to 2013, as part of General Programme on Security and Safeguarding Liberties, the Specific Programme "Prevention of and Fight against Crime"', *Official Journal*, L:58, 7

Council of the European Union (2007c) 'Implementation of the EU counter-terrorism strategy—discussion paper', 15448/07

Council of the European Union (2008a) 'Council conclusions on enhancing cooperation in the area of countering radicalisation and recruitment to terrorism', 10928/08

Council of the European Union (2008b) 'Summary of discussions', 12072/08

Council of the European Union (2009a) 'Report on the activities of the Working Party on Terrorism', 16882/09

Council of the European Union (2009b) 'Revised EU radicalisation and recruitment action plan', 15374/09

Council of the European Union (2009c) 'Council decision 2009/902/JHA of 30 November 2009 setting up a European Crime Prevention Network (EUCPN) and repealing Decision 2001/427/JHA', *Official Journal*, L:321, 44–46

Council of the European Union (2010a) 'Council conclusions on the use of a standardised, multidimensional semi-structured instrument for collecting data and information on the processes of radicalisation in the EU', 8570/10

Council of the European Union (2010b) 'Council conclusions on the role of the police and civil society in combating violent radicalisation and recruitment of terrorists', 16178/10

Council of the European Union (2012) 'Preventing lone actor terrorism—food for thought', 9090/12

Cronin, Audrey K (2009) *How terrorism ends: understanding the decline and demise of terrorist campaigns* (Princeton: Princeton University Press)

Cross, Mai'a (2011) *Security integration in Europe: how knowledge-based networks are transforming the European Union* (Michigan: University of Michigan Press)

Dalgaard-Nielsen, Anja (2010) 'Violent radicalization in Europe: what we know and what we do not know', *Studies in Conflict and Terrorism*, 33:9, 797–814

den Boer, Monica (2007) 'Wake-up call for the Lowlands: Dutch counterterrorism from a comparative perspective', *Cambridge Review of International Affairs*, 20:2, 285–302

Den Boer, Monica, Claudia Hillebrand and Andreas Noelke (2008) 'Legitimacy under pressure: the European web of counter-terrorism networks' *JCMS: Journal of Common Market Studies*, 46:1, 101–124

Dittrich, Mirjam (2007) 'Radicalisation and recruitment: the EU response' in David Spence (ed) *The European Union and terrorism* (London: John Harper Publishing), 54–70

Dyre, A and S Belaala (2008) Les facteurs de création ou de modification des processus de radicalisation violente, chez les jeunes en particulier. Une étude réalisée par CEIS pour la Commission Européenne. Compagnie Européenne d'Intelligence Stratégique (CEIS)

Egene, JO (2004) *Terrorism in Western Europe: explaining the trends since 1950* (Cheltenham, UK; Northhampton, MA: Edward Elgar)

Enders, Walter and Todd Sandler (2006) *The political economy of terrorism* (Cambridge: Cambridge University Press)

European Council (2004) 'Declaration on combating terrorism', <http://consiliumeuropaeu/uedocs/cmsUpload/79635.pdf>, accessed 25 November 2011

European Council (2005) 'The Hague Programme: strengthening freedom, security and justice in the European Union', *Official Journal of the European Union*, C:53, 1–14

European Council (2010) 'The Stockholm Programme—an open and secure Europe serving and protecting citizens', *Official Journal of the European Union*, C:115, 1–37

Expert Group on Violent Radicalisation (2008) 'Radicalisation processes leading to acts of terrorism: a concise report prepared by the European Commission's Expert Group on Violent Radicalisation', <http://www.rikcoolsaet.be/files/art_ip_wz/Expert%20Group%20Report%20Violent%20Radicalisation%20FINAL.pdf>, accessed 28 November 2011

Foley, Frank (2009) 'Reforming counterterrorism: institutions and organizational routines in Britain and France', *Security Studies*, 18:3, 435–478

Freeman, Richard (2007) 'Epistemological bricolage: how practitioners make sense of learning', *Administration and Society*, 39:4, 476–496

Frey, Bruno and Simon Luechinger (2003) 'How to fight terrorism: alternatives to deterrence', *Defence and Peace Economics*, 14:137, 237–249

Githens-Mazer, Jeremy and Richard Lambert (2010) 'Why conventional wisdom on radicalization fails: the persistence of a failed discourse', *International Affairs*, 86:4, 889–901

Hooghe, Lisbeth and Garz Marks (2001) *Multi-level governance and European integration* (Lanham: Rowman and Littlefield)

Institute for Strategic Dialogue (2010) 'The role of civil society in counter-radicalisation and the de-radicalisation: a working paper on the European Policy Planners' network on countering radicalisation and polarisation', <http://wwwstrategicdialogueorg/PPN%20Paper%20-%20Community%20Engagement_FORWEBSITE.pdf>, accessed 25 November 2011

Jackson, Richard (2005) *Writing the war on terrorism, language, politics, and counter-terrorism* (Manchester: Manchester University Press)

Jenkins, B (2012) 'Al Qaeda in its third decade: irreversible decline or imminent victory?', *RAND Occasional Paper*, 362

Kaunert, Christian (2007) 'Without the power of purse or sword: the European arrest warrant and the role of the Commission', *Journal of European Integration*, 29:4, 387–404

Kern, Kristine and Harriet Bulkeley (2009) 'Cities, Europeanization and multi-level governance: governing climate change through transnational municipal networks', *Journal of Common Market Studies*, 47:2, 309–332

King, Michael and Donald M Taylor (2011) 'The radicalization of homegrown Jihadists: a review of theoretical models and social psychological evidence', *Terrorism and Political Violence*, 23:4, 602–622

Lord Carlile of Berriew (2011) 'Report to the Home Secretary of independent oversight of prevent review and strategy', <http://wwwhomeofficegovuk/publications/counter-terrorism/prevent/prevent-strategy/lord-carlile-report?view=Binary>, accessed 25 November 2011

Lum, Cynthia, Christoper Koper and Cody Telep (2011) 'The evidence-based policing matrix', *Journal of Experimental Criminology*, 7:1, 3–26

Mellinger, Lauren (2010) 'Illusions of security: why the amended EU framework decision criminalizing "incitement to terrorism" on the internet fails to defend Europe from terrorism', *Syracause Journal of International Law and Commerce*, 37:2, 339–368

Meyer, Christoph (2009) 'International terrorism as a force of homogenization? A constructivist approach to understanding cross-national threat perceptions and responses', *Cambridge Review of International Affairs*, 22:4, 647–666

Monaghan, Mark (2010) 'The complexity of evidence: reflections on research utilisation in a heavily politicised policy area', *Social Policy and Society*, 9:1, 1–12

Mueller, John (2010) 'Assessing measures designed to protect the homeland', *Policy Studies Journal*, 38:1, 1–21

Neumann, PR and R Brook (2007) *Recruitment and mobilisation for the Islamist militant movement in Europe: a study carried out by King's College London for the European Commission* (London: King's College London)

Pantazis, Christina and Simon Pemberton (2009) 'From the "old" to the "new" suspect community', *British Journal of Criminology*, 49:5, 646–666

Peters, Rudolph (2011) 'Dutch extremist Islamism: van Gogh's murder and his ideas' in Rik Coolsaet (ed) *Jihadi terrorism and the radicalisation challenge*, second edition (Farnham: Ashgate), 145–160

Pisoiu, Daniela (2012) *Islamist radicalisation in Europe: an occupational change process* (Abingdon: Routledge)

Pisoiu, Daniela and Eric van Um (2011) 'Effective counterterrorism: what have we learned so far?', *EUSECON Working Paper*, 55

Richards, Anthony (2011) 'The problem with "radicalization", the remit of "prevent" and the need to refocus on terrorism in the UK', *International Affairs*, 87:1, 143–152

Ronen, Yael (2010) 'Incitement to terrorist acts and international law', *Leiden Journal of International Law*, 23:3, 645–674

Sageman, Marc (2008) *Leaderless jihad: terror networks in the twenty-first century* (Philadelphia: University of Pennsylvania Press)

Schmitt, E (2012) 'Intelligence report lists Iran and cyberattacks as leading concerns', *New York Times*, <http://www.nytimes.com/2012/02/01/world/intelligence-chief-sees-al-qaeda-likely-to-continue-fragmenting.html>, accessed 4 May 2012

van Dongen, Teun (2009) 'Break it down: an alternative approach to measuring effectiveness in counterterrorism', *Economics of Security Working Paper*, 23

van Um, Eric (2009) 'Discussing concepts of terrorist rationality: implications for counterterrorism policy', *EUSECON Working Paper*, 22

Vidino, Lorenzo (2009) 'Europe's new security dilemma', *Washington Quarterly*, 32:4, 61–75

Wilner, AS and C-J Dubouloz (2011) 'Transformative radicalization: applying learning theory to Islamist radicalization', *Studies in Conflict and Terrorism*, 34:5, 418–438

Whither the withering democratic deficit? The impact of the Lisbon Treaty on the Area of Freedom, Security and Justice

John D Occhipinti
Canisius College

Abstract   *This article examines how the Lisbon Treaty's changes to the European Union's (EU's) Area of Freedom, Security and Justice (AFSJ) have affected its 'democratic deficit'. How this issue is perceived depends on one's conceptual understanding of democratic legitimacy. This article reviews key scholarly perspectives on this matter and organizes these according to Schmidt's concepts of 'inputs', 'throughputs' and 'outputs'. The article then applies this framework to specific innovations of the Lisbon Treaty, including new roles for the European Parliament and Court of Justice in the AFSJ. The article concludes that the EU's latest treaty has improved its democratic deficit in some regards, but that many issues of democratic legitimacy remain.*

Introduction

The European Union's (EU's) third and most recent multi-year agenda for its Area of Freedom, Security and Justice (AFSJ), the Stockholm Programme, provides a set of guiding principles and objectives regarding the full range of issues connected with justice and home affairs (JHA). In substance, but especially in tone, this agenda for the AFSJ is distinct from its forerunners due to its focus on citizens and emphasis on fundamental rights. The section on 'Political priorities' begins,

> The European Council considers that a priority for the coming years will be to focus on the interests and needs of citizens. The challenge will be to ensure respect for fundamental freedoms and integrity while guaranteeing security in Europe. It is of paramount importance that law enforcement measures and measures to safeguard individual rights, the rule of law, international protection rules go hand in hand in the same direction and are mutually reinforced. All actions taken in the future should be centred on the citizen and other persons for whom the EU has a responsibility. (European Council 2010, 3–4)

Though its ultimate outcome may indeed vary from its lofty intentions, the Stockholm Programme's emphasis on fundamental rights means that the time is right to consider a related issue, namely the very democratic nature of the AFSJ.

Over the years, there has been much debate among political theorists of European integration about the EU's so-called 'democratic deficit', but this discussion has rarely focused on or even mentioned its AFSJ. The same was the case during the era of the EU's original 'third pillar' dealing with JHA. All of this is surprising because it could be argued that the democratic deficit has long been

45

more pronounced concerning JHA and the AFSJ than any other aspect of the EU due to the long-standing marginal role of the European Parliament (EP). This has changed under the Treaty of Lisbon (ToL), but does it mean that the democratic deficit has been significantly addressed? This article argues that the answer to this question depends on one's conceptual understanding of democratic legitimacy, and so the perceived impact of the ToL's changes to the AFSJ on the democratic deficit will vary according to the various perspectives that are discussed in this article.

The article begins with an account of the general scholarly debate on the EU's democratic deficit, focusing on the main ways that it has been conceptualized in the literature. This, in turn, provides an analytical framework for examining whether and how the ToL has addressed the democratic deficit regarding the AFSJ. Then the specific innovations brought by the ToL regarding the AFSJ will be examined, especially the new roles for the EP. The article also describes how the ToL has further addressed the democratic deficit by changing the role of national parliaments and granting new jurisdiction to the renamed Court of Justice of the European Union (CJEU) concerning the AFSJ. The concluding sections of this article examine the democratic deficit regarding the AFSJ according to the framework established earlier in the article and elucidate areas for future research, including many topics connected with the Stockholm Programme.

Conceptualizing the democratic deficit

Critics who point out a democratic deficit in the EU are essentially questioning its democratic legitimacy. The contemporary scholarly and theoretical debate on this issue has its roots in the 1990s and includes the much cited work of Giandomenico Majone (1998). Majone argued that critiques of the democratic deficit were overblown, given that the EU is best conceptualized as a kind of regulatory state that should not be judged according to the same kind of legitimizing criteria as a traditional nation state. While this assertion is supported by some more recent scholarship, another one of his claims is not, namely, that 'arguments about the democratic deficit are really arguments about the nature, function, and goals of the EC [European Community]' (Majone 1998, 6).

To the contrary, the contemporary debate on the democratic deficit stems mostly from different philosophical understandings of 'democracy' itself (Scharpf 2009). Thus, examining whether and how the ToL has addressed the democratic deficit concerning the AFSJ requires some precision as to the general nature of the perceived democratic deficit itself. In her recent work, Vivien Schmidt has usefully conceptualized the main dimensions of this issue as (1) participation-oriented 'inputs', (2) process-oriented 'throughputs' and (3) policy outcome-oriented 'outputs' (Schmidt 2013). The institutional changes brought on by the ToL, especially regarding AFSJ, can be examined from these and related conceptual perspectives.

A good place to start is what Follesdal and Hix (2006) refer to as the 'standard version' of the democratic deficit, citing the early work of Joseph Weiler et al (1995), which illustrates inputs, throughputs and outputs. This standard version of the democratic deficit has been summarized as (1) increased executive power at the expense of national parliamentary control, (2) a weak policy-making role for the European Parliament, (3) the lack of 'European' elections that are truly about

EU-related leadership positions or policy agendas, (4) too much 'distance' between the EU institutions and citizens regarding understanding and identity, (5) EU policies that eventually drift from those of the majority of citizens and member states and (6) the inadequate role played by interest groups in general, but particularly trade unions, consumer groups and other non-governmental organizations (NGOs) representing diverse interests (Follesdal and Hix 2006, 534–537; Hix 2008, 67–71).

Using the framework suggested by Schmidt, the first two dimensions of the democratic deficit in the standard version can be categorized as types of throughputs. The same is true of the sixth dimension of the standard version on democratic shortcomings of the EU regarding NGOs, which is an issue that has been explored by Sabine Saurugger (2008). The third problem area of European elections deals with inputs, while the divergence between EU policies and the preferences of citizens and governments refers to the connections between outputs and inputs, and will be discussed in greater depth below. In sum, if the conclusion is to be reached that the ToL has improved the EU's democratic legitimacy regarding its AFSJ, then, from the perspective of the standard version of the democratic deficit, the changes it has brought about will have to have addressed at least one of these areas and not worsen the situation regarding others.

Follesdal and Hix (2006) actually reject the standard version of the democratic deficit, favouring instead a perspective that strongly emphasizes inputs. Specifically, they stress that the most serious problem with the EU's democratic legitimacy is its lack of competitive elections and governmental structures that would allow citizens to choose from among opposing political leaders with alternative policy agendas and form their opinions based on these mechanisms (548–552). More recently, Hix argued that the EU has many of the procedural elements of healthy democracy, but 'what's missing is the substantive content of democracy: a battle for control of political power and the policy agenda at the European level, between rival groups of leaders with rival policy platforms, where the winners have a reasonable chance of losing next time round and the losers have a reasonable chance of winning' (2008, 85). The key questions are whether the ToL's alterations to the AFSJ have changed any of this and whether these modifications have improved the link between the policy preferences of European citizens and the policy agendas pursued by key actors at the EU level, especially those in the Commission and EP?

Similar questions will have to be asked concerning the perspective of Andrew Moravcsik, who has taken a 'liberal' point of view on democracy which emphasizes both throughputs and outputs. Writing after the entry into force of the Amsterdam Treaty but before the Nice Treaty, Moravcsik reached the conclusion that concerns at the time about the EU's democratic deficit were misplaced. In his view, the EU embodies sufficient 'constraints' to ensure that an undemocratic European 'superstate' cannot emerge. In fact, the power of governmental institutions is more constrained than any national polity (Moravcsik 2002, 606–607, 611). These limitations include (1) the EU's treaty-based constraints that limit its encroachment on national sovereignty, (2) substantive constraints on policy-making competence vis-à-vis its member states, including its small budget and administrative staff relative to the those of member states, (3) the EU's reliance on member states' governments and their courts to implement most legislation and policies, (4) constraints on treaty reform and the separations of powers and checks and balances among Commission, Council, EP and Court of Justice and (5) the constraints provided by alternative legal norms, such as those provided by broader international organizations or interactions among sub-sets of member states (Moravcsik 2002).

While the separation of power and checks and balances in the policy-making process highlighted by Moravcsik are rightly characterized as throughputs, other dimensions of democratic legitimacy valued by Moravcsik are categorized as outputs by Schmidt (2013). Specifically, these are the policy outputs produced by semi-autonomous institutions, including efficiency based on expertise, justice, equality and rights for individuals and minorities, and unbiased representation of majorities in the face of powerful, yet particularistic, interests (Moravcsik 2002, 614). Moravcsik discounts concerns for the democratic deficit not only because of his views on constraints—throughputs *and* outputs—but also because of the progressively increased power of the EP in providing democratic accountability regarding the latter. One task of this article is to examine whether these attributes of the EU have been strengthened or weakened by the changes of the ToL to the AFSJ.

Another scholar who takes the outputs perspective and views critiques of the democratic deficit as overblown is Majone. Specifically, he has argued that the EU's democratic legitimacy can be evaluated according to its ability to produce positive results regarding the collective action problems facing its member states (Majone 1998). In this regard, Majone contends that it is appropriate for the EU to delegate tasks aimed at this goal to institutions that are independent of the political process, provided that they are supported by an adequate system of accountability (1998, 28). He reached this conclusion because he chose to view the EU not as a traditional state, but rather as a 'regulatory state'. As such, the legitimacy of the EU should not be measured according to traditional democratic criteria but rather by standards connected to efficiency-orientated policies. Thus, the pertinent question at hand is whether and how the ToL's changes to the AFSJ have affected the EU's legitimacy in this regard—from the output- and efficiency-oriented perspective of Majone.

Just as Majone and Moravcsik's perspectives are connected because they both deal with outputs, Majone's work is also connected with Vivien Schmidt's regarding the calls of each to reconceptualize the EU when evaluating the nature and extent of the democratic deficit. According to Schmidt (2004; 2006), the EU should not be compared to the ideal of the nation state, but should be reconceived as a 'regional state' in which, among several defining attributes, sovereignty is shared with its constituent member states and governance is compound in nature. Whereas the EU, as a regional state, mainly provides democracy 'for the people' through effective government and 'with the people' in the sense of including interest groups in policy-making, ideal nations states *also* provide democracy 'by the people' through political participation, especially voting, and 'of the people' through citizen representation (Schmidt 2006, 977). Where others view it as problematic that the EU does not match up to the kind of democracy afforded by traditional nation states (see Zweifel 2002), Schmidt, similar to Majone and Moravcsik, sees the problems of the democratic deficit at the EU level to be not as great as they are sometimes made to appear (Schmidt 2006, 977).

For Schmidt, however, it is not the case that she necessarily disregards the democratic deficit at the EU level. Indeed, her views on the inadequacy of input legitimacy, for example, are not unlike those of Hix. Yet what distinguishes Schmidt's viewpoint from others is that she sees the far more serious problems with the democratic shortcoming of the EU lying in the member states themselves and not at the EU level per se (Schmidt 2004; 2006). Specifically, Schmidt critiques national governments for not fostering democratically healthy 'communicative discourse' on the EU, by speaking to their constituents in a way that misrepresents the significance of the EU vis-à-vis the policy-making authority of the member states. In short, the impact of the EU has been profound, and yet national politicians typically engage in public policy debate as if they have retained their former authority and citizens their influence (Schmidt 2006, 36). This not only prevents communicative discourse that could allow national polities to re-evaluate their own national democracies in light of Europeanization, but also dooms efforts to address the democratic deficit at the EU level (Schmidt 2006, 2–3). In fact, Schmidt develops this notion further by pointing out that this problem is more serious in simple polities (that is, unitary governments) than in compound ones (such as federal governments) because the effect of the EU is greater in the former than the latter (Schmidt 2006, chapter 2). In light of this perspective, this article will also consider whether the ToL's changes to the AFSJ have altered the democratic deficit concerning communicative discourse by national governments on EU policy-making in this area.

An additional noteworthy conclusion reached by Schmidt is that the three dimensions of democratic legitimacy—inputs, throughputs and outputs—are connected in such a way that affecting positive change in one area can actually harm democratic legitimacy in another (Schmidt 2006, 20–29; 2013). For example, input legitimacy might be improved by making electoral campaigns for the EP more about EU issues and less about national issues. However, this could lead to the politicization of EU public policy, and, potentially at least, to policies that are less effective, which would diminish the EU's output legitimacy.

Fritz Scharpf is another scholar who points out the potential problems with the interconnectedness of the various dimensions of EU legitimacy. For Scharpf (2009, 181), 'what matters foremost is the willingness and ability of member states to implement EU law and to assume political responsibility for doing so'. In this regard, Scharpf's main concern is that European law is difficult to change or correct once in place. This means that the EU's legislation can undermine its legitimacy when law and policies fail to match politically salient interests, and normative convictions in national polities cannot be justified in communicative discourse or are at odds with notions of the common good, from a 'republican' point of view on democracy à la Aristotle or Rousseau (Scharpf 2009; 2004; and compare Beetham 1991). In short, there is a problem of legitimacy when EU policy outputs do not match with inputs. Indeed, the powerful role of the EU's Court of Justice, which is viewed positively by liberals, such as Moravcsik, is a source of much concern for Scharpf, who sees the potential for judge-made EU law and policies to undermine the legitimacy of the EU (198–199). This article will examine whether the changes to the EU's AFSJ brought on by the ToL contribute to this phenomenon, regarding the role of the CJEU, but also the general issue of the interconnectedness among inputs, throughputs and outputs and how changes in one area could impact on democratic legitimacy in another. In sum, the nature of the EU's democratic deficit should be examined in terms of inputs, throughputs and outputs, as well as interconnections among these dimensions. Following the case made by Schmidt, scholars should be attentive to problems of democratic legitimacy stemming from discourse by national leaders regarding EU issues. Thus, the ToL's changes to the AFSJ and its potential impact on the EU's democratic deficit should be examined according to this entire analytical framework, rather than from just one point of view.

The democratic deficit and JHA

The initiatives of the Stockholm Programme, including those directed at the protection of fundamental rights, are being operationalized under the EU's latest legal basis, the ToL (Common Market Law Review 2010). As is by now fairly well known, the ToL has strengthened the role of the EP, Court of Justice and national parliaments in the AFSJ. What are the implications of these recent developments for the democratic legitimacy of the EU?

To address this issue, the innovations of the ToL must be understood in their proper historical context. The democratic nature of the EU, and specifically the AFSJ, has been changing gradually over the years, beginning with the direct elections of the EP in 1979 and its eventual legislative empowerment via the Maastricht Treaty in 1993. Despite the expansion of the co-decision procedure since this time, critics of the EU's legitimacy can still point to a democratic deficit regarding JHA due to the continued marginal role of the EP. However, just as the overall role of the EP in the EU has evolved, so has the AFSJ itself, including the power of the EP in this policy domain.

The first step in the direction came with the Amsterdam Treaty, which established the AFSJ as a goal and transformed the original third pillar when it took effect in 1999 (Peers 2011, 662–664). Specifically, the legal basis of the policy areas dealing with civil law and border management were shifted from the Treaty on European Union (TEU) to a new Title IV of the Treaty Establishing the European Communities (TEC). The resulting, abridged third pillar henceforth referred only to 'Police and Judicial Cooperation in Criminal Matters'. The JHA policies based in the first pillar would, after a transitional period, be handled according to the so-called 'community method': decision-making in the Council would be by qualified majority voting (QMV), the EP would have the right of co-decision and the European Court of Justice (ECJ) would have jurisdiction to make preliminary rulings and hear cases of infringement brought by the Commission. In contrast, third pillar matters would be handled 'intergovernmentally', whereby decision-making in the Council would be through unanimity, the EP would merely have to be consulted (but could be ignored) and the ECJ would lack competence.

However, what is often overlooked by even some seasoned observers of the EU is that the entry into force of the Amsterdam Treaty did not mean that all of the items of the former third pillar were immediately handled under the terms of the first. Instead, the implementation of the co-decision procedure and stronger powers for the EP was, in fact, delayed in several regards. Not only did the provisions of the Amsterdam Treaty potentially postpone this until the formal deadline of 2004, but several key items affected by this change remained handled by the consultation procedure until well after this, meaning that the new role for the EP on border issues was much delayed beyond 1999. This was notably the case for several items related to asylum policy which were eventually altered by changes prescribed by the Nice Treaty, which was agreed upon by the end of 2000 but did not enter into force until 2003. In effect, the Council was first allowed to finish its work on common rules and basic principles for asylum policy, and only then was the co-decision procedure implemented for new initiatives. This did not happen until 2005.

By the time it did, the EU had progressed from its original Tampere Agenda to the Hague Programme for creating its AFSJ (Council of the European Union 1999; European Council 2005). Work on the Hague Programme thus took place more or less as envisioned under the Amsterdam Treaty, meaning that most new legislative matters dealing with civil law, visas and asylum policy were handled using the co-decision procedure, giving the EP a new, stronger role. Meanwhile, issues pertaining to family law and police and judicial cooperation in criminal matters continued to be handled intergovernmentally. The series of reforms ending with the Nice Treaty resulted in a third pillar that could still be criticized in terms of its lack of efficiency, ineffectiveness, complexity and problems of legitimacy (Ladenburger 2008).

Monica Den Boer et al (2008) examined the legitimacy of EU governance at this stage of its developments by focusing specifically on its network of counter-terrorism (CT) structures, including 'vertical' arrangements such as the European Police Office (Europol), Eurojust and the Joint Situation Center (SitCen), as well as 'horizontal' forums such as the Police Working Group on Terrorism. In one of the very few attempts to merge some of the literature on the democratic deficit with that on the AFSJ, their analysis considered the legitimacy of this network from three perspectives, namely, democratic, legal and social (Den Boer et al 2008, 109). They concluded that the more formalized vertical arrangements for CT raise fewer legitimacy questions than the horizontal ones and also highlighted the connection between input and output legitimacy for EU governance of CT to move forward (Den Boer et al 2008, 119).

Concerns about the AFSJ regarding its legitimacy and effectiveness were commonly expressed throughout the era of the Hague Programme from 2004 onwards. During the same period, the EU experienced a series of mini-crises and delays with its next round of treaty reform, which included further changes to the third pillar. In the end, what was supposed to be a true constitution for the EU turned out to be merely revisions of its two founding treaties, though both modified significantly by the ToL, which took effect in December 2009 (DeVuyst 2008; Occhipinti 2008; Ladenburger 2008; Sieberson 2008; Kaunert 2010, chapter 8; Peers 2011). Contrary to the popular view on the issue, the ToL has not truly eliminated the pillar structure of the EU with regard to JHA, at least not its effects.

All AFSJ items are now handled under Title V of the Treaty on the Functioning of the European Union (TFEU),[1] which essentially replaces the old TEC. The new Title V is entitled 'Area of Freedom Security and Justice', contains Articles 67–89 of the TFEU, and is housed in five chapters that cover the full range of AFSJ items, including general provisions, policies on border checks, asylum and immigration, judicial cooperation in civil matters, judicial cooperation in criminal matters, and police cooperation. There are no longer any items directly connected to the AFSJ with their legal basis in the revised TEU. In this sense, the third pillar has indeed been eliminated. Moreover, more decision-making on AFSJ than ever before is

---

[1] See 'Consolidated version of the Treaty on the Functioning of the European Union', *Official Journal of the European Union*, 2010/C 83/49.

handled using co-decision, referred to as the 'ordinary legislative procedure' by the TFEU.

It should also be noted that, since its inception in the Maastricht Treaty, the EU's pillar structure has always implied that decision-making on JHA would be handled differently than most other policies. This remains at least partially the case for the AFSJ in the EU today under the TFEU. For example, decision-making pertaining to *operational* police cooperation (Article 87, paragraph 3, TFEU) and the operation of law enforcement in foreign jurisdictions (Article 89) are handled according to the terms of the old consultation procedure, which is now known as the 'special legislation procedure'. In addition, legislative proposals under Chapter 4 (Judicial Cooperation in Criminal Matters) and Chapter 5 (Police Cooperation) may be initiated not only by the Commission, but also by at least one-quarter of the member states acting collectively. Thus, at least in part, the handling of AFSJ continues to diverge from other policy areas even under the TFEU. In this sense, the third pillar is not completely dead.

Nevertheless, the ToL is indeed noteworthy for the ways in which it addresses some long-standing issues related to democratic deficit on JHA. This entails key changes for the EP, but also new roles in EU decision making for national parliaments and the EU's Court of Justice, as well great potential significance for the new Charter of Fundamental Rights. In addition, the entry into force of the ToL coincided with the EU's Stockholm Programme, which was endorsed by the European Council in December 2009 and provided the agenda for the EU on JHA from 2010 until 2014. Finally, all of these developments have happened simultaneously with not only a new political leadership in the College of Commissioners on the AFSJ, but also a new bureaucratic structure (that is, directorates-general) for handling the AFSJ. In sum, the time is right to take stock of the democratic deficit on JHA in light of all of these significant developments.

Impact of the ToL

The latest treaty comprises a mix of stability and change compared with the EU's former legal basis (Occhipinti 2008). The TFEU contains some paragraphs that merely reword or even replicate existing provisions, entailing no substantive change over the consolidated, post-Nice version of the treaties while other provisions of the TFEU contain new items designed to provide a more explicit legal basis for what the EU was already doing or what the member states had already agreed to do. And some provisions of the TFEU are truly new and have meaning for the EU's democratic deficit.

Substantive changes

Many of the innovations of the ToL regarding the EU's AFSJ pertain to police and judicial cooperation in criminal matters, which were formerly covered by the TEU in the third pillar and are now based in Title V of the consolidated version of the TFEU. Interestingly, some of these changes will not go as far as measures that were originally in the draft treaty produced by the European Convention which preceded the Intergovernmental Conference of 2003–2004 or in the failed constitution itself. A few of these eventual treaty provisions serve to protect national sovereignty in various ways and do not necessarily pertain to the democratic deficit.[2] However, the approximation ('harmonization') of criminal law is an area that has been altered by the ToL (Articles 67, 82 and 83, TFEU) and marks a significant development for the democratic deficit. This area was previously handled intergovernmentally through so-called 'framework decisions', which served as legislative 'blueprints' needing to be transposed into national law, similar to the 'directives' of the old first pillar. Under the TFEU, the harmonization of substantive and procedural criminal is now carried out via directives under the ordinary legislative procedure. A member state can use an emergency brake provision built into the new treaty to potentially block a measure via a consensus vote in the European Council, but then nine or more members can proceed without them via enhanced cooperation. In any case, the new treaty has significantly addressed the democratic deficit by granting the EP new authority in this area.

Decision-making regarding Europol is also covered by the ordinary legislative procedure under the TFEU (Article 88). Originally, this was supposed to be a true innovation of the constitution, but was superseded by a political agreement reached in the Council at the end of 2006 to make Europol a genuine EU agency. It took over two years to work out the legislative details to make this happen, culminating in a Council decision of April 2009 that entered into force in 2010, just one month after the entry into force of the much delayed ToL. Previously, Europol's structure, powers and crime-fighting remit were determined by its intergovernmental convention and several related protocols—it often took years to negotiate and ratify revisions to these accords, as reflected in the length of time it took for the Council to make Europol's agency status a reality. Today, with Europol's agency status and new legal basis in the TFEU, a bit more of the democratic deficit has been addressed. Although sweeping changes to Europol's structure and function are unlikely, the EP will now play a greater role in scrutinizing its operations and an integral part in drafting any new legislation concerning its mandate and powers (Busuioc et al 2011, 859–861).

Article 87 TFEU also provides a new legal basis for law enforcement cooperation unrelated to Europol for police, customs and other specialized services. This entails lawmaking at the EU level to facilitate the collection, storage, processing, analysis and exchange of data and intelligence, as well as mechanisms to support the training and exchange of staff, cooperation on equipment and research on investigative techniques concerning serious forms of organized crime. In all of these areas, the ordinary legislative procedure now applies, giving the EP new authority, and yet matters of operational police cooperation are still handled intergovernmentally, protecting national sovereignty through the continued use of both consensual decision-making in the Council and merely a consultative role for the EP.

Meanwhile, decision-making regarding Eurojust—the EU's liaison network for criminal prosecutors—is also handled through the ordinary legislative procedure under the TFEU (Article 85). The governance of Eurojust was already dealt with via Council decisions under terms set out in the Nice Treaty, rather than

---

[2] This includes the opt-outs created via Protocols 21 and 22 to the ToL for the United Kingdom, Ireland and Denmark on Title V measures, revised provisions on 'enhanced cooperation' (that is, flexibility), 'emergency brakes' for states to delay or block new legislation and the limited nature of a possible European Public Prosecutor (Peers 2011).

through conventions and protocols (though Eurojust was operational prior to that). Until the ToL, decisions on Eurojust's structure, operations and tasks were taken intergovernmentally. Now, under Article 85 TFEU, regulations providing the legal basis for these aspects of Eurojust are dealt with through the ordinary legislative procedure, including, of course, new powers for the EP in this regard. In addition, should the Council decide to create a European Public Prosecutor's Office from Eurojust to protect the EU's financial interests (foreseen under Article 86), it can only do so with the 'consent' of the EP. However, this is one area in which a democratic deficit remains, because the EP's power of consent here is unlikely to be as influential as its power to amend legislation under the ordinary legislative procedure, based on the experience of other EU policy areas where the now defunct 'assent' procedure has been used, such as cohesion policy.

The new treaty includes the democratic deficit in AFSJ among the areas of the EU's policy competence for which the role of national parliaments has been strengthened. As with other policy areas, legislative proposals made by the Commission or groups of member states under Title V of the TFEU must first be reviewed by national parliaments (Protocol 1 to the ToL and Article 69 TFEU), which could potentially lead to a revision of these prior to the continuation of the rest of the ordinary or special legislative procedures. National parliaments, along with the EP, are now to be included in monitoring and evaluating the activities of both Europol and Eurojust, while Article 70 TFEU requires that national parliaments be kept informed of evaluations of the implementation of EU policies under Title V conducted by the Commission or the Council. In this way national parliaments have a new role in JHA provided by the ToL, addressing some conceptualizations of the democratic deficit.

Limitations of the previous treaties on the jurisdiction of the CJEU on JHA are removed by the ToL. Depending on one's views of throughput- or output-oriented democratic legitimacy, the new role for the CJEU is significant for evaluations of the EU's democratic deficit. The new treaty accomplishes this for the Court by simply omitting the pre-existing stipulations forbidding the Court's competence in the AFSJ. At least potentially, the main effect of this change will be the improved implementation of EU laws pertaining to the AFSJ, which has been problematic over the past decade, such as with various pieces of legislation relating to counter-terrorism, including the European Arrest Warrant (Kaunert 2010). Under the TFEU, the Commission can now bring infringement procedures against member states that fail to implement directives related to the AFSJ properly or on time. This applies as well to measures dealing with police and judicial cooperation in criminal matters approved under the TEU (third pillar) before the entry into force of the ToL, but only after a five-year transitional period (Protocol 36, Title VII), unless an existing item is amended under the terms of the new treaty (Peers 2011, 666).

Judicial scrutiny of the AFSJ has also been strengthened by the alteration of Commission portfolios and the related directorates-general dealing with the AFSJ. For the first time, the Commission has separated its work on citizens' rights and justice from its activities on internal security and borders. The first step in this transformation was the appointment of Viviane Reding as commissioner for justice, fundamental rights and citizenship and Cecilia Malmström as commissioner for home affairs. Subsequently, the Directorate-General for Justice, Freedom and Security was divided into two directorates-general on 1 July 2010. The

Directorate-General for Justice (DG Justice) now consists of directorates on civil justice, criminal justice and equality, while the Directorate-General on Home Affairs (DG Home) consists of directorates on internal security, immigration and asylum, migration and borders. While it remains to be seen how the new Commission portfolio and structure will affect policy outcomes, it is likely that the change will increase the Commission's propensity to utilize the Court of Justice to scrutinize the implementation of EU law when fundamental rights are at issue. This too has implications for the democratic deficit.

The new power for the Court of Justice under the ToL is also noteworthy in the context of the democratic deficit. First, the EP now shares in the ability to bring members states to the Court of Justice for infringing EU law in JHA. From its perspective as a frequent champion of fundamental rights, this can be significant when the EP needs to pressure a member state that has missed a legal deadline for implementing a directive designed to protect such rights or has implemented a measure in a way that threatens these rights. This could be the case, for example, in matters pertaining to the harmonization of criminal procedure concerning defendants' rights or privacy and data protection regarding information-sharing among law enforcement agencies for crime-fighting, counter-terrorism or border management.

Secondly, the new power of the Court of Justice further impinges on the democratic deficit by expanding the scope of its powers of judicial review. The Court now has the competence to give preliminary rulings on police and judicial cooperation in criminal matters regarding questions submitted by a wider range of national courts. Previously, based on Article 35 of the old third pillar (TEU), member states had to make, in advance, individual declarations to accept the Court's competence to issue preliminary rulings. Only 17 member states had done so prior to the entry into force of the ToL, including two with restrictions on this. Today, only the three member states with opt-outs on Title V are beyond the scope of the Court of Justice's preliminary rulings when it comes to the AFSJ, but the Court's new power will impact even on these countries if and when they choose to participate in a particular legislative measures related to the AFSJ (that is, opt in). Moreover, the ToL has increased access to judicial review regarding visas, asylum, immigration and judicial cooperation in civil matters by eliminating Article 68 of the old first pillar (TEC), which had stipulated that appeals to the ECJ could only come from member states' highest courts of appeal.

Early studies of the Court's new role have revealed a significant increase in the number of cases referred to it on civil law and immigration and asylum law, but no change on criminal law. According to Steve Peers, this can be explained by the transitional rules that continue to limit the role of the CJEU. So far, the Court of Justice has not been overburdened by an explosion of cases related to the AFSJ, though national courts may become more active in seeking rulings as more measures in this policy area miss their transpositions deadlines or are adopted in the future (Peers 2011, 684–685).

The new powers of the Court of Justice on the AFSJ are not without their limits. Article 276 of TFEU clarifies that on exercising its powers regarding the provisions of Chapters 4 and 5 of Title V (on judicial cooperation in criminal matters and on police cooperation) the Court of Justice has 'no jurisdiction to review the validity or proportionality of operations carried out by the police or other law-enforcement services of a member state or the exercise of the responsibilities incumbent upon Member States with regard to the maintenance of law and order and the safeguarding of internal security' (Part Six, Title I, Chapter 1, Section 5). This restriction could serve to restrict judicial scrutiny of both Eurojust (specified in Chapter 4) and Europol (specified in Chapter 5) and is supported by limits placed on Title V itself, namely, that it 'shall not affect the exercise of the responsibilities incumbent upon Member States with regard to the maintenance of law and order and the safeguarding of internal security' (Article 72). This is a provision that has always narrowed the scope of EU competence on JHA under the previous treaties in policy areas founded in the first and third pillars via Article 64(1) (TEC) and Article 33 (TEU).

Despite these persistent limitations, the new role of the Court of Justice has been strengthened by the attachment of the Charter of Fundamental Rights to the ToL. The new Charter is not the 'bill of rights' of a true EU constitution which many had hoped it would be, but when combined with the new powers of the Court of Justice, the impact of the Charter can be significant. This may especially be the case regarding principles closely related to the AFSJ that are specified in the Charter, which itself has been given a somewhat firmer basis through its attachment to the new treaty.

Article 8 of the Charter on the protection of personal data and Article 42 on the right of access to documents have implications for border management and exchanges of information among law enforcement authorities, just as Article 11 on the freedom of expression and information pertains to EU measures aimed at restricting the use of the internet to promote radicalization. Meanwhile, Article 4 on the prohibition of torture and inhuman or degrading treatment or punishment, Article 18 on the right to asylum, Article 19 on protection in the event of removal, expulsion or extradition and Article 45 on freedom of movement and of residence all have implications for EU policies on relations with third countries, border management, the handling illegal immigration and the treatment of third country nationals regarding internal security. Article 49 on the principles of legality and proportionality of criminal offences and penalties also pertains to the future development of judicial cooperation in criminal matters, as does Article 50 on the right not to be tried or punished twice in criminal proceedings for the same criminal offence.

The ToL also brings changes to the nature of some of the EU's international agreements, something that also has implications for the democratic deficit concerning the AFSJ. The new treaty essentially maintains the key pre-existing principle embodied in Article 300 TEC, that for agreements negotiated between the EU and third countries or international organizations, the Council can approve these only after obtaining the consent of the EP when the agreement covers fields in which either the ordinary legislative procedure is used or the special legislative procedure applies but where the consent of the EP is still needed (TFEU Article 218). In other words, where the EP has power on the EU's internal agenda, its approval is also required for international agreements in this area.

As the EP's power has been widened by the ToL to include most areas of police and judicial cooperation in criminal matters, international agreements that impinge on these areas require parliamentary approval. An early illustration of the EP's new authority in this regard came when it rejected an agreement reached between the EU and the United States (US) that would allow US authorities to have access to data on financial transactions involving EU-based financial institutions. The

Terrorist Finance Tracking Programme (TFTP) agreement was previously and better known as the 'SWIFT agreement', named for the Society for Worldwide Interbank Financial Telecommunication, which has some of its computer servers in the EU and must therefore abide by European law on data protection. With the entry into force of the ToL, the EP gained the power to block the transatlantic SWIFT agreement, based not only on Article 218 TFEU, but also Article 82(1)(d), which authorizes cooperation in criminal matters, as well as Article 87(2), which permits the collection, storage, processing, analysis and exchange of relevant information. At least in some regards, this demonstration of the EP's new authority shows that the EU's democratic deficit has been at least partly addressed.

Lastly, Article 71 of the TFEU creates a new body in the AFSJ with implications for the democratic deficit: the Standing Committee for Operational Cooperation on Internal Security (COSI). Unlike the 'Article 36 Committee' (known as CATS), which has helped prepare the legislative work of the JHA Council, COSI's work is specifically aimed at improving the *operational* effect of EU policy. In doing so, it has essentially replaced the now defunct EU's Police Chiefs Task Force and includes some of the same national personnel that once met in that forum. Moreover, since 2011, COSI has been given a central role in the EU's new, multi-year 'policy cycle', which aims to implement the goals of the EU's International Security Strategy (European Commission 2010). The ability of COSI to deliver on this task—especially through the promotion of better coordination among the member states—will affect whether the ToL will improve legitimacy in the AFSJ from an outputs- and efficiency-oriented perspective (Scherrer et al 2011).

Superficial developments

Beyond the substantive changes implemented by the ToL regarding the AFSJ, the new treaty also contains a number of provisions that are superficial in nature yet have implications for the democratic deficit. Under the ToL (Title V, Chapter 2), decision-making on border checks, asylum and immigration is handled using the ordinary legislative procedure. However, this was already provided for under the existing treaties in Article 67 of the TEC and was implemented following agreement on the Hague Programme. As a result, all matters pertaining to illegal immigration and the control of the EU's external borders have been handled using the Community method since 1 January 2005.

Concerning visas, the Amsterdam Treaty had already implemented Article 67, calling for the shift away from the intergovernmental method for the four components of this policy domain. For two of these aspects of visa policy (the list of third countries whose nationals need visas and a uniform format for visas), the changes took effect immediately upon the entry into force of the Amsterdam Treaty, the Commission gaining the sole right to initiate policy and shifting voting in the Council to QMV. On these matters, however, the EP needed only to be consulted, and this situation was left unchanged by the Nice Treaty. Thus, these are areas where the ToL has brought some greater authority for the EP and further implications for the democratic deficit. Concerning the other aspects of visa policy, the shift to the Community method occurred on 1 January 2005 via the decision to use Article 67 (TEC), so the ToL is not innovative here. The new treaty does indeed establish an explicit legal basis for a 'common visa policy' (Article 77, TFEU), but the Hague Programme had already identified a need for this, so this was also not really new and is not directly connected to the democratic deficit at any rate.

The ToL also brings little real change to asylum policy, owing to a new paragraph that had already been added under Article 67 (TEC) by the Nice Treaty. This called for the Community method to be applied to asylum policy as soon as the Council had agreed upon 'minimum rules' for member states to follow in each of the main five main components of this policy area. Ultimately, the Council's work on this continued throughout 2006, meaning that employing the Community method for asylum policy was delayed until all of the legislative proposals were completed using the intergovernmental method. By the time they had done so, the European Council had already endorsed the Hague Programme, which called for the EU to move beyond the minimum rules established in the initial package of asylum measures and create a common policy on asylum and related issues, such as subsidiary protection and temporary protection. Thus, the TFEU's prescriptions under its Article 78 that 'the Union shall develop a common policy on asylum, subsidiary protection and temporary protection', as well as its provisions that this should be established using the ordinary legislative procedure, do not entail any real change regarding the democratic deficit. In addition, decision-making on burden-sharing among member states regarding refugees (noted in Article 63.2[b] TEC) had already been shifted to the Community method via Article 67, effective 1 January 2005. Regarding this issue, the TFEU includes 'the principle of solidarity and a fair sharing of responsibility' in its Article 80.

Finally, the ToL entails no real change for the handling of civil law by the EU. As under the previous treaties, the new treaty (Article 81) calls for this to be handled via the Community method and not intergovernmentally, meaning real power of co-decision for the EP. This had already come into force under the terms established by the same new paragraph in Article 67 created by the Nice Treaty. The ToL has not changed this and leaves the sensitive matter of family law in intergovernmental hands, just as the Nice Treaty had done. Consequently, under the ToL, there is nothing new for the democratic deficit concerning family law.

Towards a withering deficit?

To investigate whether the above changes, substantive and superficial, wrought by the ToL upon the AFSJ have in fact reduced the democratic deficit, we return to the questions posed near the start of this article and focus on whether the democratic legitimacy of the EU has been improved with regard to inputs, throughputs and outputs, as well as connections among these and communicative discourse at the national level.

As previously discussed, some of the changes brought on by the ToL are merely superficial and have simply streamlined or codified developments that were already in the works. However, other innovations are quite substantial indeed, including roles for the EP, national parliaments and the Court of Justice in the AFSJ. But what do these changes really mean for the democratic deficit?

Inputs and democratic legitimacy

Starting with inputs, we can consider the dimension of the 'standard version' of the democratic deficit which deals with the lack of true European elections. Clearly, the ToL has not addressed this important issue. Moreover, returning to the perspective of Follesdal and Hicks, we can contemplate whether the changes brought on by the ToL have improved the democratic deficit regarding the contestation for political leadership or debate on issues and policy agendas related to matters handled at the EU level. One way to do this is to examine whether the new treaty brought about any of the prescriptions suggested by Hix (2008) that would promote 'limited democratic politics' in the EU. On one level, it is evident that the ToL has not instituted the major areas of reform suggested by Hix, namely creating a 'winner-take-all' system for electing the EP's president and allocating its committee chairs, transforming the Council into a proper and transparent legislature and bringing about an open contest for the Commission president based on clear policy manifestos and policy debate (Hix 2008, 186).

However, the ToL's changes to the AFSJ have improved the democratic deficit from the inputs perspective in some regards, at least at the margins. Hix has argued that granting the EP more power in areas such as taxation policy would increase political contestation, though he is pessimistic about achieving this through treaty reform and worries about its impact on outcomes, namely the harmful politicization of EU politics (Hix 2008, 190). Nevertheless the ToL has strengthened the role of the EP in several regards when it comes to AFSJ. According to the logic espoused by Hix, this has to be viewed as an improvement for democratic legitimacy regarding inputs, given its potential to promote political contestation in an area such as police and judicial cooperation in criminal matters, for which the EP previously had little real authority vis-à-vis the Council. Hix has not only prescribed greater openness in the Council to the media and public but also suggested that this EU body develop more legislature-like debate and coalition-building. While the ToL does little in practice for transparency, it has extended the use of QMV to most of areas of police and judicial cooperation in criminal matters, as noted above. Although the consensus norm still endures in the Council for its decision-making, this increased use of QMV can only promote more debate and coalition-building and surely not less. Thus, the expansion of QMV in the AFSJ must be viewed as a positive, albeit still inadequate, step regarding democratic legitimacy from the inputs perspective.

Hix has suggested more coalition-building in the Council could be achieved if the right to amend Commission proposals were restricted to groups of member states acting together. While the ToL has not implemented this prescription, it has instituted new rules for member states to initiative new proposals for the AFSJ where the Commission's right to do so is not exclusive. As discussed in the previous section, national governments can no longer unilaterally propose legislation but must be part of a group of at least one-quarter of all member states acting collectively. Early studies of the policy-making under the ToL indicate that member states are indeed utilizing this provision (Peers 2011, 679–680). Although this may be insufficient from the viewpoint of Hix, it does indeed promote more and not less coalition-building and debate in the Council, which should also be viewed a positive step towards democratic legitimacy from the inputs perspective.

In sum, the changes brought on by the ToL for the AFSJ improve the democratic deficit regarding inputs in some regards, but ultimately fail to address adequately the core concerns of this perspective. Above all, the new treaty has not improved democratic legitimacy in the EU regarding the contestation for leaders or policy agendas regarding the AFSJ and has not met Hix's suggestions for creating 'limited democratic politics'. Nevertheless, it would be wrong to claim that the changes of the ToL regarding the AFSJ have done nothing to improve the democratic deficit of the EU from the inputs perspectives. To the contrary, the situation has been at least marginally improved in three noteworthy ways.

Throughputs and democratic legitimacy

In contrast to its effect on inputs, the impact of the ToL on the EU's AFSJ regarding throughputs has been more substantial. From this perspective, as expressed in some dimensions of the 'standard view' on the EU's democratic deficit, the ToL has improved democratic legitimacy in two ways. First, the inclusion of national parliaments by the ToL in the review of EU legislation, including measures pertaining to the AFSJ, has addressed the issue of increased executive power at the expense of national parliamentary control. By the end of 2010, a large proportion of opinions from national parliaments had come on issues related to the AFSJ (Peers 2011, 681). Yet, it remains to be seen how this power will matter in practice for the EU under the ToL, particularly whether it will lead to legislation being delayed or blocked.

Second, and certainly more significant, is the new role for the EP in the AFSJ under the terms of the ToL, which clearly strengthens the Parliament's policy-making role across a wide range of not only internal matters, but also related external polices, as illustrated most famously by the mini-crisis over the SWIFT data-sharing agreement with the US. However, regarding the other dimension of the standard version of the democratic deficit dealing with throughput, namely the inadequate role played by NGOs, the ToL does nothing to improve the situation.

The ToL should also be viewed as improving the democratic deficit from the liberal perspective of Moravcsik, which can also be conceived in terms of throughputs. Although he may not be terribly convinced about the severity of this problem in the first place, Moravcsik's assessment of democratic legitimacy places value on checks and balances among the main institutions of the EU, and this has always been lacking on JHA compared with other policy areas. One can guess that Moravcsik's published views on democratic deficit (2002) were formed prior to the explosion of EU legislation on policies on the AFSJ, which only began in late 2001. In light of the heightened significance of EU policy-making in this area today, one could also surmise that empowerment of the EP and Court of Justice on AFSJ by the ToL would be viewed as a positive development from Moravcsik's liberal point of view because these changes enhance checks and balances among the EU institutions. Meanwhile, constraints preventing a European superstate are preserved through the use of opt-outs, emergency breaks and the endurance of the old third pillar and its intergovernmental decision-making on *operational* police cooperation, the activities of law enforcement in foreign jurisdictions and family law.

These illustrations show that the ToL has significantly addressed the EU's democratic deficit from a throughputs perspective. However, as pointed out by

Peers, one consequence of the EP's new power has a been a lack of transparency, because the EP and Council now reach more informal deals out of the public light, leading to measures being adopted without much debate at the first-reading stage (Peers 2011, 677–678). Thus, from a throughputs perspective, improved democratic legitimacy in the AFSJ resulting from an empowered EP is somewhat offset by reduced transparency in EU decision-making.

Outputs and democratic legitimacy

Turning to outputs, the direct impact of the ToL is not as strong, but there still appears to be a positive effect on the democratic deficit regarding the AFSJ. The first way to approach this issue is from the perspective of Majone and Moravcsik and focus on whether and how the ToL has promoted more efficient outcomes regarding the AFSJ. In this regard, the new authority given to the Commission to initiate infringement proceedings against member states in order to pressure them to implement legislation for the AFSJ properly or on time has improved efficiency. In principle, this should reduce the problems that the EU has experienced in the regard, as illustrated by the cases of the European Arrest Warrant and framework decision on terrorism.

The effects of the ToL on Europol and Eurojust can also be considered. Although efficiency cannot be examined here with respect to the actual contribution of these organizations to the fight against cross-border crime, we can consider how each agency is governed and can be adjusted to meet the changing needs of the member states in this endeavour. In this respect, the ToL's main contribution to each is to eliminate national vetoes when it comes to altering their structure, mandate and power. On the one hand, this shift to the normal legislative procedure could be viewed as more efficient, allowing the member states to modify each more easily than in the past as conditions dictate. On the other hand, this change also means the EP has gained real authority in doing so, which could delay or water down needed changes, leading to greater inefficiency. The same situation now exists for many areas of law enforcement cooperation covered by Article 87 TFEU to which the ordinary legislative procedure applies, such as the collection, storage, processing, analysis and exchange of data and intelligence, and training measures. Lastly, more time is needed to determine whether COSI can improve effectiveness and efficiency in the AFSJ by successfully promoting more operational coordination among member state authorities and helping the EU to deliver results under its Internal Security Strategy (European Commission 2010). It is not entirely certain whether the ToL will improve democratic legitimacy from an efficiency-oriented outputs perspective, but several of its innovations provide some reason for optimism.

What is clearer, however, is that the ToL has improved democratic legitimacy regarding accountability, which is valued by both Majone and Moravcsik in their consideration of outputs. While both scholars consider efficiency to be important, they also emphasize that technocratic or independent authorities must be held accountable. In this regard, the strengthened role of the EP on law enforcement cooperation in general, and in the work of Europol and Eurojust in particular, must be viewed as a positive step regarding the democratic deficit by improving democratic accountability concerning policy outcomes in the AFSJ (Busuioc et al 2011, 859–861). Of course, as with other areas of recent change involving the ToL, the practical effect of the EU's new legal basis in this policy area remains to be seen. One issue to consider is whether this new role of the EP will actually politicize Eurojust and Europol or expose them to new pressures from NGOs via their influence in the EP. If so, then their efficiency and ability to resist narrow interests might be reduced, along with their democratic legitimacy from the perspective of Majone and Moravcsik.

Open questions remain as well for another area in which the ToL has made a significant impact on the democratic deficit, namely, the protection of justice, equality and rights, when viewed as outputs. In this regard, at least in principle, the impact of the new treaty has been substantial, given both the relevance of the Charter of Fundamental Rights to the AFSJ and the enhanced role of the Court of Justice on European law in JHA. In addition, the empowered EP and new DG Justice may use both the Charter and Court to protect individual rights. More time is needed to see whether rights are indeed protected by these new developments, but the formal changes brought on by the ToL move the EU in this direction, which contributes to the fact the ToL's changes to AFSJ have improved democratic legitimacy regarding outputs.

Connections, member states and democratic legitimacy

Next, we turn our analysis to the connections among the dimensions and, especially, the concerns raised by Scharpf as discussed in the previous section. This examination differs from the previous consideration of inputs, throughputs and outputs because the impact of the ToL on these connections is indirect and the analysis is entirely speculative. Nevertheless, the potential consequences of the ToL can be shown.

The effect of the ToL on inputs regarding the AFSJ is marginal at best. Yet we must consider the impact of the potential increase in political debate in this policy area which could result from expansion of both the EP's power and the use of QMV in the Council. Here, the most worrisome possible outcome, as previously noted, is that this new debate could politicize issues connected with the AFSJ, which could harm democratic legitimacy regarding outcomes. Specifically, it is possible that the more debate in the EP and Council becomes politicized, the harder it will be for compromises to be reached on new legislation, which could make EU policy-making function less efficiently. Moreover, if debate in the Council, but especially the EP, were to become more politicized, then there could be increased pressure on the semi-autonomous agencies in the AFJS to operate in response to political concerns, rather than on the basis of their specialized expertise. This could be the case for Europol, Eurojust or Frontex (the EU's external border management agency, which is not mentioned in the ToL).

It is important to note that it is mere speculation how the politicization of inputs will affect outcomes in the AFSJ, and the particular impact may depend on the nature of the debate itself. For example, outcomes could differ if the salient political debate prioritizes security over civil liberties or human rights, as opposed to the reverse. The point here is that addressing the democratic deficit on inputs might actually worsen outputs and leave democratic legitimacy in the EU no better off overall.

The same is also true for the improvement of throughputs. In this regard, the EP's new powers in the AFSJ may have improved democratic legitimacy from the liberal perspective that values checks and balances, but this might only create policy-making gridlock that would work against efficiency from an outputs point of view. Moreover, even after legislative deals are concluded by the Council and the EP, these can potentially be overturned by national parliaments through their new powers of review. While inefficiency may take the form of new policies that are delayed, weakened by compromise or never implemented at all, this problem could also stem from a proliferation of different approaches to shared policy challenges among the member states. This could result from the preservation of national vetoes in some areas of the AFSJ under the ToL, such as for operational police cooperation, allowing contending national approaches to endure. In addition, the ToL's inclusion of op-outs and flexibility provisions also encourage member states to respond differently to policy challenges that are the same or linked. In sum, the ToL's improvements to the democratic deficit from a throughputs perspective can potentially harm democratic legitimacy that is defined in terms of efficient outcomes.

We can consider potential problems with outcomes themselves and focus on the particular concerns of Scharpf. As noted above, the ToL has improved the democratic deficit regarding outcomes in several regards, including the strengthened the role of the Court of Justice in the AFSJ. This entails both the ability of the Commission to use the Court in infringement proceedings brought against member states that violate EU law, as well the enhanced role of the CJEU in making preliminary rulings in this policy area, such as those that might be founded on some aspect of the new Charter of Fundamental Rights.

From the liberal viewpoint this new power of the Court might be viewed as an additional healthy democratic check on policies of the member states. In fact, Clifford Carrubba (2003) explores how national governments can become increasingly constrained by rulings of the CJEU, as citizens come to believe that the Court's ruling should be followed and the 'legitimacy costs' for failing to do so rise for their governments. However, from the perspective of Scharpf, the increased power of the Court is potentially damaging to democratic legitimacy.

In making this point, Scharpf elucidates that once EU law is in place, it is nearly irreversible (Scharpf 2009, 178). Moreover, the Court of Justice is highly immune from political correction (Scharpf 2009, 176). While these features of the EU's legal system may serve liberal agendas well in the protection of individual rights, Scharpf argues that this can actually undermine legitimacy by creating incongruence between EU policy outcomes and notions of the common good at the national level (Scharpf 2009, 174–178).

Although he does not mention it, Scharpf's concerns in this area have implications for the AFSJ. For example, just as its agenda of economic liberalization and deregulation might undermine the EU's legitimacy in some member states by neglecting redistributive policy goals (see Habermas 2001), so too EU policies of free movement or fundamental rights might fail to correspond with national notions of the common good defined in terms of tighter border management or greater security against crime or terrorism. In both instances, Scharpf's concern would be that policy outcomes can become entrenched due to the mostly immutable nature of EU law, buttressed by the role of the CJEU. Should these outcomes occur in areas of high political salience within member state polities in a way that cannot be justified by national leaders in communicative discourse with their citizens, then the input legitimacy of the EU will suffer. While this is only a hypothetical example, it demonstrates how improving the outputs legitimacy of the EU by strengthening the role of the Court of Justice can potentially worsen the democratic deficit from an inputs perspective at the level of the member states.

As noted earlier, Schmidt identifies a related, yet different, type of a problem for legitimacy at the national level. Whereas Scharpf worries that member states' governments will be unable to justify policy outcomes fostered by the EU's legal system, Schmidt is concerned that an informed discourse between national leaders and their citizens on EU policies will not happen at all. The inclusion of national parliaments by the ToL in the review of EU legislation, including measures pertaining to the AFSJ, may help to address this concern by changing the nature of the communicative discourse among political leaders and their constituents. Of course, the actual impact of this will be shaped by many factors, including country-specific public policy concerns, political parties' views on European integration, media coverage of EU issues, and so on. In fact, one possibility is that the formal inclusion of national parliaments in EU policy-making will not alter the nature of communicative discourse in the member states, and national leaders will simply continue to misrepresent the true significance of the EU on JHA. However, another plausible outcome is that any improved communicative discourse in this regard could lead to the legitimacy issues raised by Scharpf. That is, national leaders might not be able to justify to their constituents why a particular policy outcome of the EU, such as its provisions of free movement in the Schengen zone or standards for treating asylum-seekers, is for the common, public good. In this way, we see yet another example of how improving the EU's democratic deficit in one regard can lead to problems for democratic legitimacy in another.

Democratic legitimacy and the Stockholm Programme

There are two ways to answer the question, 'Whither the withering democratic deficit?' One is to examine the particular ways in which the ToL's provisions regarding the AFSJ contribute to changes in the behaviour and outcomes of the key institutional actors and processes involved in the work on the Stockholm Programme. In that regard, this article has already suggested a number of avenues for future research, but several key issues can be summarized here. The most important empirical questions deal with the new policy-making role of the EP in the AFSJ, as well as new scrutinizing mechanisms implemented by the ToL.

Concerning the EP, future research can examine how its new role impacts on specific legislative initiatives under the Stockholm Programme. Another set of questions deals with the EP's enhanced role in scrutinizing the work of Europol. Regarding both endeavours, a key issue is whether the EP will place greater weight on fundamental rights versus effectiveness when dealing with perceived security threats. In fact, similar questions can also be asked about civil society and whether democratic legitimacy in the EU will be improved through a greater role for NGOs across the full range of issues in the AFSJ. This too could affect outcomes in the Stockholm Programme.

Along with these issues, researchers of the democratic deficit can also examine whether JHA will emerge as salient issues among voters in European elections. If so, will coherent and enduring policy distinctions emerge among the EP's political groups on AFSJ issues that will truly distinguish one group from another? Moreover, how would this politicization of the AFSJ affect the implementation of the Stockholm Programme or its successor agenda?

Additional research topics might deal with new forms of scrutiny implemented by the ToL, which could also impact on the outcomes of the Stockholm Programme. For example, what will be the impact of national parliaments' new role in reviewing legislation or monitoring the work of Europol and Eurojust? Will the impact of this be substantive or merely symbolic? In general, how will national parliaments affect the work of the Stockholm Programme?

Related research questions on scrutiny mechanism apply as well to the Court of Justice. For example, will the threat or use of infringement proceedings in new areas improve the implementation of legislation dealing with police and judicial cooperation in criminal matters? Likewise, how will citizens or groups in civil society challenge new initiatives in the Stockholm agenda via national courts and through preliminary rulings of the CJEU? Overall, how important will the Charter of Fundamental Rights be for the work of the Court on the areas pertaining to the AFSJ in general and the initiatives of the Stockholm Programme in particular?

With so many open empirical questions, the answer is unclear with regard to the first way of addressing the query, 'Whither the withering democratic deficit?' In contrast, this article has shed more light on the second way of approaching this question, namely by exploring the very nature of the EU's democratic legitimacy and how this has been impacted on by the ToL's changes to the AFSJ. Nevertheless, the most concise answer to this way of approaching the question in this article's title is, 'It depends on who you ask!'

Evaluating how the ToL has affected the democratic deficit regarding the AFSJ requires attention to the various conceptual points of view on the fundamental issues at hand. From the inputs perspective, the EU's latest treaty has brought some noteworthy improvements for democratic legitimacy, though, all in all, the effect of this has been quite limited. Meanwhile, the impact of the ToL on throughputs and outputs has been much more substantial. However, this article has also pointed out that the positive changes brought by the ToL in any of these dimensions can potentially be offset by new problems that these same developments can foster. Moreover, the ToL offers little prospect of changing the nature of communicative discourse on the AFSJ among national politicians and their citizens in the EU's member states.

The ToL's changes to the AFSJ have improved the state of the EU's democratic deficit in some regards, though many issues of democratic legitimacy remain. In the short run, researchers can explore both how these improvements affect the implementation of the Stockholm Programme, but also how the enduring democratic deficit continues to impact policy outcomes. In the long term, scholars can focus on whether and how future treaty reforms could help improve democratic legitimacy in the AFSJ where it is still lacking.

Notes on contributor

John D Occhipinti is Professor of Political Science and Department Chair at Canisius College in Buffalo, New York. In 2003, he wrote the first scholarly book on the evolution of Europol (Lynne Rienner). More recently, he has published on EU information-sharing in Kaunert and Leonard (eds), *European security, terrorism and intelligence* (Palgrave, 2013). His forthcoming article in *Intelligence and National Security* is 'Still moving toward a European FBI?' Occhipinti has presented his research at the US State Department and briefed newly appointed US ambassadors to the EU. In 2013, he was elected to the Executive Committee of the European Union Studies Association and co-founded its section on the EU's AFSJ.

References

Beetham, D (1991) *The Legitimation of Power* (London: Palgrave)

Busuioc, M, D Curtin and M Groenleer (2011) 'Agency growth between autonomy and accountability: the European Police Office as a "living institution"', *Journal of European Public Policy*, 18:6, 101–124

Carrubba, C (2003) 'The European Court of Justice, democracy, and enlargement', *European Union Politics*, 4:1, 75–100

Common Market Law Review (2010) 'Editorial comment. The EU as an Area of Freedom, Security and Justice: implementing the Stockholm Program', 48:5, 1307–1316

Council of the European Union (1999) 'Presidency conclusions, Tampere European Council, 15–16 October 1999', 16 October

Den Boer, M, C Hillebrand and A Nölke (2008) 'Legitimacy under pressure: the European web of counter-terrorism networks', *Journal of Common Market Studies*, 46:1, 101–124

DeVuyst, Y (2008) 'The European Union's institutional balance after the Treaty of Lisbon: "community method" and "democratic deficit" reassessed', *Georgetown Journal of International Law*, 39:3, 247–326

European Commission (2010) 'Communication from the Commission to the European Parliament and the Council, the EU Internal Security Strategy in action: five steps towards a more secure Europe', COM (2010) 673 final, Brussels, 22 November

European Council (2005) 'The Hague Program: strengthening freedom, security and justice in the European Union', *Official Journal of the European Union*, 2005/C 53/01

European Council (2010) 'The Stockholm Program—an open and secure Europe serving and protecting citizens', *Official Journal of the European Union*, 2010/C 115/01

Follesdal, A and S Hix (2006) 'Why there is a democratic deficit in the EU: a response to Majone and Moravcsik', *Journal of Common Market Studies*, 44:3, 533–562

Habermas, J (2001) 'The postnational constellation and the future of democracy', *The postnational constellation—political essays*, trans and ed Max Pensky (Cambridge, Massachusetts: MIT Press), 58–112

Hix, S (2008) *What's wrong with the European Union and how to fix it* (Cambridge: Polity Press)

Kaunert, C (2010) *European internal security: towards supranational governance in the Area of Freedom, Security and Justice* (Manchester: Manchester University Press)

Ladenburger, C (2008) 'Police and criminal law in the Treaty of Lisbon; a new dimension for the Community method', *European Constitutional Law Review*, 4:1, 20–40

Majone, G (1998) 'Europe's democratic deficit', *European Law Journal*, 4:1, 5–28

Moravcsik, A (2002) 'Reassessing legitimacy in the European Union', *Journal of Common Market Studies*, 40:4, 603–624

Occhipinti, J (2008) 'Securing a way out of the constitutional impasse' in Michael O'Neill and Nicolae Paun (eds) *Explaining the European Union's constitutional crisis: international perspectives* (Cluj-Napoca: Foundation for European Studies)

Peers, S (2011) 'Mission accomplished? EU justice and home affairs law after the Treaty of Lisbon', *Common Market Law Review*, 48:5, 661–693

Saurugger, S (2008) 'Interest groups and democracy in the European Union', *West European Politics*, 31:6, 1274–1291

Scharpf, FW (2004) 'Legitimationskonzepte jenseits des Nationalstaats', MPIfG Working Paper 04/6, Max-Planck-Institut für Gesellschaftsforschung, Cologne, November, <http://www.mpifg.de/pu/workpap/wp04-6/wp04-6.html>

Scharpf, FW (2009) 'Legitimacy in multilevel European polity', *European Political Science Review*, 1:2, 173–204

Scherrer, A, J Jeandesboz and E-P Guittet (2011) 'Developing an EU Internal Security Strategy, fighting terrorism and organised crime', Directorate General for Internal Policies, Policy Department C: Citizens' Rights and Constitutional Affairs Civil Liberties, Justice and Home Affairs, European Parliament, Brussels, November

Schmidt, VA (2004) 'The European Union: Democratic Legitimacy in a Regional State?', *Journal of Common Market Studies*, 42:4, 975–999

Schmidt, VA (2006) *Democracy in Europe* (Oxford: Oxford University Press)

Schmidt, VA (2013) 'Democracy and legitimacy in the European Union revisited: input, output, and "throughput"', *Political Studies*, 61:1, 2–22

Sieberson, S (2008) 'The Treaty of Lisbon and its impact on the European Union's democratic deficit', *Columbia Journal of European Law*, 14:3, 445–465

Weiler, JHH, UR Halstern and F Mayeerm (1995) 'European democracy and its critique', *West European Politics*, 18:3, 4–39

Zweifel, T (2002) '... Who is without sin cast the first stone: the EU's democratic deficit in comparison', *Journal of European Public Policy*, 9:5, 812–840

Tacit procedural politics: institutional change and member states' strategies in police and judicial cooperation in criminal matters

Marat Markert
European University Institute

Abstract   *This article analyses the dynamics of procedural politics in the EU's Police and Judicial Cooperation in Criminal Matters across subsequent Treaty regimes (Amsterdam and Lisbon). In the course of legislative policy-making in this area, member states and the European Commission engage in strategic interactions with respect to procedural rules, whereby specifically member states attempt to contain integrationist legislation coming from the Commission through legislative preemption strategies. Drawing on Joseph Jupille's procedural politics approach, the article hypothesizes that member states' strategies are conditioned by several scope conditions, notably jurisdictional ambiguity, influence difference between different decision-making procedures, and prointegrationist case law from the European Court of Justice. I test these hypotheses by analysing the legislative process on a number of selected cases.*

Introduction

A challenge for researchers studying the European Union (EU)'s policy area of Police and Judicial Cooperation in Criminal Matters (PJCCM) is to make sense of the pattern of EU integration in this area. PJCCM has been a 'dynamic' field of cooperation. Over the last decade, member states and the European Commission have come up with a plethora of legislative instruments, aimed at facilitating cross-border cooperation between national judicial and law enforcement authorities. Yet, this dynamism presents a puzzle as to who, or what, drives EU integration in this area of PJCCM: are member states successful in strengthening their governance autonomy in law and order policies by instrumentalizing EU institutions and organs in the field of PJCCM, as some have argued (Lavenex 2007; Wagner 2011)? Or, are they losing their autonomy and incrementally giving up sovereignty due to the evolution of EU institutions and supranational actors that increasingly escape governments' collective control (Herschinger et al 2011; Kaunert 2007)?

I would like to thank the participants of the 2011 'Policy Change in EU Internal Security' Workshop, held at the European University Institute in Florence, in particular Christian Kaunert, Julian Siegl, Adrienne Héritier, Monica Den Boer, Valsamis Mitsilegas and Wolfgang Wagner for their useful comments on an earlier version of this article. Likewise, I would like to thank the three anonymous reviewers and the editors of this journal for their suggestions and advice on this manuscript. All remaining errors are mine.

Neither current neofunctionalist accounts (Sandholtz and Stone Sweet 2012; Stone Sweet and Sandholtz 1997), nor (liberal) intergovernmentalism (Moravcsik 1994; Wolf 1999) fit squarely with institutional and policy developments in PJCCM. One finds evidence that would give weight to either argument. For example, despite successive institutional reforms in PJCCM that increasingly come to resemble a supranational mode of governance, intergovernmental elements continue to persist on questions of competences and decision-making procedure due to member states' reservations. At the same time, it was during the period when intergovernmental institutional rules dominated PJCCM (1993–2009) that first supranationalist inroads were made by the Commission and the European Court of Justice (ECJ)[1] into this policy area (Fletcher 2007; Kaunert 2007; Mitsilegas 2009).

In this article, I show that integration dynamics in PJCCM arise from strategic interactions between actors in the policy-making process. In particular, the institutional rules governing the policy-making processes provide opportunities for strategic interactions between member states and the Commission regarding the initiation of legislation. Examining member states' strategies underlying their legislative proposals, I show how member states have been successful in deliberately countering prointegrationist Commission legislation. More specifically, rather than just vetoing Commission initiatives, member states advance legislative proposals with the aim to preempt prointegrationist policies from the former. Drawing on the theoretical framework of 'procedural politics' (Jupille 2004), I show how member states engage in a game of 'tacit procedural politics' when deploying strategies of legislative preemption. In advancing this argument, this article's broader aim is to contribute to current debates on theories of EU integration by providing a theoretical perspective of how member states can influence the course of EU integration *against* the preferences and strategies of supranational actors.

The article is structured as follows: first, an overview on theories of interstitial institutional change and procedural politics within the EU's legislative process will be provided, followed by a section on formulating hypotheses regarding the scope conditions under which member states deploy strategies of legislative preemption. Second, I will test these hypotheses, drawing on cases of preemption selected from the population of legislative initiatives advanced by member states and the Commission over the last 12 years (1999–2011), as well as illustrate the strategy of legislative preemption in more detail based on two selected case studies. The article concludes with a discussion on implications of these findings for EU integration theories and the future of the area of PJCCM.

Procedural politics in the EU's decision-making process

In explaining the EU's institutional design and dynamics of change, 'classic' accounts of EU integration have focused on dynamics at treaty negotiations (Moravcsik and Nicolaidis 1999; Thurner and Pappi 2009). Yet, these accounts treat the 'process of institutional creation [in isolation] from the day-to-day political

---

[1] Throughout the article I will refer to the Court of Justice by its pre-Lisbon name, that is European Court of Justice (ECJ).

interactions that takes place within these institutions' (Farrell and Héritier 2007, 229) and thereby miss an important factor of how actors' preferences can change. Actors' institutional choices resulting from interactions in the policy-making process under given institutional rules are not taken into consideration.

More recently, attempts to develop theories of endogenous institutional change in the EU have gained momentum (Farrell and Héritier 2007; Jupille 2004; Stacey and Rittberger 2003). These accounts postulate that higher order institutional rules (general Treaty provisions on a given policy area) can change as a result of strategic interactions among different EU actors under given lower order institutional rules (procedural rules). These changes occur *ex ante* to Treaty negotiations and become institutionalized even without formal Treaty changes and have been termed *interstitial institutional change*.[2] There are two main mechanism by which such interstitial change occurs: either actors resort to informal procedural rules that substitute formal procedural ones (Farrell and Héritier 2007); or actors contest unfavourable institutional rules through litigation before the European Court of Justice (ECJ) (Jupille 2004; Moral Soriano 2007). In turn, and depending on the intensity of use of informal rules and/or judicial contestation, change in higher order institutional rules can ensue. The analysis of such interstitial dynamics focuses on conflicts over procedures, unfolding in the course of the policy-making process and the subsequent effects thereof on institutional choices of actors. These dynamics can be subsumed under what Joseph Jupille (2004) has labelled 'procedural politics'.

The procedural politics approach is based on several rational choice institutionalist assumptions. Actors are assumed to be utility maximizers with 'derived preferences [over institutional rules] as a function of the outcomes they generate' (Jupille 2004, 223), whereby 'outcomes' refers to institutional influence in the policy-making process, rather than achieving a specific policy outcome (Stacey and Rittberger 2003). In addition, actors are assumed to prefer procedurally the most efficient ('fastest') way to reach a final decision (Héritier and Reh 2012; Jupille 2004). Moreover, actors act strategically (as opposed to sincerely) by anticipating the moves of other actors, taking into consideration institutional and environmental constraints.

Legislative preemption as a tacit procedural politics strategy

One limitation of the procedural politics approach is that it has been applied only to cases where actors revealed their preferences, that is on cases where judicial contestation before the ECJ occurred. Cases in which actors made choices based on procedural consideration, yet no overt contestation occurred, cannot be accounted for. This constitutes a potential form of selection bias for the study of procedural politics.[3] I will focus on such cases of 'covert' conflict between actors regarding institutional rules in the policy-making process. In doing so, I suggest to distinguish between different kinds of procedural politics, played by the different actors. First,

---

[2] The term interstitial is derived from the Latin word *interstitium*, which means to stand in between. In the context of EU studies it is used to denote institutional changes in between Treaty negotiations.

[3] I am grateful to the anonymous reviewer who pointed this out.

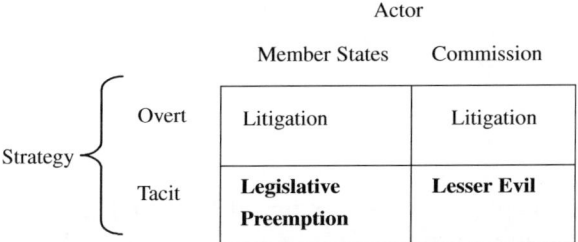

Figure 1. Possibilities of procedural politics by actors (member states and commission).

one can distinguish between overt and tacit procedural politics. Overt procedural politics take place when actors resort to litigation before the European Court, whereas tacit procedural politics take place without litigation. Second, member states on the one hand, and the Commission on the other deploy different strategies of tacit procedural politics: the former rely on what I call here 'legislative preemption', and the latter on what Susanne K Schmidt has termed strategies of 'lesser evil' (2000, 39). Figure 1 illustrates these different types of procedural politics.

The 'lesser evil' strategy as elaborated by Susanne K Schmidt (2000) postulates that, in the face of opposition in the Council of Ministers (hereinafter Council) to a Commission proposal, the latter can pressure the former to adopt its proposals by implicitly or explicitly threatening member states with litigation before the ECJ. In turn, the Council adopts the Commission proposal, even if the scope is beyond what individual member states would otherwise accept, given that a more supranational/ integrationist outcome is expected to arise from a potential Court ruling.

Legislative preemption, on the other hand, is a member states' strategy to counter proposals by the Commission. What motivates such strategic interactions is the divergence of actors' preferences (Frieden 1999). Preference divergence in PJCCM can occur regarding the level of integration entailed by a specific legislative proposal (Lavenex 2007). Accordingly, member states will preempt more 'integrationist'[4] Commission proposals by tabling legislative initiatives parallel to, or in anticipation of Commission initiatives in order to contain the integrationist scope of legislation. This implies that preemption is not merely a blocking or vetoing strategy: preemptive strategies necessitate proactive engagement by member states, whereas inaction in response to a Commission proposal does not reveal the preemptive logic. Likewise not all member states' proposals in PJCCM represent instances of preemption: issues on which the Commission has been deliberatively inactive while member states took initiative cannot be counted as instances of preemption. Methodologically, preemption can be identified whenever a member state(s) proposal is advanced, while having evidence for the existence of a Commission proposal, or plans to advance such a proposal.

The rationale behind preemption is the same as behind procedural politics: in opting for preemption, member states choose a path in the decision-making procedure that gives them more leverage over the final outcome. Preemption

---

[4] 'Integrationist' refers here to the placement of a given issue on a one- dimensional policy space ranging from 'exclusive national competence' to 'exclusive EU competence' (see Börzel 2005), whereby integrationist proposals are situated closer to the 'exclusive EU competence' end of the continuum.

provides member states with the possibility to diminish the influence of other actors in the decision-making process, contain policy drift and ultimately avoid litigation before the ECJ.

Limitations

The analysis on legislative dynamics in PJCCM sets limits on our ability to extrapolate the findings to other EU policy areas. PJCCM is a policy area with distinct institutional rules, particularly regarding the formal right initiative of member states (*ex* article 34(2) TEU; Article 76(b) TFEU). This shared right of initiative allows for strategies of preemption to be deployed in the first place. In contrast, for policy areas in which the Commission retains an exclusive right of initiative, member states can only block, contest judicially or simply ignore proposals. They cannot set the basis for subsequent negotiations through their own proposal (Rasmussen 2007).

Secondly, focusing exclusively on interactions between member states and the Commission, the role of the European Parliament (EP) is omitted here. Yet, the strategic interaction between Commission and member states at the proposal stage is a different step in the legislative procedure than interactions between Commission, Council and EP when interinstitutional negotiations on a given piece of legislation are underway, and thus merits a separate analysis.

Thirdly, I do not address transactions costs associated with member state(s)' proposals, that is resources member states invest at the prenegotiation stage to gather a group of like-minded peers in the Council who will support their initiative. There are plausible reasons to assume that transaction costs for member states' proposals are lower than for Commission proposals. Firstly, member states' proposals do not go through the same process as Commission proposals at the preparatory stage, such as public consultations with stake-holders, Impact Assessment studies etc. Secondly, the structure of the Council in PJCCM has several specialized subcommittees (such as the standing Committee on Internal Security [COSI]) and working groups that foster frequent and intensive contacts between the representatives from member states' Justice and Interior ministries (Nilsson and Siegl 2010), thereby reducing transaction costs at the preparatory stage. Bearing these limitations in mind, under what scope conditions do member states deploy the strategy of preemption?

Scope conditions for tacit procedural politics

Three institutional scope conditions under which procedural politics are likely to be triggered have been identified by Jupille (2004): the presence of an arbitrator that decides on procedural disputes, the degree of jurisdictional ambiguity and the influence difference among available institutional alternatives. I will consider each in turn.

Case law

The most straightforward scope condition is the existence of an (independent) ultimate arbitrator (Court) that decides in the 'endgame' which institutional alternative is the correct one. Procedural disputes before the ECJ are not isolated one-shot games, but develop path-dependent effects on future rounds of contestation (Burley and Mattli 1993; Pierson 1996; Sandholtz and Stone Sweet 2012; Scharpf 1999). The area of PJCCM does not create an exception in this regard (Fletcher 2007; Mitsilegas 2009). Expectations of actors about resolving successfully litigations concerning procedural disputes before the Court in their favour are strongly influenced by past case law. Moreover, case law might not only refer to contestations about the correct procedural rule (such as actions of annulment). Case law impacting institutional rules in PJCCM might as well arise from preliminary references originating from national courts. Through preliminary rulings, the ECJ might clarify the interpretation of ambiguous provisions in the Treaty or secondary law (for example, the legal effect of instruments), providing a more integrationist interpretation and thereby foster 'interregnum integration' (Stacey and Rittberger 2003, 863). In turn, the Commission can rely on such rulings to justify more integrationist legislation subsequently,[5] effectively threatening member states to accept it (see Schmidt 2000). To counter this, member states can preempt such proposals by advancing proposals on their own that are more limited in scope.

Thus, one would expect that strategies of legislative preemption are deployed when integrationist ECJ case law is used as the basis for Commission proposals (Hypothesis 1).

Jurisdictional ambiguity

Jurisdictional ambiguity is defined by Jupille (2004) as the amount of available institutional alternatives under which a given legislation in a policy area can be adopted. It is measured by the number of possible legal bases for any given piece of legislation. The choice of a legal basis, in turn, determines which actor can initiate legislation, which decision-making procedure applies and which *ex post* enforcement mechanisms exist. The more viable legal bases exist, the more likely actors will engage in procedural politics (Jupille 2004). Jurisdictional ambiguities do not arise from the Treaty texts by default, given that the EU's constitutional system is based on 'attributed competences' (20). Rather, the general formulation of Treaty provisions (that is, competences) can give rise to 'a lack of correspondence between political issue and the rules used to process them' (20). In turn, specific issues to be addressed through EU legislation might not fit unambiguously into one specific legal provision of the EU Treaty, but could be equally adopted under various legal bases. This potential misfit between legal text and concrete political issue can give rise to jurisdictional ambiguity, triggering strategic interactions between actors regarding the choice of the legal basis. In turn, this ambiguity could be exploited by any one actor to further its own particular interest.

Accordingly, one would expect that, in cases where a Commission proposal substantively deals with PJCCM matters, yet relies on a legal basis outside PJCCM, member states will preempt such proposals (Hypothesis 2).

---

[5] See, for example, COM (2005)583.

Influence difference

However, the mere 'existence of procedural alternatives ... does not suffice to produce procedural politics' (Jupille 2004, 23). Actors might be indifferent between the various institutional alternatives, if these alternatives do not entail a difference in terms of influence for any one actor over the legislative process. Consider the following example: a Commission proposal is based on a different legal basis than member states would prefer; yet, the legislative procedure and enforcement mechanisms under this legal basis are the same as under the legal basis member states would prefer. Accordingly, no procedural politics should be triggered. Thus, actors consider the difference in influence in the legislative process resulting from different alternatives, and choose the alternative that provides them with a maximum influence over the final outcome in the decision-making process. Influence difference might arise due to the existence cross-sectional alternatives at any point in time (legislation that cuts across different policy areas entailing different decision-making procedures) or procedural alternatives arising over time (imminent change in Treaty rules).

Therefore, we should observe that the influence difference accorded to actors through different available decision-making procedures—within as well as across subsequent Treaty periods—leads member states to preempt Commission proposals (Hypothesis 3).

Scope conditions in PJCCM: institutional change and case law

How do these scope conditions manifest themselves in PJCCM and how do they impact strategic interactions between member states and the Commission? The following section will operationalize the scope conditions that are hypothesized to drive tacit procedural politics.

Treaty provisions in PJCCM: from Amsterdam to Lisbon

During the post-Amsterdam Treaty period (1999–2009), the institutional rules governing PJCCM were set out in Title VI in the Treaty of the European Union (TEU). Member states and Commission shared the right of initiative to propose legislation (article 34(2) TEU). The interinstitutional legislative procedure foresaw Consultation with the EP (article 39 TEU and article 40a TEU), while the default voting procedure was unanimity. Furthermore, the direct effect of Decisions and Framework Decisions has been explicitly excluded (article 34(2) b, c TEU), thereby ensuring the scope of legislation remained intergovernmental, meaning that is was applicable only to states, not individuals. The role of the ECJ was limited to review the legality of instruments (Decisions, Framework Decisions and Conventions), interpreting the content and application of these measures and resolving procedural disputes between Commission and member states (articles 35(6) and 35(7) TEU). The Court's right to give preliminary rulings (article 35(1) TEU) was restricted and conditional on member states' explicit consent by way of a formal declaration (article 35(2)). A formal infringement procedure for nonimplementation did not exist.

These rules changed fundamentally with the entry into force of the Treaty of Lisbon. Commentators stated that the new decision-making rules would lead to 'higher degree of efficiency, legal certainty, accountability and democratic control' (Carrera and Geyer 2007, 2). Henceforth, the ordinary legislative procedure would apply to PJCCM (codecision and qualified majority voting), ultimately elevating the role of the EP in the legislative process. Likewise, the role of the Court and Commission had been elevated to give preliminary rulings on all PJCCM matters, as well as commence infringement procedures against member states respectively, albeit only after the end of a transition period of five years. The competence on legislative initiatives continues to be shared between member states and Commission (article 76 TFEU). However, a *quorum* rule has been introduced, requiring that member states' proposals have to comprise at least one quarter of the member states. How did these institutional rules and changes thereto affect the scope conditions of tacit procedural politics? With regard to jurisdictional ambiguity, there are no new substantive issue areas added to PJCCM that have previously fallen into the exclusive competence of the Community Pillar. Thus, theoretically, the institutional alternatives to propose legislation under a different Title than those governing PJCCM have not changed. However, a more general provision on substantive criminal law approximation was added in the Lisbon Treaty, allowing for 'approximation of criminal laws and regulations of the member states [if such approximation] proves essential to ensure the effective implementation of a Union policy in an area which has been subject to harmonization measures' (article 83(2) TFEU). Hence, a generic possibility for jurisdictional ambiguity has been added, which did not exist previously in the Treaty texts.

Regarding influence difference, we can observe a convergence from Amsterdam to Lisbon. Under the Treaty of Amsterdam, influence difference between procedures adopted under the former Third Pillar (Consultation + Unanimity + Shared Right of Initiative + No ECJ) and procedures applicable to 'communitarized' policies (Codecision + QMV + Exclusive Right of Initiative + ECJ) were greater than the influence differences between the procedures envisaged by the Treaty of Lisbon across the formerly separated policy areas (Codecision + (mostly) QMV + Quorum Shared Right of Initiative + ECJ). Some influence differences across policy areas remain also under the Lisbon Treaty (in particular regarding the shared right of initiative), albeit less crass than under the Amsterdam Treaty.

Interstitial institutional changes through case law

During the last decade, several ECJ rulings have addressed questions relating to the interpretation of provisions in the Treaties and secondary legislation concerning PJCCM matters. I will restrict myself to the two most important types of rulings, namely (1) horizontal disputes concerning the relationship between the First and Third Pillar of the EU and thus competences of the European Communities in criminal law, and (2) vertical disputes regarding the relationship between PJCCM measures and national legal orders. I will consider each in turn.

The Treaty of Amsterdam contained an explicit provision regarding the relationship between the Community and Third Pillar. These provisions, stipulated in article 47 TEU, proved to be a source of jurisdictional ambiguity, triggering several interinstitutional procedural disputes. Article 47 TEU stated that 'nothing in this Treaty [TEU] shall affect the Treaties establishing the European Communities or the subsequent Treaties and Acts modifying or supplementing them'. While intended to be a delimiting clause, defining an independent relationship between the Pillars and thereby isolating PJCCM matters from Community policies, it has been interpreted by the ECJ as a one way relationship,[6] manifesting a hierarchy of the First over the Third pillar (Mitsilegas 2009; Randazzo 2009). The Commission could henceforth propose legislation relating to criminal sanctions used for the effective implementation of the *acquis communautaire* to be implemented evenly across EU member states, even though harmonization of national criminal law was excluded by provisions in Title VI TEU. Furthermore, since the legal basis for such measures fell formally under the Community Pillar, the legislative procedure (Codecision) and enforcement mechanism (infringement procedures) would favour the Commission over individual member states. Consequently, Community policies could intrude the sphere of PJCCM, providing an additional jurisdictional alternative regarding legal basis and ultimately legislative procedure.

In addition to these horizontal disputes, ECJ case law also affected the Third Pillar vertically. The relevant case law concerns the establishment and development of the principle of 'indirect effect', originating from a series of cases (*Pupino*,[7] Dell'Orto,[8] Eredics[9]) (Fletcher 2007; Hatzopoulos 2008; Spaventa 2007). In the *Pupino* judgment the ECJ was asked, by way of reference for preliminary ruling from an Italian court, to clarify the relationship between national criminal procedural law and EU framework decisions. The case involved the Framework Decision on the standing of victims in criminal procedure.[10] The Court's interpretation changed two fundamental rules in the EU Treaty with regard to Title VI TEU. First, there was a question of admissibility posed by the Italian court. Could the ECJ provide a ruling that would interpret national criminal procedural law in the light of the provisions of an EU framework decision? The ECJ held that this was possible by invoking the principle of loyal cooperation between national and EU institutions as established in the former first Pillar (ex-Art. 10 TEC). Accordingly, national courts needed to interpret national criminal procedural law (as far as possible) in the light of EU law, and, if necessary call upon the ECJ to give an interpretation to this end.

Second, the ECJ held that framework decisions entailed 'indirect effect', despite the fact that member states explicitly excluded 'direct effect' of Framework Decisions and Council Decisions in the Treaty provisions under former Title VI TEU. The Court argued that such an EU conform interpretation of national criminal law was warranted since otherwise the Court's right to give preliminary rulings would be without effect. Consequently, individuals standing trial in national criminal proceedings could rely on framework decisions before national courts and judges would need to interpret national criminal procedure provisions as far as possible in the light of these Framework Decisions.

---

[6] Case C-176/03, *Commission v Council* [2005] ECR I-7879.

[7] Case C-105/03, *Criminal proceedings against Maria Pupino* [2005] ECR I-5285.

[8] Case C-467/05, *Criminal proceedings against Giovanni Dell'Orto* [2007] ECR I-5557.

[9] Case C-205/09, *Eredics and others* [2010] ECR I-10231.

[10] Framework Decision 2001/220/JHA, OJ L 82, 22 March 2001, p. 1.

The *Pupino* judgment constitutes an interstitial institutional change, since it changed Treaty provisions without formal Treaty amendment. Henceforth, it was clear that measures adopted in the Third Pillar—in particular measures concerning rights of individuals—could be screened by national courts (in cooperation with the ECJ) for correct implementation. In turn, member states needed to pay more attention to the substance of proposals relating to rights in criminal procedures, coming from the Commission.

Considering overall the evolution of case law in PJCCM, it affected all three scope conditions that trigger tacit procedural politics: (1) setting precedence for expansive interpretation of intergovernmental Treaty provisions (indirect effect); (2) increasing the jurisdictional ambiguity across the Pillars by making new institutional alternatives available (article 47 TEU interpretation); and (3) thereby increasing the influence difference of available institutional alternatives in the legislative process. How did these changes affect dynamics in the decision-making procedure?

Patterns of legislative policy-making in PJCCM

Data on legislative proposals (from Commission or member states) has been gathered from official EU databases (Pre-Lex and Legislative Observatory of the European Parliament). The cases selected fall within the period between the entry into force of the Treaty of Amsterdam (1 May 1999) and the most recent legislative file available (last checked in November 2011). Cases have been selected on the basis of a legalistic criterion: only measures adopted under the relevant Treaty Articles of PJCCM (Title VI TEU and Chapter 4 and 5 TFEU respectively, where member states could propose legislation) and only legally binding measures have been considered. The total population of cases comprises 162 legislative proposals. Looking at the evolution of legislative process in PJCCM, we can observe an increase in proposals advanced by the Commission and a decrease of member states' initiatives (Figure 2).

However, considering the adoption rate of member states and Commission proposals (see Table 1), we can see that member state initiatives fared better (81 per cent) than Commission proposals (52 per cent). The biggest share of failed Commission proposals have been withdrawn or lapsed due to the entry into force of the Lisbon Treaty (2009), since the Commission considered proposing reformed initiatives, based on the new legal bases provided in the Lisbon Treaty. At the same time, it is noteworthy that a large part of member states' initiatives still due have been adopted one day before the entry into force of the Lisbon Treaty.[11] Although these figures account only for a small fraction in the overall population of measures adopted from 1999 to 2011, this pattern indicates that anticipated changes in influence difference across subsequent Treaty regimes mattered for actors' strategic calculations: by adopting legislation shortly before the entry into force of the Lisbon Treaty, member states were not only able to avoid the less preferred Codecision procedure under the Lisbon rules, but were also able to push the shadow of ECJ enforcement far ahead into the future (until the end of the transition period in November 2014), while maintaining the ambiguous legal

---

[11] Council Doc. 5474/2/10, REV 2, pp. 10–14.

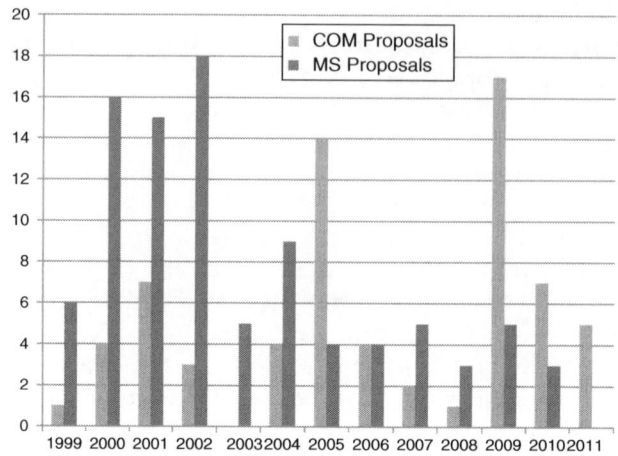

Figure 2. Number of Commission and member state legislative initiatives by year (N = 162).
Note: Year refers to the date of the proposal.
Source: European Parliament Legislative Observatory (search filter: legal basis on Criminal Justice and Police Cooperation: all Treaty Articles under Title VI TEU (Amsterdam) and Chapter 4 and 5 TFEU (Lisbon)) and Pre-Lex.

Table 1. Proposals: adopted, ongoing and withdrawn/lapsed by actor (1999–2011)

Actor	Adopted	On-Going	Withdrawn/Lapsed	Total
COM	36 (52%)	13 (19%)	20 (29%)	69
MS	75 (81%)	2 (2%)	16 (17%)	93

Source: European Parliament Legislative Observatory (search filter: legal basis on Criminal Justice and Police Cooperation: all Treaty Articles under Title VI TEU (Amsterdam) and Chapter 4 and 5 TFEU (Lisbon)) and Pre-Lex.

status of the effect of these post-Amsterdam instruments indefinitely (Peers 2009). Likewise, the Commission's choice to withdraw several of its proposals, only to reintroduce them under the Lisbon Treaty rules, can be explained by the influence difference in procedural rules: with a *quorum* rule for member states' proposals and qualified majority voting, chances that a Commission proposal would be preempted were lower than under institutional rules that allow for single member state proposals and unanimity voting in the Council.

Zooming in on member states' initiatives, one can see that the ratio between collective and individual initiatives of member states has increased already before the Lisbon Treaty *quorum* rule, despite an enlarging EU membership and an increasingly constraining institutional environment (Figures 3 and 4). The ratio in the EU27 column is roughly 3:1 (11 collective initiatives and four individual initiatives).

To what extent these patterns reflect strategic considerations on the side of the member states to contain Commission proposals and whether/how these strategies are influenced by the hypothesized scope conditions will be the main focus of the next sections.

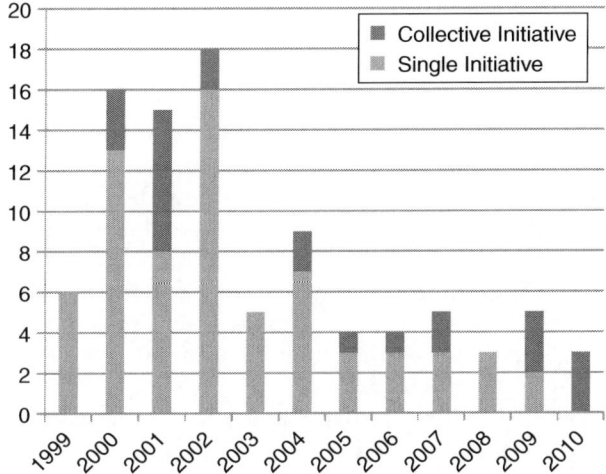

Figure 3. Evolution of collective and individual initiatives of member states over time (*N* = 93).

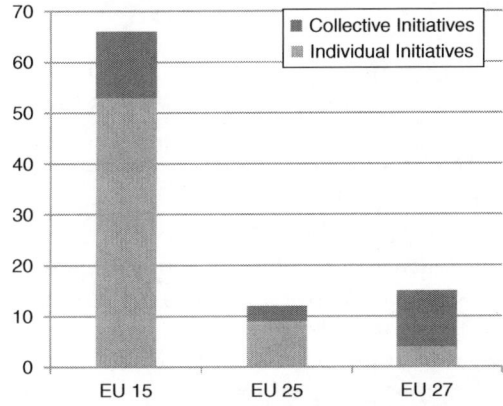

Figure 4. Individual and collective initiatives across different EU sizes.

Patterns of legislative preemption

How were cases of preemption identified? Cases of preemption can be found whenever two parallel legislative dossiers (one initiated by the Commission and one by member states) listed in the official EU databases, or whenever a given legislative dossier has been planned by the Commission, but eventually proposed by member states. To identify these instances, various databases monitoring the decision-making procedure (Pre-Lex and EP Legislative Observatory) have been cross-checked with various Commission databases (DORIE,[12] Green Papers,[13] Impact Assessments,[14] Commission's Work Programme[15]) across all 162 issues.

---

[12] <http://ec.europa.eu/dorie/home.do>.
[13] <http://europa.eu/documentation/official-docs/green-papers/index_en.htm>.
[14] <http://ec.europa.eu/governance/impact/index_en.htm>.
[15] <http://ec.europa.eu/atwork/key-documents/index_en.htm>.

From the population of member states' legislative initiatives presented above, I could identify seven instances of legislative preemption. These are the Directive on the Right to Interpretation and Translation in Criminal Proceedings[16] (RTI), the Framework Decision on Prevention and Settlement of Conflicts of Exercise of Jurisdiction in Criminal Proceedings[17] (FD NeBis), the Council Decision on setting up Eurojust[18] (CD Eurojust), the Council Decision on the stepping up of cross-border cooperation (Prüm Decision),[19] the Framework Decision on simplifying the exchange of information and intelligence between law enforcement authorities (the so-called 'Swedish Initiative'),[20] the proposal for a Directive on the European Protection Order[21] (EPO) and a proposal for a Directive on the European Investigation Order[22] (EIO). Overall, successful attempts of legislative preemption account for slightly less than eight per cent of cases from the entire population of member states' proposals ($n = 93$).

In all but one case (EPO), the Commission launched its own initiatives prior to that of member states or was preparing to do so; and all but one (the 'Swedish Initiative') are based on collective member states proposals. Three of these instruments (RTI, EIO, EPO) had been proposed by member states shortly after the entry into force of the Lisbon Treaty, of which two (RTI and EIO) had been already envisaged by the Commission under the Amsterdam Treaty. The other four were preempted under the Treaty of Amsterdam (FD NeBis, CD Eurojust, Prüm and Swedish Initiative).

Turning to the three hypotheses, which of the three scope conditions had an impact on member states' preemptive strategies? With regard to the effect of ECJ case law (H1), two cases were affected by previous case law, notably RTI and FD NeBis. The ruling in *Pupino* had implications for the substantive scope of the RTI, since it concerned rights of individuals in criminal proceedings and ultimately could be influenced by the principle of 'indirect effect'. More specifically, a large scope of an instrument addressing rights of individuals in criminal proceedings would have put pressure on national courts to interpret national criminal procedural law in conformity with these provisions. In turn, this would have created potentially more preliminary questions arising from national courts directed towards the ECJ, thereby providing further opportunity for Court driven integration in PJCCM against the preferences of member states. In fact, the original proposal from the Commission on procedural rights in criminal proceedings[23] contained a wider range of rights than member states wanted. Likewise, the long thread of ECJ cases created by the *Ne Bis in Idem* provision (article 54 of the Convention Implementing the Schengen Agreement [CISA] created an obligation for the legislators to take account of these cases in future legislation; Fletcher 2007). These rulings stood in stark contrast to certain member states' preferences in this

---

[16] Directive 2010/64/EU, OJ L 280, 26 October 2010, p. 1.
[17] Framework Decision 2009/948/JHA, OJ L 328, 15 December 2009, p. 42.
[18] Decision 2002/187/JHA, OJ L 63, 6 March 2002, p. 1.
[19] Decision 2008/615/JHA, OJ L 210, 6 August 2008, p. 1.
[20] Framework Decision 2006/960/JHA, OJ L 386, 29 December 2006, p. 89.
[21] Initiative for a Directive on the European Protection Order (2010/C 69/02), OJ C 69, 18 March 2010, p. 5.
[22] Initiative for a Directive regarding the European Investigation Order in criminal matters, (2010/C 165/02), OJ C 165, 24 June 2010, p. 22.
[23] COM(2004)328.

area. The Commission made extensive reference to this case law in its preparatory work for a proposal on settlement of conflicts of jurisdiction (FD NeBis). Among others, its proposal suggested a centralized mechanism for settling conflicts through Eurojust.[24] These prointegrationist plans thus provided an incentive for member states to preempt potentially integrationist Commission proposals, replacing it with a more flexible instrument.

Jurisdictional ambiguity (H2) affected directly only one case (EPO), where the Commission was planning to adopt it under a civil law cooperation legal basis (Lambermont 2012), but member states opted for a legal basis under criminal law cooperation. This pattern supports Hypothesis 2 in the post-Lisbon period. What about the pre-Lisbon period? The four pre-Lisbon cases identified here as instances of preemption do not reveal evidence that the Commission would have sought to adopt them under a legal basis outside the PJCCM Title (under the former 'first Pillar'). Yet, as the case of the Prüm Decision shows, jurisdictional ambiguity might also be created when legislative proposals are 'fused' strategically (Jupille 2004). In this case, the Commission's plans to propose a Framework Decision on the exchange of information among law enforcement authorities,[25] parallel to the Prüm Treaty, coincided with its plans on introducing reformed rules on Data Protection in the context of PJCCM.[26] Since the benchmark for data protection standards has always been the data protection legislation adopted under the former 'first pillar',[27] the potential for 'cross-pillarization' existed also in this case. Member states, in turn, opted for taking the Prüm Treaty as the basis for adopting a legal instrument in PJCCM, instead of pursuing negotiations on the Commission's proposal. In doing so, member states were successful in limiting the scope of the instrument (House of Lords 2007; Kietz and Maurer 2007), as well as separating the issue of data exchange from questions of data protection. In sum, jurisdictional ambiguity could be identified in two out of seven cases underlying member states preemption strategies.

Regarding influence difference (H3), in a sense all cases of preemption support this hypothesis, since part of the influence of each actor over the decision-making procedure starts with who proposes legislation. Aside from this general effect of influence difference, one case reveals that difference in decision-making procedure would have mattered (EPO). Had the Commission proposed the EPO successfully under its preferred legal basis (Judicial Cooperation in Civil Matters), member states would have been prevented from adopting their proposal on the EPO, as well as prevented from vetoing the legislative proposal through an 'emergency brake' mechanism. Since influence difference arises also in the transition from one Treaty period to the next, it is useful to consider those cases of preemption that have been timed around the period of the entry into force of the Lisbon Treaty. Two cases can be attributed to this change in influence difference across Treaties, whereby one has been adopted shortly before the transition date (FD NeBis), and the other one shortly afterwards (RTI, see below).

Due to reasons of space, an in-depth description of the processes from each single preemption case cannot be provided here. Therefore, the following section

---

[24] SEC (2005)1767.
[25] COM (2005)490.
[26] COM (2005)475.
[27] Data Protection Directive 95/46/EC.

will elaborate more thoroughly on the process of preemption, drawing on two cases as illustrative examples (RTI and EIO). These two cases provide interesting variation on the hypothesized scope conditions: Both have been proposed by the Commission during the Amsterdam Treaty period and were subsequently preempted by member states under the Lisbon Treaty rules.

Case I. Directive on rights to interpretation and translation in criminal proceedings

Shortly before the entry into force of the Lisbon Treaty, the Commission advanced a proposal[28] on the rights to interpretation and translation in criminal proceedings for persons standing trial in another member state. The Commission proposal was already the second attempt, following a failed proposal from 2004.[29] The first proposal failed to pass Council negotiations due to its broad scope, since it included a package of rights for individuals in criminal proceedings.[30] At that time, several member states' delegation—including the UK, Maltese and Cypriot delegations—could not accept such a broad scope.[31] In giving justification to the UK House of Commons' Justice Committee, Lord Bach explained the decision to block the Commission proposal and support the member states proposal on the procedural rights framework decision:

> [w]e think there was a real danger of that a few years ago, which is the main reason why we, with some other countries, were not prepared to accept the decision on procedural safeguards and pulled out of it. ... Now, with the Swedish roadmap and the way in which the framework decisions are to emerge one by one—the first having emerged really, and I was happy to speak in favour of it .... (House of Commons 2009, Ev 2)

Shortly after the entry into force of the Lisbon Treaty and parallel to a new Commission proposal, several member states advanced their own initiative,[32] thereby effectively preempting a new proposal by the Commission.

The failure of the first Commission proposal should be seen in the light of the institutional changes brought about by ECJ rulings. Following the *Pupino* judgment, Framework Decisions were established to entail indirect effect, making these instruments enforceable in national courts. Henceforth, adopting the Commission proposal would have entailed an obligation on the side of the member states to not only transpose the framework decision into national criminal procedural law, but also oblige national courts to interpret existing national criminal procedural law through the lens of EU law. Consequently, national courts could invalidate provisions of national criminal procedural law on the basis of broadly defined Framework Decision provisions (Lööf 2006). Moreover, in cases where ambiguities of interpretation would arise, national criminal procedural law provisions could give rise to further preliminary references and thus interpretations by the ECJ, potentially expanding the jurisdiction of the Court in PJCCM. Member states that blocked the Commission

---

[28] COM (2009)338.
[29] COM (2004)328.
[30] COM (2004)328.
[31] Council Doc. 10287/07, p. 3.
[32] Council Doc. 16471/09.

proposal (United Kingdom, the Czech Republic, Ireland, Malta and Slovakia) feared that granting procedural rights through the framework decision would leave them less flexibility in accommodating such rights in their national systems.[33]

Although the constraining institutional context of the Amsterdam Treaty provided incentives to block a Commission proposal, the allegedly 'enabling' institutional context under Lisbon Treaty can account for why member states eventually advanced their own proposal. A glance at the Impact Assessment conducted by the Commission prior to the second proposal reveals that the preferred option under the Lisbon Treaty would have been the reintroduction of a comprehensive proposal, covering all the procedural rights as stipulated in the original 2004 proposal:[34]

> [i]f the Lisbon Treaty comes into force, unanimity will no longer be required in order to adopt legislation in the Council and the European Parliament would play a role in codecision. Since 21 member states supported the 2004 proposal and the European Parliament has been calling for a measure of this type for some time, both these factors make it more likely that a broader instrument could be adopted.[35]

It is difficult to ascertain whether the Commission would have tabled a different proposal under the Lisbon Treaty, encompassing more rights as its original proposal envisaged. However, considering that member states had reservation about the scope, a far-reaching Commission proposal might have divided the Council. Thus, even if a vast majority of member states had accepted a new Commission proposal under the Lisbon Treaty, they opted rather for their own, limited proposal. This corroborates Hypotheses 1 and 3: expansive ECJ case law made member states wary of Commission proposals on rights enhancing measures. Likewise, changing influence difference must have played a role. In this regard, the effect of influence difference across subsequent Treaty regimes seems to be stronger than within a single Treaty regime.

Case II. European investigation order

A second instance in which member states preempted a planned Commission proposal concerns the Directive on the European Investigation Order (EIO). At the time of writing (November 2011) the proposal is still subject to negotiation in the Council. The EIO seeks to establish a comprehensive mutual recognition instrument in the area of obtaining and transferring evidence, replacing all other existing instruments in this area.[36] Previous instruments proved to be impracticable, since either these were wrongly transposed into national law,[37] or not transposed at all. Furthermore, given that the Mutual Legal Assistance Convention of 2000 was still in force and could be used for requesting evidence from other member states, national authorities would be more likely to use one

---

[33] Council Doc. 11788/06.

[34] SEC (2009)915.

[35] SEC (2009)915.

[36] Framework Decision 2003/577/JHA, OJ L 196, 2 August 2003, p. 20, and Framework Decision 2008/978/JHA, OJ L 350, 30 December 2008, p. 72.

[37] COM (2008)885.

legal channel for all requests, rather than different channels for 'requests' and 'orders' (Bachmaier-Winter 2010).

In the Stockholm Multiannual Policy Programme (2010–2014), the European Council envisaged to replace this patchwork of different instruments with a comprehensive system, inviting the Commission to draft a proposal.[38] Subsequently the Commission launched a consultation process by issuing a Green Paper.[39] The Commission envisaged broadening the scope of the EEW by including all types of evidences,[40] as well as reducing the grounds for refusal in order to ensure an effective functioning of the principle of mutual recognition of evidence orders. Furthermore, the Commission sought to receive input from stake-holders and interested parties on the whether establishing common standards on the admissibility of evidence in criminal trials would be desirable— with its own preference clearly in favour of such a regime.[41]

Following the Green Paper, a group of seven member states tabled its own proposal for a measure that would repeal the EEW and related acts. The Commission referred to the Stockholm Programme, where it was explicitly stated that such a comprehensive system was to be proposed by the Commission.[42] Although we lack a comparable final draft proposal by the Commission, evidence that institutional ambiguity played a role can be found in member states' reactions to the Green Paper. A particularly contentious element in the Green Paper was the question concerning common standards for gathering evidence. The Treaty of Lisbon provides an explicit legal basis for the approximation of criminal procedural law, but only for minimum rules (article 82(2) TFEU). Introducing common standards on how to gather evidence would have touched upon core questions of law enforcement authorities' competences and procedures in criminal trials.

Considering the responses to the Green Paper by the preempting member states, several indications for an opposition to common standards become apparent. The Austrian, Swedish and Spanish responses referred to the lack of EU competences to introduce such common standards in the Lisbon Treaty[43] and the conflict such standards would create with regard to the principle of mutual recognition respectively.[44] Governments from the 'new' member states sponsoring the EIO welcomed the introduction of such standards, but remarked that 'diversity of criminal procedures in the various member states should also be taken into account'.[45] Other member states had serious misgivings about a new

---

[38] The Stockholm Programme, OJ C 115/1, 4 May 2010, p. 12.
[39] COM (2009)624.
[40] *Ibid.*, p. 5.
[41] *Ibid.*
[42] <http://ec.europa.eu/justice/news/intro/doc/comment_2010_08_24_en.pdf>.
[43] <http://ec.europa.eu/justice/news/consulting_public/0004/national_governments/sweden_en.pdf>.
[44] <http://ec.europa.eu/justice/news/consulting_public/0004/national_governments/spain_en.pdf>.
[45] <http://ec.europa.eu/justice/news/consulting_public/0004/national_governments/bulgaria_en.pdf>, <http://ec.europa.eu/justice/news/consulting_publ ic/0004/national_governments/estonia_en.pdf>, <http://ec.europa.eu/justice/news/ consulting_public/0004/national_governments/slovenia_en.pdf>.

legislative initiative, including Germany, France, Cyprus and Poland, albeit for different reasons than the avant-garde group.[46]

In sum, member states, even if diverging on the question whether a new measure should be introduced or not, agreed at least to preempt a proposal by the Commission. Yet, neither jurisdictional ambiguity, nor past ECJ case law affected member states decision to preempt in the case of the EIO. However, and as already pointed out above, the influence difference across subsequent Treaty regimes seems to matter more than within a single Treaty regime in PJCCM. Thus, the post-Lisbon rules might have made a comprehensive proposal of the Commission more likely, consequently leading member states to preempt it.

Conclusion

What do these patterns of policy-making tell us about the processes and mechanisms underlying EU integration in PJCCM? The effects of (changing) institutional rules on member states' strategies in PJCCM provides a promising empirical field for testing and complementing theoretical approaches to EU integration that focus exclusively on strategies of supranational agents and neofunctionalist logics. I want to conclude with a discussion on possible implications of these findings for EU integration theory debates and to what extent the legislative dynamics in PJCCM can enrich these debates.

First, legislative preemption challenges neofunctionalist arguments about the positive feedback mechanism underlying EU integration, that is integrationist case law leading to subsequent integrationist legislation (Schmidt 2000; Stone Sweet and Sandholtz 1997). Legislative dynamics in PJCCM reveal that integrationist case law has led to more prointegrationist proposals by the Commission. However, such case law has led member states to advance legislation in an attempt to contain integrationist initiatives by the Commission. Thus, there seems to be evidence for a 'negative' feedback loop, whereby member states aim to correct for 'unwanted' integration steps.

Second, an important point in the debate between neofunctionalism and intergovernmentalism is the 'unintended consequences' of institutions that unfold over time (Stone Sweet and Sandholtz 2001; Tsebelis and Garrett 2001). While 'unintended' usually refers to effects of EU institutions escaping member states' collective control, legislative dynamics in PJCCM reveal the opposite development. The original intention behind introducing a *quorum* for member states initiatives was to contain individual member state proposals that would reflect narrow national interests. However, member states proved to be able to use this restrictive institutional rule as a corrective device against supranational actors' policies and decisions. Hence, despite increasing environmental constraints, member states are able to exert collective control over EU institutions and the course of EU integration.

Third and finally, considering the evidence from PJCCM in the light of more recent debates regarding member states' ability to influence ECJ rulings through a collective 'threat of legislative override' (Carrubba et al 2008, 436): preemption can

---

[46] <http://ec.europa.eu/justice/news/consulting_public/0004/national_governments/germany_en.pdf>.

be seen as a strategy that is sensitive to expansive ECJ jurisprudence and aims at containing its effects in future Commission legislation. Through a series of cases in PJCCM, the Court raised the stakes for member states in negotiating future legislation that deal with rights of individuals in criminal procedure. Legislative preemption proves to be one option for member states to control the substantive scope of legislation following an 'unfavourable' ECJ ruling.

To what extent strategies of legislative preemption will continue to be deployed in the future and have a lasting effect on the pattern of integration in this area remains to be seen. Considering current and future developments in PJCCM, we should see more rather than less procedural politics (tacit or overt) in this area. Recent plans by the Commission to establish an EU criminal law policy[47] (using criminal law approximation to ensure effective implementation of other EU policies) will certainly cause conflict between Council and Commission regarding the scope of integration in substantive criminal law, potentially triggering legislative preemption strategies. Likewise, several upcoming institutional changes in PJCCM might trigger further strategic action on the side of member states: the impending expiry of the transitional period on both Commission and ECJ competences in PJCCM[48] will bring about changes regarding these actors' enforcement powers. Until then, the old, pre-Lisbon PJCCM legislations will need to be reformed to give full effect to ECJ jurisdiction over them (Gocmen 2012). Given the number of Framework Decisions to be reformed, some speculate that this will give rise to more case law in PJCCM. It is expected that individuals in criminal procedures will rely on the principle of direct effect to either claim protection of their fundamental rights flowing from the EU level (vis-à-vis national provisions), or, on the contrary, contest EU acts that infringe upon their national rights in criminal procedure (Gocmen 2012, 17–30). Thus, the reform of pre-Lisbon measures might trigger strategies of member states to contain the substantive scope of post-Lisbon instruments. In short, the coming two years will provide an empirical basis for testing the validity of the legislative preemption arguments.

Notes on contributor

Marat Markert is a PhD candidate at the Political and Social Sciences Department, European University Institute. His main research interests are related to the analysis of institutional and policy dynamics in the area of EU criminal justice and police cooperation.

References

Bachmaier-Winter, Lorena (2010) 'European investigation order for obtaining evidence in the criminal proceedings: study of the proposal for a European directive', *Zeitschrift für Internationale Strafrechtsdogmatik*, 5:9, 580–589

Börzel, Tanja A (2005) 'Mind the gap! European integration between level and scope', *Journal of European Public Policy*, 12:2, 217–236

Burley, Anne-Marie and Walter Mattli (1993) 'Europe before the court: a political theory of legal integration', *International Organization*, 47:1, 41–76

---

[47] COM (2011)573.
[48] Article 10, Protocol 36 on transitional provisions (OJ C 115, 9 May 2008, p. 322).

Carrera, Sergio and Florian Geyer (2007) 'Thereform treaty and justice and home affairs—implications for the common area of freedom, security and justice', CEPS Policy Brief 141, Centre for European Policy Studies, <http://www.ceps.be/ceps/dld/1365/pdf>

Carrubba, Clifford James, Matthew Gabel and Charles Hankla (2008) 'Judicial behavior under political constraints: evidence from the European Court of Justice', *American Political Science Review*, 102:2, 435–452

Farrell, Henry and Adrienne Héritier (2007) 'Introduction: contested competences in the European Union', *West European Politics*, 30:2, 227–243

Fletcher, Maria (2007) 'The European Court of Justice: carving itself an influential role in the EU's Third Pillar', Paper presented at EUSA tenth biennial international conference, <http://aei.pitt.edu/7818/1/fletcher-m-08i.pdf>

Frieden, Jeffry (1999) 'Actors and preferences in international relations' in David A Lake and Robert Powell (eds) *Strategic choice and international relations* (Princeton: Princeton University Press), 39–76

Gocmen, Ilke (2012) 'Keeping a(n) (un)fair balance between the judicial cooperation in criminal matters and fundamental rights: the contributions of the Court of Justice of the European Union', Paper presented at UACES 42nd annual conference, <http://events.uaces.org/documents/papers/1201/gocmen.pdf>

Hatzopoulos, Vassilis (2008) 'With or without you ... judging politically in the field of Area of Freedom, Security and Justice', *European Law Review*, 33:1, 44–65

Héritier, Adrienne and Christine Reh (2012) 'Codecision and its discontents: intra-organisational politics and institutional reform in the European Parliament', *West European Politics*, 35:5, 1134–1157

Herschinger, Eva, Markus Jachtenfuchs and Christiane Kraft-Kasack (2011) 'Scratching the heart of the artichoke? How international institutions and the European Union constrain the state monopoly of force', *European Political Science Review*, 3:3, 445–468

House of Commons (2009) Great Britain Parliament Justice Committee. Justice Issues in Europe. Seventh Report. Session 2009–2010, Vol. II

House of Lords (2007) 'Prüm: an effective weapon against terrorism and crime?', House of Lords European Union Committee 18th report with evidence, <http://www.publications.parliament.uk/pa/ld200607/ldselect/ldeucom/90/9002.htm>

Jupille, Joseph (2004) *Procedural politics: issues, influence and institutional choice in the European Union* (Cambridge: Cambridge University Press)

Kaunert, Christian (2007) 'Without the power of purse or sword: the European arrest warrant and the role of the Commission', *Journal of European Integration*, 29:4, 387–404

Kietz, Daniela and Andreas Maurer (2007) 'Folgen der Prümer Vertragsavantgarde: Fragmentierung und Entdemokratisierung der europaeischen Justiz- und Innenpolitik?', SWP Diskussionspapier, SWP Berlin, <http://www.swp-berlin.org/fileadmin/contents/products/arbeitspapiere/Pruem_KS__JBOES_final_word.pdf>

Lambermont, Frank (2012) 'The member states' initiatives: an inter-institutional turf war after the Treaty of Lisbon', EIPA Scope Article, EIPA Maastricht, <http://www.eipa.eu/files/repository/eipascope/20120710143731_FRL_Eipascope2012.pdf>

Lavenex, Sandra (2007) 'Mutual recognition and the monopoly of force: limits of the single market analogy', *Journal of European Public Policy*, 14:5, 762–779

Lööf, Robin (2006) 'Shooting from the hip: proposed minimum rights in criminal proceedings throughout the EU', *European Law Journal*, 12:3, 421–430

Mitsilegas, Valsamis (2009) *EU criminal law* (London: Hart Publishing)

Moral Soriano, Leonor (2007) 'Contested procedures: ambiguities, interstices and EU institutional change', *West European Politics*, 30:2, 321–337

Moravcsik, Andrew (1994) 'Why the European Union strengthens the state: domestic politics and international cooperation', CES Working Paper 52, Center for European Studies Harvard, <http://aei.pitt.edu/9151/>

Moravcsik, Andrew and Kalypso Nicolaidis (1999) 'Explaining the Treaty of Amsterdam: interests, influence, institutions', *Journal of Common Market Studies*, 37:1, 59–85

Nilsson, Hans G and Julian Siegl (2010) 'The Council in the Area of Freedom, Security and Justice' in Jörg Monar (ed) *The institutional dimension of the European Union's Area of Freedom, Security and Justice* (Brussels: PIE Peter Lang), 53–82

Peers, Steve (2009) 'The 'Third Pillar acquis' after the Treaty of Lisbon enters into force', Statewatch Analysis, <http://www.statewatch.org/analyses/no-88-analysis-third%20pillar-ver2.pdf>

Pierson, Paul (1996) 'The path of European integration: a historical institutionalist analysis', *Comparative Political Studies*, 29:2, 123–163

Randazzo, Vincenzo (2009) 'EU security policies and the pillar structure: a legal analysis', *Perspectives on European Politics and Society*, 10:4, 506–522

Rasmussen, Anne (2007) 'Challenging the Commission's right of initiative? Conditions for institutional change and stability', *West European Politics*, 30:2, 244–264

Sandholtz, Wayne and Alec Stone Sweet (2012) 'Neofunctionalism and supranational governance' in Erik Jones, Anand Menon and Stephen Weatherill (eds) *Oxford handbook of EU politics* (Oxford: Oxford University Press), 18–33

Scharpf, Fritz W (1999) *Governing Europe: effective and democratic?* (Oxford: Oxford University Press)

Schmidt, Susanne K (2000) 'Only an agenda setter? The European Commission's power over the Council of Ministers', *European Union Politics*, 1:1, 37–61

Spaventa, Eleanor (2007) 'Opening Pandora's Box: some reflections on the constitutional effects of the decision in Pupino', *European Constitutional Law Review*, 3:1, 5–24

Stacey, Jeffrey and Berthold Rittberger (2003) 'Dynamics of formal and informal institutional change in the EU', *Journal of European Public Policy*, 10:6, 858–883

Stone Sweet, Alec and Wayne Sandholtz (1997) 'European integration and supranational governance', *Journal of European Public Policy*, 4:3, 297–317

Stone Sweet, Alec and Wayne Sandholtz (2001) 'No foundations, no edifice: a comment on Tsebelis and Garrett', <http://www.socsci.uci.edu/~wsandhol/>

Thurner, Paul W and Franz Urban Pappi (2009) *European Union intergovernmental conferences—domestic preference formation, transgovernmental networks and the dynamics of compromise* (London and New York: Routledge)

Tsebelis, George and Geoffrey Garrett (2001) 'The institutional foundations of intergovernmentalism and supranationalism in the European Union', *International Organization*, 55:2, 357–390

Wagner, Wolfgang (2011) 'Negative and positive integration in EU criminal law co-operation', *European Integration Online Papers*, <http://eiop.or.at/eiop/texte/2011-003a.htm>

Wolf, Klaus Dieter (1999) 'The new raison d'état as a problem for democracy in world society', *European Journal of International Relations*, 5:3, 333–363

Tempering the EU? NGO advocacy in the Area of Freedom, Security, and Justice

Emek M Uçarer
Bucknell University

Abstract *The European Union's (EU) area of Freedom, Security and Justice (AFSJ) portfolio comprises policy areas such as immigration and asylum, and police and judicial cooperation. Steps were taken to bring this field into the mandate of the EU first by the Maastricht Treaty, followed by changes implemented by the Amsterdam and Lisbon Treaties, the last one 'normalizing' the EU's erstwhile Third Pillar. As the emergent EU regime continues to consolidate in this field, NGOs of various kinds continue to seek to influence policy-making and implementation, with varying success. This article seeks to establish the context in which NGOs carry out their work and argues that the EU-NGO interface is impacted both by the institutional realities of the European Union and the capacities of EU-oriented NGOs to seize and expand opportunities for access and input into the policy cycle. Using EU instruments representing three different policy bundles in AFSJ (immigration, asylum and judicial cooperation in criminal matters), the article seeks to map out NGO strategies in engaging and oftentimes resisting European Union policy instruments.*

Introduction

Nongovernmental organizations (NGOs) have long had the European Union (EU) in their sights. Kohler-Koch observes that 'over the last two decades civil society has gained a prominent place in the programmatic re-orientation of EU integration' (Kohler-Koch 2009, 48; Saurugger 2010), not least because of the EU's desire to address its so-called democratic deficit. The European Union's (EU) Area of Freedom, Security and Justice (AFSJ; previously Justice and Home Affairs, JHA) is a latecomer in this respect. The AFSJ portfolio comprises cooperation on immigration, asylum, police and judicial matters. This field was brought into the mandate of the EU by the Maastricht Treaty, followed by institutional changes implemented by the Amsterdam and Lisbon Treaties, the last one 'normalizing' the EU's erstwhile Third Pillar. AFSJ deals with concepts of state sovereignty and is tinged with negative attitudes towards outsiders, so policy output in this field has been slow and often riddled with controversy. Despite the institutional progress and 'normalization' of the field with the Lisbon Treaty, AFSJ has certain characteristics (lowest common denominator policy output, resistance to transparency) that make it a target for criticism for its democratic deficit as well as a difficult arena to penetrate by civil society actors. A review of the engagement of prominent Brussels-based NGOs with this field through various access points and strategies and their experiences in that process are instructive in highlighting the lingering peculiarities of AFSJ despite its evolution.

The analysis is based on process-tracing of four recent key AFSJ policy instruments of the European Union and is augmented by 40 semistructured and anonymized[1] elite interviews conducted in October–November 2005, June 2011 and October–November 2011 with NGO staffers[2] and EU officials.[3] These four instruments are the Family Reunification Directive, the Asylum Procedures Directive, the Returns Directive and the Trafficking Directive. Collectively, these four instruments span all four subfields of AFSJ, namely immigration, asylum and judicial and police cooperation. Two of the instruments (Family Reunifications Directive and the Asylum Procedures Directive representing legal migration and asylum) were negotiated before the move to co-decision and Qualified Majority Voting (QMV), arguably presenting rather narrow opportunities for NGO input and impact. The other two instruments (the Returns Directive, the first major instrument on irregular migration, and the Trafficking Directive, the first major criminal law instrument in AFSJ) were concluded in post-Lisbon AFSJ, presenting potential for better leverage for NGOs. Yet, as the narrative below will illustrate, while NGO access might have improved over the last 10 years, the same cannot be said of their impact, characterized by the increasing distance between NGO positions and policy outcome throughout the policy cycle. Why? This article argues that this has to do with the negotiating behaviour of EU actors to which NGOs have better access, especially the European Parliament (EP). Even though the post-Lisbon institutional framework improved its stature in decision-making, the EP has not lived up to NGOs' expectations of being a forceful ally.

Because of the sensitive nature of the issues involved in this portfolio, cooperation has been slow and difficult. Furthermore, AFSJ is has gone through significant institutional restructuring. In such a setting in which governmental cooperation was difficult, nongovernmental actors have found it even more challenging to penetrate the policy-making cycle. Unlike in other fields, such as the environment (Green 2010; Zito and Jacobs 2009; Bomberg 2012) and business (Bouwen 2002) and trade union organization (Martin and Ross 2001), NGO interface with the EU in AFSJ is recent and unrobust. This is largely to do with the nature of the issues captured in this field and the institutional peculiarities that set this portfolio apart.

---

[1] Because of the sensitive nature of the portfolio, the relatively tentative access that NGOs have been working hard to establish and the ongoing nature of the work in a number of the instruments that were used in this study, NGO staffers talked on condition of anonymity.

[2] The principal Brussels-based NGOs working on the AFSJ portfolio are Churches Committee on Migrants and Exiles (CCME), European Council on Refugees and Exiles (ECRE), Amnesty International EU Office, the European Women's Lobby (EWL), Migration Policy Group (MPG), Jesuit Refugee Service (JRS), Caritas Europa, Solidar and the Platform for International Cooperation on Undocumented Migrants (PICUM), all of which were interviewed.

[3] Of these, 17 were with NGOs based in Brussels, nine were NGOs based nationally, five were with UNHCR, six were with European Union officials (four European Commission civil servants, one European Parliament staffer and one MEP) in the Commission and Parliament and one was a national bureaucrat.

The EU–NGO interface is impacted both by the institutional realities of the European Union (which result in the variable opening of the political opportunity structures for NGOs) and the capacities of EU-oriented NGOs to seize expanding opportunities while at the same time seek or push for new openings. Joachim and Locher (2009) argue that NGOs are embedded in political opportunity structures (POSs), that these impact various mobilization resources, which in turn are deployed within particular frames to convince others. POSs are themselves shaped by the context. During the last two decades, AFSJ issues have increasingly Europeanized (Lavenex and Uçarer 2002; 2004; Tholen 2005; Geddes 2003; Lavenex 2001; Oxfam 2005). The POSs for this field, both for NGOs and for some key EU institutions, display significant flux over the same period of time, usually in tandem with the institutional maturation of the AFSJ dossier, the proliferation of the substantive content of EU-level cooperation or both. Major stakeholders (member states, EU institutions as well as NGOs) have had to navigate this fluid institutional and policy-specific terrain, which has significantly shaped the resources and strategies of individual actors.

Transnational activism, political opportunity structures and human rights

Tarrow (2011, 2005) argues that dissenting movements emerge as a response against the central monopoly of states which seeks to consolidate power in the capitals and demand that contentious dialogues between the state and its citizens occur within an exchange that is sanctioned and controlled by the state. Keck and Sikkink (1998) demonstrate that, when such dialogues are blocked, domestic actors can seek to circumvent the coercive authority of the state by establishing international networks and enlisting international allies to exert pressure on the target state. Recent research also persuasively argues that NGOs and other elements of civil society have been influential in development of international norms, especially in the field of human rights (Keck and Sikkink 1998; Brysk 1993; Clark 2001; Florini 2003; Burgerman 2001; Friedman et al 2005; Risse et al 1999).

Often, NGOs seek to leverage their moral authority (Risse 2000) and engage in naming and shaming. They flank their moral authority by laying claim to political legitimacy and emphasize and/or offer their expertise in a particular field, all the while taking pains to retain their credibility *vis-à-vis* the other salient actors in the field (Florini 2000b). However, although not all transnational advocacy efforts are successful, the burgeoning literature on third sector activity in the human rights field captures successes both in terms of policy output and in terms of effective strategies for nonstate actors (Brysk 2005; Clark 2001; Florini 2003; Risse et al 1999; Price 1997; 1998).

Price (2003, 584) discerns four useful types of activities, which involve corresponding sets of achievement strategies, for civil society activism: '(1) agenda setting—identifying a problem of international concern and producing information; (2) developing solutions—creating norms and recommending policy change; (3) building networks and coalitions of allies, and (4) implementing solutions— employing tactics of persuasion and pressure to change practices and/or encourage compliance with norm.' Price's categorization implies activity in various stages of the policy cycle, from the identification of an issue to implementation of policy outcomes. NGOs can and do insert themselves into each (or all) of the stages of the policy cycle. Such activity and activism often challenge established norms and the development of new ones, but it might also involve protection of established norms ignored, undermined, or violated by a variety of actors. What Keck and Sikkink (1998) have termed information politics and accountability politics are key to the work of NGOs. The first involves effective deployment of pertinent information towards key actors and the second hinges on persistent monitoring of discrepancies between the commitments and actual performance of targeted actors and creates the feedback loop through which renewed activism efforts can be launched when noncompliance and shirking is evident or forthcoming.

Engaging in information and/or accountability politics involves framing the specific in terms of inconsistencies with broader overarching commitments. This is an especially useful strategy for human rights cases and can serve to deploy shaming strategies by highlighting inconsistencies between proclaimed liberal identities and possibly illiberal conduct (Risse 2000). The EU, whose self-professed identity rests on commitments to democracy (and, implicitly, accountability and transparency), rule of law, and respect for human rights, can thus become a target.

Successful advocacy must also be appropriately connected to 'local reality' (Florini 2000a; Burgerman 2001). As we will see below, however, it is also important to recognize the importance of 'local knowledge' of the international scene, especially if activism involves targeting the (undesirable) behaviour of opaque IGOs. Predictably, such activism invites some resistance from the targeted actors that might display intransigence, ignore activists' overtures or actively pursue the disruption of activists' work. In the European Union context, access by NGOs is not institutionalized, which further complicates matters. As a result, factors exogenous to NGOs, such as the changing institutional dynamics of the EU, become pivotal to NGO advocacy.

The playing field: AFSJ institutional terrain

In 1993, just before Justice and Home Affairs (JHA) became part of the EU mandate, the European Communities had 12 members. It had no authority to make policy in the realm of immigration or engage in judicial cooperation in criminal matters. Internal borders were still mostly intact and no set of comparable policies existed for the external borders. In 2013, the picture is significantly different. The EC has given way to the EU, which now has competence in immigration, asylum and certain police and judicial matters. JHA has been transformed into AFSJ. The institutional changes that resulted from Maastricht, Amsterdam and Lisbon are well-documented (Bache et al 2011; Acosta Arcarazo and Geddes 2013; Uçarer 2013) and broadly capture the following: enhanced competence for the European Commission (including the transform-ation from a shared right of initiative to an exclusive right of initiative) and the European Parliament (in particular a move to co-decision or ordinary legislative procedure [OLP] that extends to all former JHA fields after Lisbon),[4] a move from

---

[4] The Parliament obtained competence to legislate on regular migration on 1 December 2009 with the entry into force of the Lisbon Treaty. In 2005, it obtained a competence to legislate on irregular migration. See Council of the European Union (2004).

unanimity in decision-making to QMV, an increased role for the Court of Justice of the EU and the step-wise communautarization of the Third Pillar.

Maastricht, Amsterdam and Lisbon represent three important institutional turning points. The first provided the EU with a mandate, the second tinkered with the Maastricht institutional arrangements and the last normalized AFSJ. The role of the four core institutions of the EU shifted over time during this normalization process. The Council and individual member states, privileged by the unanimity rule under Maastricht and to a lesser extent by Amsterdam, technically suffered a decline relative to other institutions during the move to QMV. The Commission's stature and agenda-setting capability was also enhanced (at least theoretically) with the move from a shared to exclusive right of initiative with Amsterdam and Lisbon. However, the Parliament experienced the greatest advancement. Even though it was relegated to a consultative level by Maastricht, it did gain co-decision rights with Amsterdam on certain portfolios, enabling it to assert colegislative stature with the Council. Parliament also gained a general competence on regular immigration in December 2009 and irregular migration in 2005 with the entry into force of the Lisbon Treaty. The European Court of Justice (now the Court of Justice of the European Union, CJEU) also for the first time received a (limited) mandate with Amsterdam, allowing it to interpret the treaties and undertake preliminary rulings in policy areas falling within the first pillar, in response to requests by, initially, highest national courts. With the Lisbon Treaty, all national courts could refer questions on migration matters. As such, it can be argued that the CJEU now constitutes another supranational instance through which domestic immigration policies can be constrained to conform to EU law (Acosta Arcarazo and Geddes 2013). The Nice Treaty made few changes to the already-communitarized immigration and asylum dossier, but expanded the role of the Commission and the Parliament in police and judicial cooperation.

Finally, the Lisbon Treaty implemented significant institutional reforms for AFSJ policy, normalizing it by subsuming the Third Pillar into the first: the treaty foresaw QMV in the Council, co-decision rights in the EP (now called the 'ordinary legislative procedure' and limited jurisdiction for the ECJ. These shifts in institutional arrangements, exogenous to NGOs, were campaigned for and welcomed by NGOs that stood to benefit from the enhancement in stature of EU actors to which they had better access, namely the Commission and Parliament. In theory, these changes enhanced achievement of NGO-preferred policy outcomes, as long as the Commission and Parliament remained close to NGO positions. As a single state could no longer hold negotiations hostage to its veto, QMV presented a move away from lowest common denominator policy outcomes, with the Commission potentially more assertive, and Parliament, traditionally demon-strating strong support for human rights issues (Kaunert 2009), keeping the more conservative and secretive Council in check as colegislator. In theory, therefore, this resulted in significantly improved political opportunity structures for NGOs, particularly those based in Brussels, as the clout of actors to which they had access was enhanced.

Playing the field: NGO access to EU institutions

NGO work in immigration and asylum at the European level predates these EU institutional developments. First, NGOs working in this field were established in the 1990s, beginning with issues related to labour and employment of migrants and eventually fanned out to include integration and later asylum—all more or less at the national level (Niessen 2002). The context for NGOs changed with Maastricht, Amsterdam and particularly Lisbon, not least because a community competence was slowly created, but also because the EU emerged as a new locus for substantial policy output. Maastricht marks a juncture when a few European NGOs begin entering the scene. Several Brussels-based NGOs emerged as actors not only lobbying at the European level but, to some extent, mediating between the regional, national and subnational levels. Brussels-based NGOs took on the additional task of convincing national NGOs of the utility of engaging in EU-level lobbying until the national consequences of EU-level decision-making became clear. EU-level NGOs are therefore not only interlocutors between the national and the regional, but also mobilize up towards the regional/EU level as well as down towards the national level. At the same time, Brussels-based NGOs need to respond to requests from below to link up.

In order to do their advocacy work, NGOs need access to relevant actors throughout the policy cycle. However, unlike the United Nations, the EU does not have an accreditation system through which NGOs are formally linked to the organization. Such lack of formal avenues along which to approach the EU can be problematic though not necessarily insurmountable (Greenwood 2009). Informal consultations and access points exist with various EU institutions, although the quality and intensity of these interactions differ by sector and the target institution. Brussels-based NGOs constantly bemoan the limits of their ability to effectively influence AFSJ policy-making; at the same time, they note and appreciate openings for access. Nonetheless, EU-level NGOs continue to engage the system and develop strategies in order to maintain the access they already enjoy, launch and expand new channels of access, and seek to develop alternatives where access is undesirably blocked. The lobbying process is often complicated and effectiveness in affecting the desired outcome is far from presumed. NGO access varies across various core institutions (Commission, Council, Parliament) of the EU and relies heavily on mostly informal personal contacts between NGOs and various EU actors. Not surprisingly, the Commission and Parliament are most receptive to NGOs given that the former are relatively resource-poor.

The European Parliament maintains the best track record for access and regularly displays a desire to consider NGO arguments, although, as will be explained below, its increasingly conservative behaviour in the post-Lisbon era (Ripoll Servent and Trauner 2012) has drawn criticism (Amnesty International and ECRE 2008b; Pollet 2011). Until the implementation of the Lisbon Treaty, the Parliament was the weakest EU institution to affect the policy process because of its relatively marginal role under the consultation procedure. This was a significant drawback for effective lobbying for NGOs that track Rapporteurs, shadow Rapporteurs, targeted MEPs and members of the EP's Committee of Civil Liberties, Justice and Home Affairs (LIBE). EU-level NGOs note that they are consulted frequently by the Parliament on their positions (and their rationale) on a variety of pending measures. Sometimes, NGO language is incorporated directly into Parliament reports.

During interviews conducted in 2005, NGOs noted their need for more time spent on advocacy efforts targeting Parliament, its LIBE committee and individual MEPs in light of the imminent move to co-decision. They also noted that the Returns Directive (discussed in more depth below) would be a test case for the degree to which access to and receptiveness by the EP coupled with its enhanced institutional stature would translate into the adoption of policies that better incorporated and reflected the advocacy points of NGOs. One NGO representative commented that the more political responsibility for the Parliament through the co-decision procedure could possibly have the adverse effect of diminished access, but on the whole NGOs remained optimistic about the prospects of an enhanced role for the Parliament, translating into an improvement in the POSs that governs this field. The interviews conducted in 2011, and policy process and output since 2005, discussed below, possibly point to a shifting trend.

With Amsterdam changes, the Commission has the power to initiate proposals. NGOs closely follow the policy cycle after the Commission launches an instrument or when it prepares communications in preparation for subsequent policy initiatives. In general, they have reasonably good access to the Commission in its various forms. Their contacts are most dense with the services of DG Justice, Liberty, Security (DG JLS) although they also seek contact with the Cabinet of the Commissioner(s) responsible for the relevant dossiers. NGOs interviewed were overwhelmingly positive about Commissioner Vitorino (Portugal, Socialist) in the Prodi Commission (widely regarded as one of the best commissioners in what was otherwise a relatively weak college) in terms of his drive, knowledge and political savvy. They were more guarded about Commissioner Frattini (Italy, People's Party) who succeeded Vitorino in the first Barroso Commission.[5] Since the second Barroso Commission was installed in 2010, the JHA/AFSJ portfolio, previously under the mandate of one commissioner, was split in two, separating home affairs from civil liberties. Currently Viviane Reding (Luxembourg, People's Party) is serving as the Justice and Fundamental Rights Commissioner and Cecilia Malmström (Sweden, Liberals) is serving as the Home Affairs Commissioner. As can be seen, there has been significant turnover in the Commission's leadership in this portfolio, and a shift from the previous centre-left commissioners (Gradin and Vitorino) to centre-right ones (Frattini, Barrot, Reding and Malmström). This latter shift corresponds to the more conservative pulse of the public on these matters.

The Commission recognizes the potential role of NGOs in the governance process (see also European Commission 2000; 2001). Given its limitations in Brussels, it needs input from NGOs to provide information through their field contacts. They can also become operational partners with the Commission (Niessen 2002). The Commission has at times acknowledged that conversations with NGOs that go beyond the ad hoc would be desirable (European Commission 2000), but consultations have largely remained in the informal arena. Predictably, NGOs have been pressing for a more regular framework for consultation (Niessen 2002).

The Council and its components, COREPER, Council Secretariat, the JHA Council and the European Council, are more difficult to penetrate and relatively impervious to NGO overtures. This could partly be to the different institutional cultures of these stake-holders and the well-circulated criticism that the Council is resistant to transparency. Additionally, the Council represents national interests

---

[5] Frattini did not end his term as he returned to serve as Italy's foreign minister after elections in 2008. He was temporarily replaced by Jacques Barrot (France, People's Party) until the end of the Barroso I commission. One could see these revolving-door developments since Vitorino as reflecting leadership instability, making it difficult for NGOs.

that are 'meant to reinforce their efforts to keep away or remove a greater number of third-country nationals' (Baldaccini 2010, 116). This frequently puts it at odds with (and therefore not particularly receptive to) positions being advanced by rights-protective NGOs. The Council is also reluctant to grant access to civil society, and both its process and its output draws NGO criticism. Many NGOs attribute this to the institutional culture of the Council as well as the privileged role that has been assigned to it when the JHA portfolio was brought into the EU's mandate. Nonetheless, efforts are made to gain access, mostly though JHA Conseillers at the permanent representations of member states in Brussels. NGOs report that while they don't have regular contacts with the Council's services (Directorate H), some of the more established NGOs make an effort to target the rotating presidency of the Council, usually before it takes office, at the stage where the upcoming presidency is formulating its dossier priorities.

How NGOs lobby: resources and strategies

Exogenous factors (such as the EU institutional framework and the willingness of targeted actors to be open to NGO overtures) paint only part of the picture. Endogenous factors, such as NGO resources and the manner in which they choose to deploy these, will also shape their advocacy strategies. Material and personnel resources for NGO mobilization in this field are modest, though these do show variance between different NGOs. Some (such as ECRE, Caritas Europe, Jesuit Refugee Service [JRS], Churches Commission on Migrants in Europe [CCME] and Amnesty International) were on the field quite early, establishing Brussels offices even before the portfolio was Europeanized. Others, such as the European Women's Lobby (EWL) and the Platform for International Cooperation on Undocumented Migrants (PICUM), have started developing their JHA portfolios quite recently. This translates into varying degrees of expertise both in institutional knowledge and in substantive policy initiatives in an exceedingly fast-changing policy-making environment. Most NGOs are financed through project funding, sometimes by the EU, which leaves them susceptible to the vagaries of grant writing. Many NGOs have no more than one or two staffers for the expansive portfolio. Yet, advocacy targets and the intensity of the required lobbying, not to mention the expanding breadth of the AFSJ portfolio, have starved NGOs of resources, resulting in a relative deterioration of personnel resources for Brussels-based NGOs. Their material resources being what they are, NGOs have become adept at deploying their nonmaterial resources, such as their substantive, testimonial and institutional expertise, as effectively as they can. They seek to leverage this expertise in setting the agenda, developing solutions, building networks and implementing/monitoring solutions.

NGOs typically engage in a number of strategies, often simultaneously to attempt desired outcomes. They use their substantive (legal) expertise to develop detailed proposals or provide law-based challenges throughout the policy cycle. They can also produce and incorporate experiential expertise by uploading first-hand accounts from their national counterparts. Often, they facilitate testimonial encounters, particularly for MEPs. They render expert opinion when requested in formal (for example, in Parliament committees) as well as informal (for example informal consultations with the Commission) settings. They produce and disseminate reasoned position papers on virtually every policy move of the EU and provide feedback for the various incarnations of these documents as they move through the policy cycle, often providing detailed articulations of appropriate human rights protective practice (see, for example, ECRE 2005). In addition to capitalizing on information technology to widen their reach given their limited financial resources, some NGOs (in particular Amnesty International) strategically engineer opportunities to get media attention both to reach a wider audience and to put pressure on decision makers. For example, NGOs often draft alternate policy initiatives in advance of the Commission's, subsequently circulating these amongst stake-holders. These are all efforts to frame the debate and dampen undesirable policy outcome at the EU level, unmistakably deployed to (re)frame AFSJ debates in human rights and civil liberties language to arrest (and reverse) the restrictionist logic prevalent in the member states and the Council. Many Brussels NGOs also have substantial institutional expertise on the ever-changing decision-making context of the EU. This allows them to track the policy cycle efficiently, identify appropriate counterparts and direct their mobilizing efforts accordingly.

NGOs not only target individual policy instruments as objects of their critique and feedback, they also advocate for institutional reform when necessary (Price 2003). After Maastricht, and particularly before Amsterdam, but also prior to Lisbon, NGOs have advocated for institutional changes that would eliminate the pillar structure and the unanimity rule, would endow the Parliament with co-decision (as opposed to consultation) rights, and would create a competence for the ECJ (ECRE 2007; Standing Committee of Experts on International Immigration 1995; ECRE et al 1999; CCME 2001), arguably to result in improved POSs for NGOs (Curtin and Peers 2002).

In contrast to Keck and Sikkink's (1998) 'boomerang pattern', in which domestic NGOs enlist the help of international allies to overcome domestic political blockage, Brussels-based NGOs engage in what might be termed a 'reverse boomerang' pattern: in response to problems of advocacy access to the Council, they frequently enlist their national partners in member states to indirectly influence the Council through domestic channels. A few of the NGOs are umbrella organizations (such as ECRE and CCME), positioning them nicely to enlist their partner/constituent NGOs to lobby national actors/politicians to then affect the desired policy output in Brussels. Other NGOs that are not umbrella organizations, but nonetheless have national offices (such as Amnesty International) are able to employ a similar strategy to reach the Council through mobilization at the national level. All these strategies can be employed to set the agenda and develop solutions.

NGOs also make networking a priority to pool their resources and expertise. The NGO Platform on EU Migration and Asylum Policy is an informal group of European nongovernmental organizations and networks. Although it started out very small (as a result of the very small number of NGOs early on), the Platform now has 22 NGO members and fosters information exchange and, at times, lobbying coordination between member organizations. The Platform also has ties with the more formal EU Social Platform, not least in the form of joint membership of several NGOs. Christian NGOs representing Catholic and Protestant churches have additionally banded together and frequently produce joint letters, press releases and common policy feedback on initiatives. Finally, after the adoption of policy instruments, NGOs can shift their attention to implementation through monitoring the transposition of EU instruments in national settings, networking with national NGOs to track compliance and publicize possible deleterious impact at national level.

In short, Brussels-based NGOs are well versed in engaging in EU policy-making by involving themselves in information and accountability politics. In particular, they regularly exert influence over agenda-setting, and the development and implementation of policy solutions.

Policy process and output in pre- and post-Lisbon AFSJ

In an effort to demonstrate their advocacy efforts, the remainder of this article presents a process overview of the development of four policy instruments and NGO involvement in the process: the Family Reunification Directive, the Asylum Procedures Directive, the Returns Directive and the Trafficking Directive. Each of these instruments involves a portfolio in which a particular issue can be framed in human rights terms. Furthermore, they represent all subportfolios (asylum, migration and cooperation in police and judicial matters) to cover the entire AFSJ portfolio. In all these cases, NGOs engaged in very active and critical campaigning, opposing what they perceived to be minimalist, restrictionist and exclusionary emphases in developing legislation. Yet, in each of these cases, NGO efforts to resist potentially regressive policy output or to insist on the adoption of rights-protective measures was counterresisted throughout the EU policy process, and, with the modest exception of the Trafficking Directive, the final policy instruments got (sometimes much) 'worse' from the perspective of NGOs as they moved through the policy cycle. Exogenous factors are comparable for the first and latter two instruments. The first instruments were concluded under unanimity and consultation, whereas the latter was subject to QMV and co-decision/OLP. With the minor exception of the Returns Directive, NGOs could also rely on relevant preexisting international and regional treaty instruments.

Pre-Lisbon AFSJ: the Family Reunification Directive

The Family Reunification Directive was the first major EU instrument on legal migration into the EU, negotiated under unanimity and subject to the consultation procedure by the European Parliament. It included claims to human rights as protection of the family unit is incorporated into the United Nations Universal Declaration of Human Rights, the 1966 International Covenant on Civil and Political Rights, the International Covenant on Economic, Social and Cultural Rights, the 1989 Convention on the Rights of the Child and the United Nations Convention on the Protection of All Migrant Workers and Members of their Families. In the EU, attempts to regulate the entry of certain family members of migrants would have to conform to obligations arising from human rights commitments. The right of EU nationals to move with their family members is already protected by the Council Regulation 492/2011. Furthermore, Directive 2004/38 provides for family reunification for EU citizens in general. Family members of citizens of non-EU countries who nonetheless reside in EU territory do not enjoy comparable rights. To partially address this, the Commission started work in December 1999 on the first draft of a Council Directive on the right of family reunification (European Commission 1999). Relevant NGOs sought to participate in and influence the policy cycle from the outset (European Commission 1999), in part at the invitation of the Commission's DG JLS (Niessen 2001). NGOs were generally pleased with this first draft produced by the Commission.

The original Commission draft met with resistance from member states, resulting in two revised drafts in October 2000 and May 2002 (European Commission 2000; 2002). The Commission's original proposal was weakened, occasioning increasing critique from NGOs that vigorously engaged in information politics (through developing point-by-point critique of drafts, and bringing their grassroots information to bear) and accountability politics (through referencing relevant instruments of international and regional law and insisting on EU's observance of its human rights obligations). During the policy negotiations, their strategies were aimed at setting or shifting the agenda in human rights terms. These efforts did not yield the intended outcome as the Council finally adopted the Directive on 22 September 2003 (Council of the European Union 2003), ignoring much of the feedback from NGOs but also, importantly, the European Parliament. This instrument drew significant criticism from NGOs and UN High Commissioner for Refugees (UNHCR) for its limited scope, its narrow definition of a family member, its exclusion of certain categories of non-EU citizens, among other things (ECRE 2003). Throughout the process, in addition to publicly criticizing the policy process and draft output, Brussels-based NGOs reached out to their domestic counterparts to put pressure on Brussels from below, a 'reverse boomerang'. At the same time, NGOs addressed letters to then-Commissioner Vitorino, asking him to shelve the instrument. Echoing some of these criticisms, and also at the urging of some NGOs, the sidelined European Parliament started annulment proceedings at the ECJ in December 2003 on procedural and substantive grounds. Procedurally, the Parliament maintained that it was not sufficiently consulted. Substantively, it argued that adopted rules were incompatible with the European Convention on Human Rights (European Court of Justice 2006). The Grand Chamber of the ECJ eventually dismissed the Parliament's action for annulment (see Uçarer 2009a). With this decision the Directive was adopted, resisted not only by NGOs but also by the UNHCR, all to little avail.

Pre-Lisbon AFSJ: the Asylum Procedures Directive

The Asylum Procedures Directive was the last piece of legislation to be put into place in the asylum subfield before the move to co-decision and QMV was to take place. Like the Family Reunification Directive, it became an immediate target of criticism based on human rights. The Commission's initial draft was issued in October 2000 (European Commission 2001). This initial draft drew some criticism from NGOs. Political agreement on the text remained elusive until June 2002 when an amended (European Commission 2002), and much watered-down (Costello 2005; Uçarer 2009b), revised proposal was issued by the Commission.

The Directive raised two (interrelated) sets of issues. First, critics, among them UNHCR and ECRE, argued that the Directive was fundamentally at odds with the EU's regional as well as international legal obligations designed to protect the ability to seek asylum, and enjoy due process. Second, there were significant questions about whether the Directive's implementation could give rise to situations where rejected asylum seekers could be sent back to dangerous situations, prohibited under the global refugee protection regime. In fact, so great was the opposition to the final draft of this directive that, in an unprecedented confrontational move mobilized through the NGO Platform, European NGOs called for it to be abandoned (Amnesty International 2004).

NGOs also concentrated their efforts on the EP, hoping to raise awareness about the problems with the draft Directive. They provided draft amendments to the EP's Rapporteur in the LIBE Committee, demonstrating their legal/technical command of the relevant regional and international legal instruments. The EP eventually rendered its opinion in September 2005 and offered no less than 102 amendments to the Draft Directive, a number of them very similar to draft texts proposed by NGOs (ECRE 2006, 2).

The proposal was adopted by the JHA Council in December 2005 (JHA Council 2005), which ignored all of the amendments proposed by the EP during the consultation process. Several NGOs then started lobbying Parliament to consider challenging the Procedures Directive at the ECJ. The goal was to strengthen the hand of the EP, perceived as an ally during this process. Parliament, still reeling from its defeat on the Family Reunification Directive, ultimately did not pursue the matter at the ECJ, leaving the Procedures Directive to be adopted over the sustained objections of NGOs and the EP.

Post-Lisbon AFSJ: the Returns Directive

This was the first major instrument on irregular migration adopted by an enlarged European Union, concluded under QMV, with the EP participating under co-decision/OLP. In contrast to the two directives briefly highlighted above, one might have expected an outcome that was in better congruence with the advocacy agenda of Brussels-based NGOs and the UNHCR as unanimity would no longer guarantee a lowest-common denominator outcome and co-decision would allow the Parliament, a perceived ally sympathetic to NGO positions, a higher profile role. This, however, was not to be.

On 1 September 2005, the Commission submitted its draft Directive to provide common rules for the removal of unauthorized persons from EU territory consistent with human rights and fundamental freedoms (European Commission 2005). The resulting negotiations were difficult in the Council and Parliament. In fact, because of differences of opinion mostly along party lines, it took the EP LIBE Committee more than two years to adopt a report on the Directive and bring it to a vote. Parliament seemed to follow NGO leads as most of the initial modifications to the Commission's first draft proposed by Parliament were interpreted as strengthening protections afforded to removable migrants (Peers 2008). A few revisions, mostly to do with the detention of such individuals, lowered the bar from the Commission's original proposal. On the eve of a 12 September 2007 vote on the draft report of the LIBE Rapporteur on the Directive, ECRE and Amnesty International sent a joint letter to the MEP members of LIBE, urging them to reconsider the provisions for detention of irregular migrants for up to 18 months on the grounds that the detention period was disproportionate and excessive (Amnesty International and ECRE 2007).

The Council undertook its own deliberations, lowering the human rights standards and procedural safeguards afforded for persons subject to return procedures while maintaining or increasing the discretion of national authorities (Acosta 2009; Baldaccini 2009; ECRE 2009; Peers 2007, 2008; Acosta Arcarazo 2011). There followed a series of so-called trilogue meetings between the Council Presidency, a Commission representative, and EP's Rapporteur (see below), resulting in a first reading compromise on 18 June 2008 in which the EP retreated from a number of positions in its 2007 report (Pollet 2011). On the eve of the adoption of this compromise text, NGOs sent a letter to all MEPs underlining the perils of the first reading compromise and arguing that '[b]y accepting this compromise text, the European Parliament will undermine its own mandate to protect human rights and allow EU law to erode existing international human rights standards ... This instrument is also the first opportunity for the European Parliament to ensure that EU asylum and immigration legislation fully respects fundamental rights by effectively using its mandate in the co-decision procedure' (Amnesty International and ECRE 2008a). The UNHCR shared similar concerns and opined that 'the compromise proposal, in its current form, does not afford a satisfactory level of procedural or substantive safeguards to ensure that removals are not effected contrary to international refugee law obligations or other fundamental rights' (UNHCR 2008a). NGOs also coordinated and staged public demonstrations in various EU cities on the eve of the Parliament's vote on the compromise text. Despite these efforts, EP plenary voted in favour of the compromise text and the instrument was formally adopted by the Council on 9 December 2008.

The Directive received unprecedented public criticism, in particular from NGOs such as ECRE and Amnesty International, and from IGOs such as the UN and UNHCR. At the heart of the criticism were the instrument's provisions for detention, involuntary removals and the reentry ban. As this instrument was designed to develop common standards rather than minimum standards, and in the absence of standstill clauses that would have prevented member states with higher levels of protection from adopting lower standards, there was widespread concern from Brussels-based NGOs as well as UNHCR (Save the Children 2008; Amnesty International and ECRE 2008b; Baldaccini 2009; ECRE 2009; UNHCR 2008b).

Why did the new rules (QMV and co-decision) not produce a more rights-protective document? To start with, appearing weak (even through the protection of certain groups of individuals) on undocumented migration is a political nonstarter in most member states, so a move to QMV did not necessarily raise the bottom line. Many of the member states had centre-right governments that generally pursued tougher approaches towards immigration. At a time when undocumented migration was being securitized and linked to terrorism, the official line of the EU was predictably the timely and effective removal of undocumented individuals, even though this could at times conflict with other human rights obligations.

The enhanced position of the European Parliament (through the OLP) offered an opening for NGOs. In this case, however, Parliament itself became a lightning rod because of its first reading capitulation to most of the Council's preferences. At the time of the adoption of this initiative, the European People's Party (typically in favour of migration restrictions) held the majority in Parliament, a majority that widened after the 2009 elections. The draft instrument was adopted 369 to 197. Amendments by the Party of European Socialists, Greens and the European

United Left-Nordic Green Left (EUL-NGL), groups seeking to improve protections for individuals subject to expulsions orders, were rejected. A proposal by the Greens and EUL-NGL to reject the directive altogether was also defeated. After the EP received co-decision powers in immigration and asylum, there developed a tendency to try to adopt legislation after a first reading by Parliament (which requires a simple majority at the EP) rather than after a second reading (which requires a qualified majority). The same applies to post-Lisbon decision-making in which the EP also has OLP rights in police and judicial matters. NGOs have very little, if any, inroads into trilogues in which first reading compromises are hammered out and, to wit, they have been vocal critics of this institutional development, bemoaning the closed nature of the trilogues, their privileging of certain actors (such as the EP Rapporteur) and the sidelining of the broader membership of the EP to which they have comparably good access (Bunyan 2007).

Post-Lisbon AFSJ: the Trafficking Directive

The Trafficking Directive is the first major criminal law instrument in post-Lisbon AFSJ, negotiated by a 27-member EU under QMV and OLP. Trafficking in human beings started to attract the attention of the EU in the mid-1990s in the aftermath of the fall of the Berlin Wall, the expansion of the EU's competences to the regulation of its external borders and the EU's enlargement. A number of influential and interested actors in the European Commission as well as the EP, many of them women, also took an interest in the issue. NGOs also contributed to the development of this portfolio, concentrating their attention on cultivating alliances with key actors within and without the EU. They did this by attempting to set the agenda, deploying their relative strengths in technical expertise as well as making available testimonials. Throughout the policy cycle, they carefully cast trafficking as a human and women's rights issue.

In post-Maastricht developments, the EU adopted a Joint Action in 1997 on the issue of sexual exploitation of women and children, and two Commission Communications in 1996 and 1998 outlining priorities. The post-Amsterdam EU also adopted a 2002 Framework Decision[6] on combating trafficking (which was all that remained of the Third Pillar after immigration and asylum matters were moved to the First), and a 2004 Council Directive on issuing residence permits to victims of trafficking. Most recently, the Commission drafted a 2010 Directive in Trafficking in Persons which repeals the 2002 Framework Decision. This was adopted after the entry into force of the Lisbon Treaty, which dissolved the third pillar.

The 2002 Framework Decision defined human trafficking in terms of sexual exploitation and labour exploitation, introducing a blueprint of measures to be adopted at European level. These included criminalization of trafficking, harmonizing the severity and nature of punishments and prosecution, as well as protecting and assisting victims. It was by and large a law enforcement document with significant emphasis on prosecution and some attention to victim protection. In 2004, responding to pressures from law enforcement officers, the EU

---

[6] Framework decisions were instruments introduced by the Amsterdam Treaty, used to align the laws and regulations of member states.

adopted a Directive that introduced a residence permit for victims who cooperate with the police, prosecution services or other competent authorities. This Directive offered a so-called reflection period, pushed for by NGOs, to non-EU national undocumented victims of human trafficking, during which the victim could make a decision on whether to cooperate with the authorities. Victims who decided to cooperate with the competent authorities could then obtain a residence permit for a fixed period, depending on how their case unfolded, which would entitle them to receive the same treatment as during the reflection period, as well as access to the labour market, vocational training and education according to national legislation. This move was partially welcomed, but human rights NGOs quickly realized that the Directive also instrumentalized the victim, and that protections were extended only to the extent that the victim could be useful to law enforcement.

The next big push came in 2009 with the Commission proposing a new Framework Decision that would repeal the 2002 one.[7] The Council, comprised of the interior ministers of member states, largely agreed on an instrument on 30 November 2009, one day before the Treaty of Lisbon entered into force. When Lisbon took effect, the Third Pillar was brought under the ordinary competence of the Union, and Framework Decisions disappeared entirely as an EU instrument. Subsequently, the Commission quickly repackaged the instrument as a Directive and tabled a proposal in March 2010. The JHA Council reached a political consensus on this Directive in June 2010. With Lisbon in force, the European Parliament now found itself with co-decision powers over most criminal law matters. The EP and Council negotiated a first reading compromise, again through a trilogue, downgrading some of the provisions that were included in the original Commission version and the Parliament finally adopted the text on 14 December 2010. The instrument was formally adopted on 21 March 2011.

To date, NGO input in this field has been varied. Due to fundamental differences of opinion between NGOs regarding the issue of prostitution, they have found it difficult to develop broad coalitions, although the antiprostitution camp led by the European Women's Lobby (EWL) appears to enjoy reasonable access to EU institutions. Bracketing the prostitution issue, advocacy have also focused on returning the criminal justice emphasis that prevailed in earlier instruments, with added attention to victim protection and the placement of the trafficking issue within a broader development framework. Providing support to NGO agenda-setting efforts to bring victim assistance and protection to the fore, international and regional instruments on trafficking, most notably the 2000 UN Convention on Transnational Organized Crime and its Trafficking Protocol, plus the 2005 Council of Europe Convention on Trafficking in Humans, have also provided support to NGO efforts to bring victim assistance and protection to the fore. NGOs such as ECPAT, Save the Children and Terre des Hommes have been very active in insisting that legislation adopted includes specific protection for minors (who represent almost half of all trafficking victims), frequently relying on existing norms of international law (such as the UN Convention on the Rights of the Child) to make their case. EWL has been particularly instrumental in

---

[7] This was after the Lisbon Treaty was signed but before it took effect, so Framework Decisions, instruments of the leftover Third Pillar, were still being used.

highlighting the gendered context of trafficking, also advocating for the protection of women migrants who are/might become victims of trafficking.

The Trafficking Directive, although it was another instrument finalized after a first reading deal, has not attracted quite the level of criticism highlighted in the other three cases, perhaps because it was widely seen, including by the NGOs involved, as a significant improvement over earlier instruments in that overemphasized prosecution of traffickers at the expense of protection of victims. Certainly because the Directive sidestepped the controversial and nonstarter issue of prostitution, it was concluded in fairly short order and incorporated a number of changes (particularly with respect to the protection of minors) that were campaigned for by NGOs. It was also helpful that, in contrast to the previously discussed cases, member states were relatively new to this issue and hence had relatively few domestic regulations that could be challenged. This resulted in a relatively unusual situation, in which NGO positions on the whole were not significantly different from those of the Council. And while the trilogue did some damage to the EP/NGO positions, this was not on the scale of what had happened as a result of the Returns Directive. That said, had the victim protections advocated by NGOs and the EP not been perceived as in the interest of member states' law enforcement services, the distance between the Council and other actors would have been significant, probably resulting in an outcome similar to the Returns Directive.

Conclusions

As Bomberg (2012) has observed, advocacy 'in multilevel systems—where power is diffused and authority contested—is especially challenging', as these decentralized settings tend to make it easy to block decisions through multiple veto opportunities. In AFSJ, this is additionally complicated by an institutional environment that was transformed significantly after Lisbon. And as the field is new to the EU, so are NGO advocacy strategies that target various EU actors. However, a number of Brussels-based specialized NGOs (such as ECRE and CCME), broader-mandate human rights NGOs with offices in Brussels (such as Amnesty International) and IGOs (such as UNHCR) have joined efforts to address and resist potentially regressive policy developments emanating from the EU. These organizations have shown the remarkable sophistication with which they can bring their technical, procedural, testimonial and networking expertise to bear in order to influence agendas, developing solutions and monitoring compliance. The instruments reviewed also reveal that factors endogenous to NGOs (resources and advocacy strategies) have remained more or less comparable in the face of changing exogenous factors, such as the decision-making framework of the EU. NGOs do spend more time lobbying the European Parliament in post-Lisbon AFSJ, but the expansion of their political opportunities through the enhanced stature of the European Commission and the European Parliament might nonetheless be mitigated by shifts in their behaviour (Farrell and Héritier 2003; 2007). Although the European Commission now has an exclusive right of initiative, it does not tend to get in the way of the Council (as was made evident by the need to draft progressively less rights-protective drafts for three of the four instruments reviewed here), even with QMV in place. The European Parliament, though now possessing OLP rights, can no longer afford to only stand on principle, and increasingly has to engage in strategic negotiations, in the process often appeasing the Council. Although unanimity was a thorn in the side of NGOs in the Maastricht and Amsterdam eras (demonstrated in the Family Reunification and Asylum Procedures Directives), trilogues and first reading compromises in a post-Lisbon European Parliament eager to portray itself as pragmatic and responsible might present new challenges for NGOs (this has already been witnessed in the form of the Returns and Trafficking Directives). These cases demonstrate that, despite its normalization, and seemingly irrespective of the type of issue in question, AFSJ continues to be a problematic area for NGO involvement as POSs expand in some respects and contract in others. However, this article has also demonstrated that NGOs have kept up the pressure on the EU by engaging in informational and accountability politics in Brussels, frequently with the help of their counterparts in national settings.

Notes on contributor

Emek M Uçarer is Professor of International Relations at Bucknell University. She holds a PhD in International Studies from the University of South Carolina. Her research interests include cooperation on immigration and asylum matters in the European Union, the role of EU institutions in cooperation, nongovernmental organizations in global and regional governance, human trafficking and smuggling, and political mobilization of ethnic diasporas in host countries. Recent publications include 'Area of Freedom, Security, and Justice' in *European Union politics* (ed Michelle Cini and Nieves Perez Solorzano Borragan, Oxford University Press, 2013), 'Safeguarding asylum as a human right: NGOs and the European Union' in *Multi-level governance and civil society: comparing the role of NGOs in the United Nations and the European Union* (ed Jutta Joachim and Birgit Locher, New York: Routledge, 2009) and 'Negotiating third-country national rights in the European Union' in *Diversity in the European Union* (ed Elisabeth Prügl and Markus Thiel, New York: Palgrave, 2009). She has previously served as an in-service trainee at the European Commission.

References

Acosta, Diego (2009) 'The good, the bad and the ugly in EU migration law: is the European Parliament becoming bad and ugly? (The Adoption of Directive 2008/115: The Returns Directive) (vol 11, p 19, 2009)', *European Journal of Migration and Law*, 11:4, 19–39

Acosta Arcarazo, Diego (2011) 'The Returns Directive: possible limits and interpretation' in Karin Zwaan (ed) *The Returns Directive: central themes, problem issues, and implementation in selected member states* (Nijmegen: Wolf Legal Publishers), 7–24

Acosta Arcarazo, Diego and Andrew Geddes (2013) 'The development, application and implications of an EU rule of law in the area of migration policy', *Journal of Common Market Studies*, 51:2, 179–193

Amnesty International (2004) 'Refugee and human rights organizations across Europe call on EU to scrap key asylum proposal', <http://www.amnesty.org/en/library/asset/IOR30/011/2004/en/ccdb3b1c-d5fb-11dd-bb24-1fb85fe8fa05/ior300112004en.pdf>

Amnesty International and European Council on Refugees and Exiles (2007) 'RE: Vote on the draft EP Report by Mr Manfred Weber (PE 374.321v02-00) Commission Proposal for a directive of the European Parliament and of the Council on common standards and procedures in Member States for returning illegally staying third-country nationals (COM(2005)0931-C6-0266 – 2005/0167(COD))', unpublished letter

Amnesty International and European Council on Refugees and Exiles (2008a) 'Joint ECRE and Amnesty International letter to the EU Parliament on the Returns Directive', unpublished letter

Amnesty International and European Council on Refugees and Exiles (2008b) *'Returns' Directive: European Parliament and Member States risk compromising respect for migrants' rights* (Brussels: Amnesty International)

Bache, Ian, Stephen George and Simon Bulmer (2011) *Politics in the European Union* (Oxford: Oxford University Press)

Baldaccini, Anneliese (2009) 'The return and removal of irregular migrants under EU law: an analysis of the Returns Directive', *European Journal of Migration and Law*, 11:1, 1–17

Baldaccini, Anneliese (2010) 'The EU Directive on return: principles and protests', *Refugee Survey Quarterly*, 28:4, 114–138

Bomberg, Elizabeth (2012) 'Mind the (mobilization) gap: comparing climate change activism in the United States and European Union', *Review of Policy Research*, 29:3, 409–430

Bouwen, Pieter (2002) 'Corporate lobbying in the European Union: towards a theory of access', *Journal of European Public Policy*, 9:3, 365–390

Brysk, Alison (1993) 'From above and below: social movements, the international system, and human rights in Argentina', *Comparative Political Studies*, 26, 259–285

Brysk, Alison (2005) *Human rights and private wrongs: constructing global civil society* (New York: Routledge)

Bunyan, Tony (2007) 'Secret trilogues and the democratic deficit', <http://www.statewatch.org/analyses/no-64-secret-trilogues.pdf>

Burgerman, Susan (2001) *Moral victories: how activists provoke multilateral action* (Ithaca: Cornell University Press)

Churches Committee on Migrants and Exiles (2001) *Safe haven not fortress* (Brussels: CCME)

Clark, Ann Marie (2001) *Diplomacy of conscience: Amnesty International and changing human rights norms* (Princeton: Princeton University Press)

Costello, Cathryn (2005) 'The Asylum Procedures Directive and the proliferation of safe country practices: deterrence, deflection and the dismantling of international protection?', *European Journal of Migration and Law*, 7, 35–69

Council of the European Union (2003) 'Council Directive 2003/86/EC of 22 September 2003 on the right to family reunification', *Official Journal of the European Communities*, L251, 12

Council of the European Union (2004) 'Council Decision of 22 December 2004 providing for certain areas covered by Title IV of Part Three of the Treaty establishing the European Community to be governed by the procedure laid down in Article 251 of that Treaty', *Official Journal of the European Communities*, L396, 45

Curtin, Deirdre and Steve Peers (2002) *Joint submission by the Standing Committee of Experts on International Migration, Refugee and Criminal Law, the Immigration and Law Practitioners Association, Statewatch, and the European Council of Refugees and Exiles to Working Group X ('Freedom, Security, Justice') of the Convention on the Future of Europe* (Utrecht: London)

ECRE (2006) "ECRE Information Note on the Council Directive 2005/85/EC of 1 December 2005 on minimum standards on procedures in Member States for granting and withdrawing refugee status", October, Brussels

European Commission (1999) *Proposal for a Council Directive on the right to family reunification* (Brussels: EC)

European Commission (2000) *The Commission and non-governmental organizations: building a stronger partnership*, <http://ec.europa.eu/transparency/civil_society/ngo/docs/communication_en.pdf>

European Commission (2001) *European governance: a white paper*, <http://eur-lex.europa.eu/LexUriServ/site/en/com/2001/com2001_0428en01.pdf>

European Commission (2002) *Amended proposal for a Council Directive on minimum standards on procedures in Member States for granting and withdrawing refugee status* (Brussels: EC)

European Commission (2005) 'Proposal for a Directive of the European Parliament and of the Council on common standards and procedures in the Member States for returning illegally staying third-country nationals' (Brussels: EC)

European Council on Refugees and Exiles (1997) *Position on the functioning of the Treaty on European Union in relation to asylum policy* (Brussels: ECRE)

European Council on Refugees and Exiles (2003) 'ECRE information note on the Council Directive 2003/86/EC of 22 September 2003 on the right to family reunification', <http://www.ecre.org/files/frdirective.pdf>, accessed 9 September 2008

European Council on Refugees and Exiles (2005) *The way forward, Europe's role in the global refugee protection system: towards fair and efficient asylum systems in Europe* (Brussels: ECRE)

European Council on Refugees and Exiles (2009) *ECRE information note on the Returns Directive* (Brussels: ECRE)

European Council on Refugees and Exiles, European Network Against Racism and Migration Policy Group (1999) *Guarding standards, shaping the agenda* (Brussels)

European Court of Justice (2006) PRESS RELEASE No 52/06: Judgment of the Court of Justice in Case C-540/03 European Parliament v Council of the European Union; The Court dismisses the action challenging the directive on the right to family reunification of nationals of non-member states, 27 June 2006, <http://curia.europa.eu/jcms/upload/docs/application/pdf/2009-02/cp060052en.pdf>

Farrell, Henry and Adrienne Héritier (2003) 'The invisible transformation of codecision: problems of democratic legitimacy', (Swedish Institute for European Policy Studies), <http://www.sieps.se/sites/default/files/9-20037.pdf>

Farrell, Henry and Adrienne Héritier (2007) 'Codecision and institutional change', *West European Politics*, 30:2, 285–300

Florini, Ann (2003) *The coming democracy: new rules for running a new world* (Washington DC: Island Press)

Florini, Ann M (ed) (2000a) *The third force: the rise of transnational civil society* (Washington DC: Carnegie Endowment for International Peace)

Florini, Ann M (2000b) 'Lessons learned' in Ann M Florini (ed) *The third force: the rise of transnational civil society* (Washington DC: Carnegie Endowment for International Peace), 211–240

Friedman, Elisabeth, Kathryn Jay Hochstettler and Ann Marie Clark (2005) *Sovereignty, democracy, and global civil society: state-society relations at UN world conferences* (Albany: State University of New York Press)

Geddes, Andrew (2003) *The politics of migration and immigration in Europe* (London: Sage)

Green, Jessica (2010) 'Private authority on the rise: a century of delegation in multilateral environmental agreements' in Christer Jönsson and Jonas Tallberg (eds) *Transnational actors in global governance: patterns, explanations, and implications* (Basingstoke: Palgrave), 155–176

Greenwood, Justin (2009) 'Institutions and civil society organizations in the EU's multilevel system' in Jutta Joachim and Birgit Locher (eds) *Transnational activism in the UN and the EU: a comparative study* (New York: Routledge), 93–104

Justice and Home Affairs Council (2005) 'Council Directive 2005/85/EC of 1 December 2005 on minimum standards on procedures in Member States for granting and withdrawing refugee status', *Official Journal of the European Communities*, L326, 13–34

Joachim, Jutta and Birgit Locher (2009) 'Transnational activism in the EU and the UN' in Jutta Joachim and Birgit Locher (eds) *Transnational activism in the UN and the EU: a comparative study* (New York: Routledge), 3–18

Kaunert, Christian (2009) 'Liberty versus security? EU asylum policy and the European Commission', *Journal of Contemporary European Research*, 5:2, 148–170

Keck, Margaret and Kathryn Sikkink (1998) *Activists beyond borders: advocacy networks in international politics* (Ithaca: Cornell University Press)

Kohler-Koch, Beate (2009) 'The three worlds of European civil society—what role for civil society for what kind of Europe?', *Policy and Society*, 28, 47–57

Lavenex, Sandra (2001) 'The Europeanization of refugee policies: normative challenges and institutional legacies', *Journal of Common Market Studies*, 39, 851–874

Lavenex, Sandra and Emek M Uçarer (eds) (2002) *Migration and the externalities of European integration* (Lanham, Maryland: Lexington Books)

Lavenex, Sandra and Emek M Uçarer (2004) 'The external impact of European integration: the case of immigration policies', *Cooperation and Conflict*, 39:4, 417–443

Martin, A and George Ross (2001) 'Trade union organizing at the European level' in Doug Imig and Sidney Tarrow (eds) *Contentious Europeans* (Lanham, Maryland: Rowman and Littlefield), 53–76

Niessen, Jan (2001) 'Overlapping interests and conflicting agendas: the knocking into shape of EU immigration policies', *European Journal of Migration and Law*, 3:3–4, 419–434

Niessen, Jan (2002) 'Consultations on immigration policies in the European Union', *European Journal of Migration and Law*, 4, 79–83

Oxfam (2005) *Foreign territory: the internationalization of EU asylum policy* (Oxford: Oxfam)

Peers, Steve (2007) 'Statewatch analysis revising the proposed EU Expulsion Directive', <http://www.statewatch.org/news/2007/apr/eu-expulsion-sw-analysis-II.pdf>

Peers, Steve (2008) 'The proposed EU returns directive', <http://www.statewatch.org/analyses/eu-returns-analysis-mar-08.pdf>

Pollet, Kris (2011) 'The negotiations on the returns directive: challenges, outcomes and lessons learned from an NGO perspective' in Karin Zwaan (ed) *The Returns Directive: central themes, problem issues, and implementation in selected members* (Nijmegen: Wolf Legal Publishers)

Price, Richard (1998) 'Reversing the gun sights: transnational civil society targets land mines', *International Organization*, 52:3, 613–644

Price, Richard M (1997) *The chemical weapons taboo* (Ithaca: Cornell University Press)

Price, Richard M (2003) 'Transnational civil society and advocacy in world politics', *World Politics*, 55:4, 579–606

Ripoll Servent, Ariadna and Florian Trauner (2012) 'Do supranational institutions make a difference? EU asylum law before and after communitarisation', paper presented at the Conference The governance of asylum and migration in the European Union, University of Salford, Manchester, 26–27 January

Risse, Thomas (2000) 'The power of norms versus the norms of power: transnational civil society and human rights' in Ann M Florini (ed) *The third force: the rise of transnational civil society* (Washington DC: Carnegie Endowment for International Peace), 177–209

Risse, Thomas, Steve C Ropp and Kathryn Sikkink (1999) *The power of human rights: international norms and domestic change* (New York: Cambridge University Press)

Saurugger, Sabine (2010) 'The social construction of the participatory turn: the emergence of a norm in the European Union', *European Journal of Political Research*, 49, 471–495

Save the Children, (2008) Letter to MEPs on the Forthcoming Plenary Vote on the Proposal for a Directive on Common Standards and Procedures for Returning Illegally Staying Third Country Nationals, 11 June.

Standing Committee of Experts on International Immigration, Refugee and Criminal Law (1995) *Proposals for the amendment of the Treaty on European Union at the IGC in 1996* (Utrecht, Netherlands: Meijers Committee)

Tarrow, Sidney (2005) *The new transnational activism* (Cambridge: Cambridge University Press)

Tarrow, Sidney (2011) *Power in movement* (Cambridge: Cambridge University Press)

Tholen, Berry (2005) 'The Europeanization of migration policy: the normative issues', *European Journal of Migration and Law*, 6, 323–351

Uçarer, Emek M (2009a) 'Negotiating third-country national rights in the European Union' in Elisabeth Prügl and Markus Thiel (eds) *Diversity in the European Union* (New York: Palgrave Macmillan), 59–75

Uçarer, Emek M (2009b) 'Safeguarding asylum as a human rights: NGOs and the European Union' in Jutta Joachim and Birgit Locher (eds) *Transnational activism in the UN and the EU: a comparative study* (New York: Routledge), 121–139

Uçarer, Emek M (2013) 'Area of Freedom Security and Justice' in Michelle Cini and Nieves Perez-Solorzano Borragan (eds) *European Union politics* (Oxford: Oxford University Press), 281–295

UN High Commissioner for Refugees (2008a) *UNHCR position on the proposal for a directive on common standards and procedures in member states for returning illegally staying third-country nationals* (Brussels: UNHCR)

UN High Commissioner for Refugees (2008b) *UNHCR position on the proposal for a directive on common standards and procedures in member states for returning illegally staying third-country nationals* (Brussels: UNHCR)

Zito, Anthony R and Jamie Elizabeth Jacobs (2009) 'NGOs, the European Union and the case of the environment' in Jutta Joachim and Birgit Locher (eds) *Transnational activism in the UN and the EU: a comparative study* (New York: Routledge), 105–120

The EU's growing external role in the AFSJ domain: factors, framework and forms of action

Jörg Monar
University of Sussex

Abstract *External action has been of growing importance for the Union's Area of Freedom, Security and Justice (AFSJ) and accounted in 2011 already for over 19 per cent of all texts adopted by the Justice and Home Affairs Council. AFSJ related external action has also added a new dimension to previously existing fields of EU external relations. This article first considers the internal and external factors which have influenced the development the external side of the AFSJ and the impact of the post-Lisbon legal and institutional framework, including the special context created by the 'opt-outs' and coherence problems within this framework. It then provides a survey and analysis of the main forms of EU action in this domain (strategy formulation, cooperation with third countries, capacity-building and cooperation with and within international organizations) before assessing—in the conclusions—the implications of this external dimension for both the EU and the Member States and its future developments prospects.*

Introduction

The objective of the European Union's (EU) 'area of freedom, security and justice' (AFSJ) is primarily an internal one: to 'offer to its citizens' an AFSJ 'without internal frontiers, in which the free movement of persons is ensured in conjunction with appropriate measures with respect to external border controls, asylum, immigration and the prevention and combating of crime' (Article 3[2] Treaty on European Union (TEU)). However, with many of the challenges of asylum, migration and serious crime within the AFSJ originating from, or being linked to, the EU's international environment, external action in this domain is not just an option but a necessity. European Union policy-makers have clearly realized this: in the latest multi-annual programme for the development of the AFSJ, the 2010–2014 Stockholm Programme, an entire section is dedicated to the 'external dimension' of the AFSJ on top of a whole range of external measures provided for in the individual policy fields (European Council 2010, 33–37). In 2011 no less than 26 out of a total of 136 texts adopted by the Justice and Home Affairs (JHA) Council, that is 19.1 per cent, were related to agreements with third countries and other external dimension issues.[1]

---

[1] Own calculations based on annual list of JHA Council texts provided by the DG Home Affairs of the EU Council Secretariat.

An assessment of the progress that the EU has made with developing this dimension, and its further potential and its limitations, seems particularly appropriate after EU external action possibilities have again been strengthened by reforms of the 2009 Lisbon Treaty. This article will first look at the factors behind the development of the external dimension of the AFSJ and at its legal and institutional framework before then analysing the progress and limitations of major forms of EU action and arriving at an overall assessment and future development prospects.

Development factors

The development of the external dimension of the AFSJ can be explained by two separate but interrelated categories of factors: external challenges, which have acted as 'driving' factors and internal 'enabling' factors. External challenges to internal AFSJ objectives have clearly been the primary 'driving' factors, as they have both necessitated and justified the use of external instruments to complement purely internal measures. They continue to provide a powerful rationale for external action in this domain; the 2011 Europol Organized Crime Threat Assessment (OCTA) report has again shown that organized crime from outside the EU contributes significantly to security threats within the AFSJ (Europol 2011a, 6–7, 16–18). As regards terrorism, the threat posed by Islamist terrorist networks based outside the EU remains important, one-third of all arrested suspects in 2010 having been born in Algeria, Egypt, Morocco and Tunisia, much of the terrorist propaganda and incitement sources being based outside the EU, and training having been provided for EU-born 'jihadists' in Afghanistan, Pakistan, Somalia and Yemen. Some third-country separatist terrorist groups, like the Kurdish Workers' Party (PKK) and the Tamil Tigers, are also carrying out extortion operations as well as drug-trafficking and trafficking in human beings in the EU (Europol 2011b, 17–20, 22–23). The extent of external challenges to the management of migration issues within the AFSJ is highlighted by the fact that the EU's external border management agency Frontex reported in its 2011 annual Risk Analysis, that there were nearly 560,000 refusals of entry, detections of illegal crossings and cases of illegal stay of third-country nationals within the EU during 2010 (Frontex 2011, 13). To this, one has to add a significant number of asylum applications, which for the whole of the EU amounted in 2010 to nearly 260,000, that is three times more than for Canada and the United States (US), the next most important asylum destination region in the developed world (United Nations High Commissioner for Refugees (UNHCR) 2011, 15).

All these external challenges for the AFSJ have in common the fact that the EU's capacity to respond effectively to them depends crucially on cooperation with third countries. European Union external borders can reduce but not stop crime and terrorism challenges threatening the EU externally, and, once these threats are inside, 'the beast is loose' (Monar and Nilsson 2009, 119) in an area of largely dismantled borders. As a result, purely national responses would be as ineffective as purely internal EU measures. Crime and terrorism challenges can only be effectively tackled if the countries from which they originate, or through which they transit, cooperate with the EU on law enforcement issues and if the EU can help them—where needed—to build up their law enforcement and judicial capabilities. The same applies to migration and asylum policy challenges. The numbers of migrants entering the EU illegally can be reduced if countries of origin or transit cooperate with the EU by better controlling their borders, building up border management capabilities and sharing relevant intelligence about migration routes, traffickers and facilitators. Perhaps even more importantly, the cooperation of third countries is essential for EU member states to be able to return identified illegal immigrants or rejected asylum seekers to countries of origin or transit. Without its external dimension, EU asylum and migration policy would face the prospect of both higher pressures on its (porous) borders and fewer possibilities to send third-country nationals in irregular situations back, which could add significantly to the domestic political problems many member states are experiencing in this policy field.

In the field of judicial cooperation in civil matters, the EU does not face external pressures of similarly political sensitivity as those impacting on internal security and migration management. Yet there are forceful reasons for common external action as well; the interests of both EU citizens and companies can be negatively affected by the absence of legal certainty and predictability in civil and commercial matters involving legal systems outside the EU. These can only be provided by international agreements, and the EU must also protect the uniform application in international negotiations which might affect the Union.[2]

External pressures on their own, however, would not have been sufficient to ensure the development of a significant external dimension of the AFSJ without a range of internal 'enabling' factors. The extension of EU internal action possibilities through the Maastricht (1993), Amsterdam (1999) and Lisbon (2009) Treaty reforms, the growth of the internal legal *acquis* and the establishment and strengthening of the special agencies Europol, Eurojust and Frontex have all contributed to a parallel growth of the rationale, possibilities and needs for EU external action.

An example of the dependency of external AFSJ action on internal progress is the visa facilitation agreements with third countries, of which the EU has been negotiating and concluding an increasing number, starting with Hong Kong in 2001/2002. It only became possible for the EU to engage negotiations with third countries on visa facilitation after the EU had completed its common visa policy with the adoption of Council Regulation (EC) 574/1999[3] 'determining which third countries nationals must be in possession of visas when crossing the external borders of the member states'. The same dependency of the external dimension on internal developments can also be observed with regard to the institutional capabilities of the EU. An example is the posting of third-country liaison magistrates to the EU, which only became possible after 2002 with the establishment of the EU cross-border prosecution unit Eurojust, to which three third-country prosecutors are currently posted.[4]

---

[2] Council of the EU, 'External relations strategy in the field of judicial cooperation in civil matters', Council document 6571/1/08 REV 1, 7 May 2008, 2.

[3] Subsequently replaced by Council Regulation (EC) 539/2001, 15 March 2001; Official Journal of the European Union L 81, 21 March 2001.

[4] From the US, Canada and Croatia. Europol fact sheet on liaison magistrates: <www.eurojust.europa.eu/coll_lmp.htm>.

The internal development of the AFSJ has also made the EU an increasingly attractive partner for third countries seeking cooperation on specific JHA issues, forcing the EU in turn to meet that demand. One can see this in the rapid and significant expansion of EU–US counter-terrorism cooperation after the US transmitted a long list of requests to Commission President Romano Prodi on 16 October 2001 in response to the 9/11 terrorist attacks.[5] Although many of the requests were not accepted by the EU counter-terrorism, cooperation with the US subsequently broke new ground through the holding of regular cooperation meetings at different levels, the conclusions of two Europol agreements on the sharing of data in 2001 and 2002, an agreement upon two agreements on extradition and mutual legal assistance in 2003, the coordination of work on terrorist lists and the posting of liaison officers in Washington and Federal Bureau of Investigation (FBI) liaison officers in The Hague and, eventually, the conclusion of the (highly controversial) EU–US agreement on the collection, transfer and storing of Passenger Name Records (PNR) (Archik 2011, 4–11).

The legal framework

Prior to the 2009 Lisbon Treaty reforms, the legal division of the AFSJ were separated between four policy areas based on Title IV TEC (asylum, migration, border controls and judicial cooperation in civil matters) and two policy areas which were based on Title VI TEU (judicial cooperation in criminal matters and police cooperation). This had the consequence not only of the need for different legal instruments and procedures to be used for internal measures, but also for external relations to be governed by substantially different rules depending on whether 'first pillar' (Title IV TEC) or 'third pillar' (Title VI TEU) matters were concerned (Monar 2004, 396–403). This not only added to the complexity of internal procedures regarding the negotiation and conclusion of AFSJ international agreements, but also allowed third countries in certain cases to question—for tactical reasons—the legal capacity of the EU to enter into binding agreements on 'third pillar' matters, due to the absence of an explicit legal personality and competence of the EU as such (De Schoutheete and Andoura 2007, 8).

The Treaty of Lisbon reforms put an end to the 'pillar divide' in the external dimension of the AFSJ by merging the formerly legally separated fields into Title V of the Third Part of the Treaty on the Functioning of the Union (TFEU). The negotiation and conclusion of agreements with third countries on AFSJ matters is now governed by a single legal framework based on a single EU legal personality (Article 47 TEU) and a single treaty-making procedure (Article 218 TFEU). As a result, the EU can now act internationally with greater legal coherence and a reduced potential for confusion or questioning of the Union's legal capacity on the part of third countries.

The treaties do not provide for an express general competence of the EU to act on external AFSJ matters. The only explicit references to external action are to be found in Articles 78(2)(g) TFEU with regard to cooperation with third countries for the purpose of managing inflows of people applying for asylum or subsidiary

---

[5] Text of the letter: < www.statewatch.org/news/2001/nov/06Ausalet.htm >, accessed 20 April 2012.

or temporary protection and 79(3) TFEU as regards the conclusion of readmission agreements with third countries. However, external action can also be based on 'implied powers' in line with the extensive case-law that the EU Court of Justice has developed since its landmark European Road Transport Agreement (ERTA) ruling of 1971[6] and which the Lisbon Treaty reforms have now fully codified. Revised Article 216(1) TFEU provides that the EU may conclude an agreement with third countries or international organizations 'where the Treaties so provide or where the conclusion of an agreement is necessary in order to achieve, within the framework of the Union's policies, one of the objectives referred to in the Treaties'. As a result, the EU can act externally on any AFSJ subject matter if there is a treaty-defined internal objective and if external action is necessary to achieve that objective (Cremona 2011, 82–87; Eeckhout 2011a, 157–163).

An important limitation of EU external powers in the AFSJ domain results from the fact that these are not exclusive. According to Article 4(2)(j) TFEU, the AFSJ is a domain of 'shared competence' between the EU and the member states. This means that member states can continue to exercise their competence on AFSJ matters to the extent the EU does not exercise its competence (Article 2[2] TFEU). So far there are very few AFSJ matters on which the EU has exercised its competence to the extent of full harmonization. One of those is the full harmonization of visa lists, which, as a result, gives the EU exclusive powers for the conclusions of visa waiver agreements (Peers 2011, 128). On most AFSJ matters, however, such full harmonization has not taken place, so that the member states retain at least partial competence and hence the right to participate in any international agreement together with the EU. As such 'mixed agreements' are more complicated to negotiate and need ratification by all national parliaments, member states have so far not insisted on their right to join AFSJ-related external agreements as contracting parties, except in the case of major multilateral legal instruments such as the 2000 United Nations (UN) Convention against Transnational Organized Crime (Palermo Convention) and the 2003 UN Convention against Corruption.[7]

In the absence of EU exclusive competences, member states can—and indeed do—continue to conclude international agreements on AFSJ-related subject matters (see below). Member states have even explicitly reserved themselves the right to continue to conclude agreements on matters relating to the crossing of external borders (Protocol 23 to the TEU and the TFEU), and a declaration attached to the Lisbon Treaty Final Act (Declaration 36 on Article 218 TFEU) does the same for agreements in the fields of judicial cooperation in civil and criminal matters as well as police cooperation.

As regards decision-making rules, the negotiation and conclusion of agreements with third countries is governed by Article 218 TFEU, which provides for a decision of the Council first on the opening of the negotiations (on the basis of a proposal by the Commission), then the authorization of the signing of any agreement and, finally, on the conclusion of negotiations. In all of these cases the Council has to act by qualified majority, except if the agreement covers a field for which unanimity is required (Article 218[8] TFEU). The extension of qualified

---

[6] Case 22/70 (AETR/ERTA) Commission vs Council [1971] ECR 263.
[7] In the case of the 2007 Convention on Jurisdiction and the Recognition and Enforcement of Judgments in Civil and Commercial Matters the ECJ ruled against 'mixity' in favour of exclusive Community competence. Opinion 1/03 (Lugano Convention) [2006] ECR I 1145.

majority voting under the 'ordinary legislative procedure' to most internal AFSJ matters by the Lisbon Treaty has therefore definitely strengthened the EU's external decision-making capacity in this domain. Of equal importance is the massive strengthening of the role of the European Parliament (EP), whose consent is now required for all international agreements covering AFSJ matters to which either the ordinary legislative procedure or a special legislative procedure with consent applies (Article 218[7] TFEU), that is, nearly all AFSJ matters.

A look at the legal framework would not be complete without considering the implications of the 'opt-outs'. Rather than removing the opt-outs granted to Ireland, the United Kingdom (UK) and Denmark, the Lisbon Treaty reforms have even expanded them, as the previously existing opt-outs, which applied only to the 'communitarized' AFSJ fields of the 'first pillar' (asylum, migration, border controls, judicial cooperation in civil matters), have been extended to the former 'third pillar' fields (police and judicial cooperation in criminal matters). Quite apart from the curious situation that the masters of the treaties have thus granted an in-principle complete opt-out to three of their number from what is defined as a fundamental common treaty objective in Article 3(2) TEU, this has serious implications for the external dimension of the AFSJ. According to Article 2 of the British, Irish and Danish opt-out protocols[8] no provision of any international agreement concluded by the EU pursuant to the provisions relating to the AFSJ is binding or applicable to these three member states). The territorial application of any such agreement is thus limited to the other member states, constituting an exception from the general principle of EU international agreements applying to the entire territory of the EU (Martenczuk 2008, 508–509). Certain opt-in possibilities for Ireland, the UK and Denmark exist, but there are major political and/or legal obstacles to their use. The most prominent example is the EU's 'common policy on visas' (Article 77[2][a] TFEU). The non-participation of Ireland and the UK in the common EU/Schengen visa system precludes their participation in any of the visa facilitation agreements concluded by the EU. The Danish position is even more complicated: Denmark is part of the Schengen group, but its opt-in possibilities do not extend to measures not building upon the original Schengen *acquis*. As visa facilitation agreements fall into the latter category, Denmark has to conclude legally separate visa facilitation agreements with the respective third countries even if the substantial provisions of these are identical with those of the respective EU/Schengen agreements (Peers 2011, 238; Trauner and Kruse 2008, 10). As a result the EU has had to negotiate such agreements with third countries without three of its member states, which is further reflected by the need to then define, at the beginning of the respective agreements, the meaning of 'member state'. It is thus stated in Article 3 of the 2007 visa facilitation agreement with the Russian Federation that

For the purpose of this Agreement:

(a) 'Member State' shall mean any Member State of the European Union, with the exception of the Kingdom of Denmark, Ireland and the United Kingdom of Great Britain and Northern Ireland. (Official Journal of the European Union L 129, 17 May 2007, 3)

---

[8] Protocols 21 and 22 to the TEU and TFEU.

The opt-outs have also forced the EU to introduce differentiation in its participation in multilateral conventions. The 2006 Council Decision on the Protocol Against the Smuggling of Migrants, supplementing the 2000 UN Convention Against Transnational Organized Crime, for instance, thus states in recital 5 that

> the UK and Ireland are not bound by this Decision to the extent that it concerns the exercise of an external power by the Community in fields where its internal legislation does not bind the UK and/or Ireland. (Council Decision 206/617/EC, Official Journal of the European Union L 262, 22 September 2006, 34)

Needless to say, such differentiation does not add to the credibility and coherence of the EU as an international actor in the AFSJ domain, especially as the opt-outs then frequently negotiate parallel bilateral agreements with the respective third countries.[9]

The institutional framework

By virtue of Article 68 TFEU, it is the European Council which 'define[s] the strategic guidelines for legislative and operational planning within the area of freedom, security and justice'. This is not a purely formal role, for although the five-year programmes for the development of the AFSJ—of which the aforementioned Stockholm Programme is the latest—have been largely finalized at the level of the JHA Council, the European Council has on several occasions (such as in relation to the adoption of the 'Global Approach to Migration' in December 2005)[10] given a significant political impetus to the development of the AFSJ. It should also be noted that, according to Article 22(1) TEU, it is the European Council which has to identify the 'strategic interests and objectives' of the EU's external action in general, which reinforces the role of the European Council as an overarching authority on any strategy involving external AFSJ issues.

The JHA Council remains the principal decision-making institution. Comprising both the ministers of the interior and those of justice, the JHA Council has to approve all programming documents for the JHA external dimension (whether these are submitted to the European Council for formal adoption or not), adopt all relevant legislative acts, take decisions on the opening, signing and conclusion[11] of international agreements in the AFSJ domain, approve the Commission's negotiation mandates, consider external risk assessments[12] and define action priorities regarding specific third countries or regions.[13]

As usual in the Council context, documents relating to the external dimension of the AFSJ are mainly negotiated, and often also finalized, by the competent Council working groups, a process that often involves several groups and requires complex

---

[9] Denmark, for instance, concluded in 2008 a bilateral visa facilitation agreement with Russia which was largely similar to the aforementioned EU–Russia agreement of 2007.

[10] 'Presidency conclusions', European Council, 14–15 December 2005, Council document 15914/1/05 REV 1, paragraphs 8–10.

[11] After the consent of the EP.

[12] An example is the 'Council conclusions on a Latin-American and Caribbean (LAC) organised crime analysis', Council document 5070/4/10 REV, 21 May 2010.

[13] An example is the 'Action-oriented paper on strategic and concerted action to improve cooperation in combating organised crime, especially drug trafficking, originating in West Africa', Council document 5069/3/10, 25 March 2010.

coordination. In the case of the 2010 'Action-oriented paper' on combating organized crime originating in West Africa,[14] for instance, no less than six different working groups were involved until the Council approved the finalized text on 26 April 2011.[15] The Council AFSJ working groups are primarily focused on internal EU AFSJ issues, which necessitates additional expertise on relations with concerned third countries. This expertise can be brought in by the group on external JHA issues (JAIEX), which regroups experts on international AFSJ issues from the national ministries, and the respective regional Common Foreign and Security Policy (CFSP) working groups. The JAIEX group finds itself in a key position below the political level of the Council as regards the preparation of decisions on the external AFSJ dimension. Yet, as the 2011 report on the implementation of the 2005 Strategy for the External Dimension of the AFSJ notes, the only monthly meetings of the group often prevent it from addressing urgent matters quickly, and JAIEX delegates tend to present only their national positions rather than really discussing issues.[16] The JAIEX group still comes hierarchically under the authority of the Committee of Permanent Representatives (COREPER), which remains the supreme coordinating body below the ministerial level. There are also other Council committees and working parties that have a key role in defining external priorities in their respective fields, such as the Strategic Committee on Frontiers, Immigration and Asylum (SCIFA), the Article 36 Committee (CATS), which deals with external aspects of police and judicial cooperation in criminal matters, and the High Level Working Group on Migration and Asylum (HLWG), which focuses on the situation in countries of origin and prepares corresponding external action plans.

A special position inside of the Council is occupied by the EU Counter-terrorism Coordinator (CTC), who works under the authority of the High Representative and Vice-President of the Commission (HRVP) but takes his or her instructions from and reports primarily to the JHA Council. The CTC not only coordinates counter-terrorism activities within the Council and monitors the implementation of EU counter-terrorism measures, but can also be described as the EU's chief counter-terrorism diplomat, as he or she has the task—re-confirmed by Stockholm Programme (European Council 2010, 24)—of ensuring the effective communication of EU objectives and cooperation offers to third countries.

Since the entry into force of the Amsterdam Treaty in 1999, the European Commission has consistently pushed for the further development of the AFSJ external dimension through general policy recommendations,[17] proposals for developing relations on AFSJ matters with specific third countries or regions,[18]

---

[14] *Ibid.*

[15] The working groups were: organized crime (CRIMORG), horizontal drugs issues (CORDROGUE), external JHA issues (JAIEX), Africa (COAFR), internal security operational cooperation (COSI) and migration (MIGR).

[16] Council of the EU, fourth implementation report of the 'Strategy for the external dimension of JHA: global freedom, security and justice' by the Council Secretariat (JAIEX working party)—period of reference: January 2010 to June 2011, Council document 11678/11, 4 July 2011, 11–12.

[17] A recent example are the proposals for external action in the April 2010 Communication on the 'Action plan implementing the Stockholm Programme' (COM(2010)171, 20 April 2010, 58–64).

[18] A major example is the 2004 Commission proposals on making the JHA domain a priority action field in relations with the ENP countries (COM(2004)373, 16–17, 21, 23).

enhanced capacity-building in third-countries, and the negotiation of agreements with third countries. Apart from substantive policy reasons, the Commission's proactivity in this domain may also have been motivated by a certain institutional self-interest, as it has allowed the Commission to develop an increasing role in a field that, in the 1990s, was still completely dominated by intergovernmental cooperation between the member states. As the executive institution of the EU, and the one responsible for the implementation of the budget, it has also often fallen to the Commission to respond fairly rapidly to crisis situations affecting the AFSJ through new proposals for external action, including the use of EU funding instruments. The most recent example of this emergency executive function of the Commission was the package of proposals presented by the Commission on 4 May 2011 in response to the surge of immigration pressure on the EU's southern borders in conjunction with the Arab Spring developments. This package included both enhanced and new forms of cooperation with the third countries concerned, including such measures as the establishment of 'trust-funds'.[19]

There are some initial indications that the recent splitting—in 2009—of the AFSJ portfolio between two commissioners (Cecilia Malmström and Viviane Reding) and the subsequent division of the old JHA Directorate-General (DG) into new 'Home Affairs' and 'Justice' DGs may have as a result a less joined-up approach of the Commission with regard to the external AFSJ dimension. In the Commission's November 2010 Communication on action for implementation of the EU's 2010 Internal Security Strategy—which was prepared by the DG Home Affairs, the section on 'Internal security in a global perspective' did not contain a single reference to international criminal justice cooperation and relegated the external role of Eurojust to a footnote.[20] There are also other commissioners and their respective DGs whose responsibilities are often affected by AFSJ external issues, such as the domains of transports (Commissioner Siim Kallas), fight against fraud (Commissioner Algirdas Semeta) and enlargement and European Neighbourhood Policy (Commissioner Stefan Füle), and who therefore need to be involved in decision-making on respective external matters.

In relation to both the Council and the Commission, a hybrid structure has to be considered which is surely the biggest institutional innovation introduced by the Lisbon Treaty: the European External Action Service (EEAS). This Service is headed by the HRVP, and its staff is drawn from the Commission (mainly from the DG External Relations and part of the DG Development), the Council (Policy Unit, DG E) and officials of the member states' foreign ministries (on temporary secondment). In spite of the comprehensive mandate that its name and the rapidly growing number of its personnel suggest, it seems unlikely that the EEAS will have any major impact on policy formulation in the external dimension of the AFSJ. Not only have the Commission's DGs Home Affairs and Justice and the Council's DG H (JHA) retained their respective external relations responsibilities, but the EEAS— which has as its main focus CFSP and the external diplomatic representation of the EU—also lacks any unit in its 'Global and Multilateral Issues' Department specifically tasked to cover external AFSJ matters. Perhaps more importantly, the

---

[19] European Commission, 'Communication on migration', COM (2011)248, 4 May 2011.
[20] European Commission, 'The EU internal security strategy in action: five steps towards a more secure Europe', COM (2010)673, 22 November 2010, 3.

HRVP (currently Baroness Catherine Ashton) has also so far steered largely clear of major external AFSJ matters, specifically, illegal immigration and the fight against international organized crime. During her high-profile visit to Tunisia in February 2011, for instance, Baroness Ashton avoided answering questions about migration challenges although thousands of Tunisian illegal immigrants had by that time already reached Italian shores.[21] While CFSP issues (and internal struggles regarding the EEAS) have no doubt kept her busy enough, her abstention on the external AFSJ side is likely to be motivated also by the wish to avoid turf wars with the JHA Council and especially the ministers of the interior, who are used to handling their external JHA issues largely amongst themselves.

The EP lost little time in demonstrating its aforementioned strengthened post-Lisbon powers when on 11 February 2010 it rejected—with an overwhelming majority of 378 to 196—the Society for Worldwide Interbank Financial Telecommunication (SWIFT) Interim Agreement between the EU and US which was intended to ensure continued access of US law enforcement authorities to the financial messaging data handled by the international SWIFT bank consortium. This Interim Agreement, which had already been concluded by the Council and provisionally entered into force on 1 February 2010, was arguably a somewhat cavalier way of dealing with the EP's newly extended powers of consent. In spite of intense lobbying not only from the Commission and member states—most of which regarded transatlantic cooperation on financial messaging data important in the fight against terrorist financing—and from the US (represented on this matter by Secretary of State Hilary Clinton personally) for whom the agreement was crucial for their Terrorist Finance Tracking Programme (TFTP), the EP's committee in charge of AFSJ matters (the Committee on civil liberties and justice and home affairs or LIBE Committee) successfully recommended the rejection of the agreement. The LIBE Committee did so on grounds of inadequate data protection provisions, especially as regards access of the US to 'bulk' rather than individually targeted data, absence of a judicial authorization requirement and lack of rules on retention and oversight. This forceful intervention of the EP in the external dimension of the AFSJ, however, lost part of its moral strength when on 7 July 2010 the EP voted through the text of a hastily re-negotiated definite EU–US agreement that provided only limited additional data protection safeguards.[22] This cleared the way for the agreement's entry into force on 1 August 2010, but made the EP's earlier stance look like it had been influenced more by an interest in affirming institutional prerogatives than by substantive policy reasons. Never-theless the SWIFT case shows that Council and Commission as well as third countries now have to reckon with the EP as an important factor in the external dimension of the AFSJ. During the re-negotiation of the SWIFT agreement the Commission, the Council Presidency and the US went to great lengths in briefing and communicating with the LIBE Committee—which is likely to set a precedent for future negotiations.

---

[21] 'Ashton weicht Frage nach Migration in Tunis aus', *Focus Magazin* (Munich), 14 February 2011.

[22] Council of the EU, 'Agreement between the European Union and the United States of America on the processing and transfer of financial messaging data from the European Union to the United States for the purposes of the terrorist finance tracking program', Official Journal of the European Union L 195, 27 July 2010.

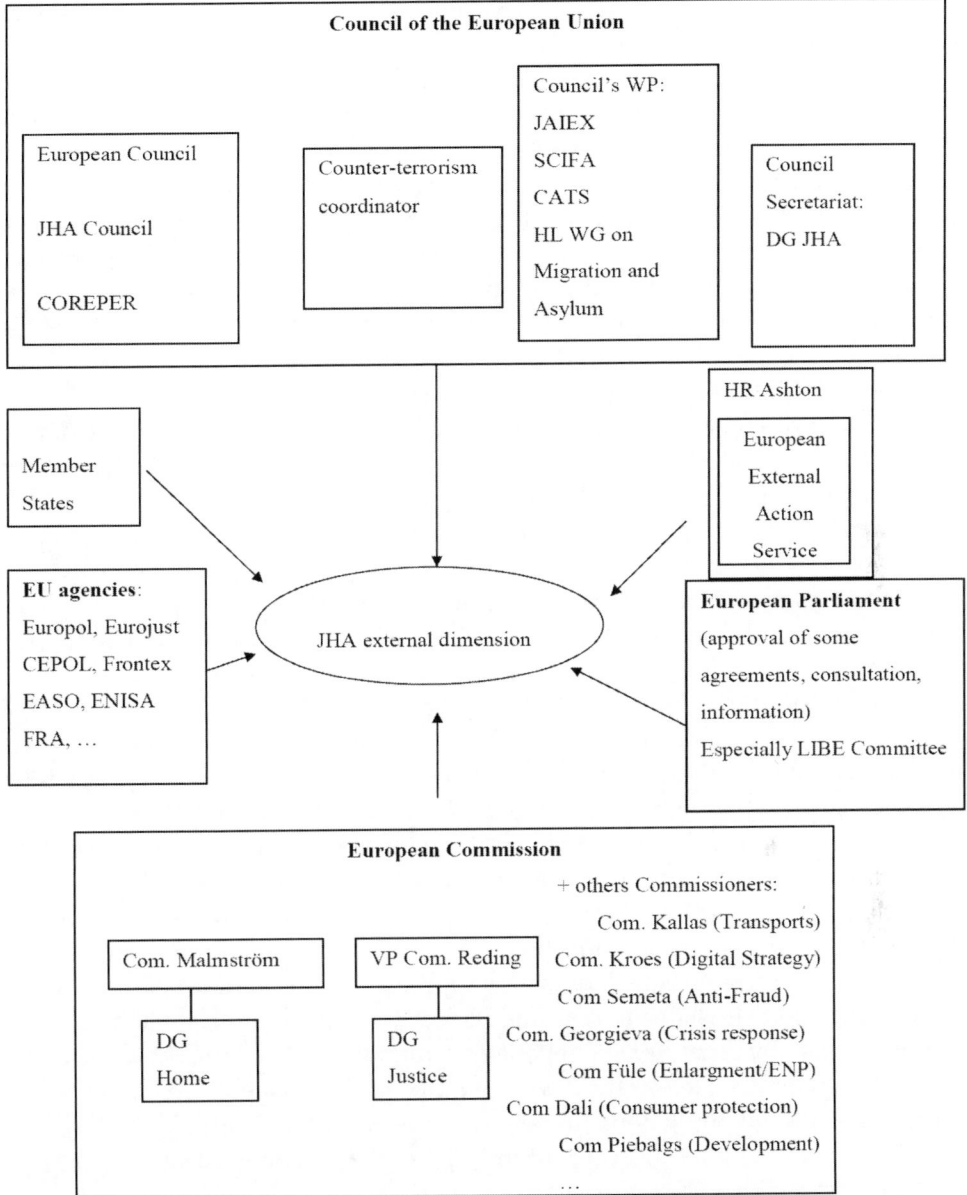

Figure 1. Unofficial chart of EU institutional actors in the AFSJ external dimension. *Source*: 2011 'JHA external relations trio programme', Council document 12004/11, 4 July 2011, 23.

Overall the institutional architecture of the AFSJ external dimension is clearly marked by considerable 'complexity', a term actually used by the 2011 JHA External Relations Trio Presidency Programme[23] with regard to the unofficial chart (Figure 1) of all actors with a role in this domain.

---

[23] Council of the EU, 'JHA external relations—trio programme', Council document 12004/11, 4 July 2011, 2.

This institutional complexity does not make it easy to ensure the 'consistency between the different areas of [the EU's] external action' provided for by Article 21(3) TEU. As regards the consistency between external actions in the different AFSJ fields, the fact that the external dimension is still under the control of a single Council formation (the JHA Council) has so far ensured adequate coordination. Yet there could be a risk of a growing 'drifting apart' of the external home affairs and external justice fields as a result of the aforementioned new separation of these fields within the Commission and also the tendency in the Council's working structure of home affairs and justice issues—even if interrelated—to be dealt with at different meetings and at different times.[24] This could reduce the potential for a comprehensive and integrated EU approach especially as regards international law enforcement cooperation issues.

The second consistency challenge, the one between the AFSJ external dimension and other EU external policies, has been identified as a challenge for quite a while. In the context of the Stockholm Programme, in December 2009 the European Council stressed again 'the need for the increased integration of these [AFSJ] policies into the general policies of the Union' (European Council 2010, 33). Tensions between external AFSJ and CFSP (or other) external policy objectives have not frequently arisen. One such case has been visa facilitation for third-country nationals, an issue on which foreign ministers have often tended to favour earlier concessions to third countries than have their colleagues from ministries of the interior, who in general have made those concessions more conditional on internal security considerations and/or the parallel conclusion of readmission agreements, which have become the EU's primary external migration management instrument. In order to overcome these tensions a 'common approach' on visa facilitation was agreed in December 2005, according to which a visa facilitation agreement would only be possible if a readmission agreement had already been agreed upon and provisions had been made for monitoring mechanisms and suspension clauses in the agreements and for the Commission to consult with member states in both the JHA and the geographical CFSP Council groups on its proposal for a negotiating mandate. It seems, however, that cooperation with the geographical working groups does have its problems, as the fourth report on the implementation of the Strategy for the External Dimension of July 2011 noted that joint meetings of the JAIEX group with geographical groups 'have not proved very successful'.[25]

---

[24] In the 2011 evaluation of the work of the senior Council committee dealing with police and judicial cooperation (CATS), it was noted that CATS meetings have been normally divided into two days, which are split between home affairs and justice delegates. While this was considered justified for a number of files, the evaluation recommended that 'more synergy should be encouraged', as it could 'provide a more comprehensive picture and avoid a fragmented approach' (Council document 13206/11, 22 July 2011, 6).

[25] Council of the EU, fourth implementation report of the 'Strategy for the external dimension of JHA: global freedom, security and justice' by the Council Secretariat (JAIEX working party)—period of reference: January 2010 to June 2011, Council document 11678/11, 4 July 2011, 11.

Main forms of action

Strategy formulation and programming

Since the Tampere European Council of October 1999, the AFSJ has been the object of a steadily increasing range of strategy and programming documents, of which four categories can be distinguished. The first are strategy documents for the development of the AFSJ as a whole, in which the external dimension appears as one field of action. The main category of these are the multi-annual (five-year) programmes. The AFSJ external dimension has so far invariably been placed at the end of these programmes, which underlines its complementary role with regard to the objectives and strategy elements defined for the individual internal policy fields which are covered in the previous sections. The 2009–2014 Stockholm Programme, however, provides in its final section, not only for general principles, but also for a list of thematic priorities with 'new tools', geographical priorities, agreements with third countries and common positions in international organizations (European Council 2010, 33–37). This can be taken as an indication of both the increased political importance of the external dimension and the desire to set clearer points of reference for implementation programming.

The second category of strategy documents has focused on the implementation of the external AFSJ dimension itself. The initial external dimension's specific 'multi-presidencies programmes' were eventually followed by the more substantial and focused 'Strategy for the external dimension of the area of freedom, security and justice' of December 2005, which still remains the main framework programming document and covers thematic priorities, principles, delivery mechanisms and tools as well as structures and processes.[26] The 2005 Strategy has survived for such a relatively long time because its elements—focused on strategic issues—have remained sufficiently general to allow periodic updating and more detailed retargeting as regards key issues, regional priorities, and changes in approaches and procedures. This retargeting is done every 18 months through a combination of assessment and new programming. These assessments come in the form of the regular 'implementation reports' on the external AFSJ strategy prepared by the JAIEX working group. The most recent report from July 2011, for instance, made recommendations on institutional and procedural changes (JAIEX methodology and topics, coordination with other EU external policies), the use of EU financial resources, capacity-building in third countries and relations with the eastern and southern neighbourhood.[27] The new programming takes the form of the 'Trio Programmes' (successor of the former multi-presidency programmes) which are mainly based on the JAIEX implementation reports, as well as on discussions at the Council level and priorities of the three incoming presidencies. The most recent Trio Programme of the Polish, Danish and Cyprus presidencies of July 2011, for instance, although addressing key issues in the 'implementation report' (such as JAIEX methodology and reports), placed a strong emphasis on

---

[26] Council of the EU, 'A strategy for the external dimension of JHA: global freedom, security and justice', Council document 15446/05, 6 December 2005.

[27] Council of the EU, fourth implementation report of the 'Strategy for the external dimension of JHA: global freedom, security and justice' by the Council Secretariat (JAIEX working party), Council document 11678/11, 4 July 2011, 11–16.

reinforcing the fight against drug-trafficking, a major Polish priority, although this had not been identified as an 'area of attention' in the 2011 implementation report.[28]

The third category of strategy and programming documents relates to individual AFSJ fields. Specific strategy and programming documents, defining objectives and priorities, have been introduced for all major AFSJ policy fields, and during the last decade external dimension elements have become an integrated part of all of them. To give only two examples: in May 2008 the Council adopted an 'External relations strategy in the field of judicial cooperation in civil matters' which defines primary areas of cooperation from jurisdiction issues to taking of evidence as well as working methods, primary target countries and preferred international forums (in particular the Hague Conference on International Private Law) (Council document 6571/1/08 REV 1, 7 May 2008). In June 2011 the Council adopted 'Conclusions on priorities for the fight against organised crime 2011–2013', which defined a range of external objectives in relation to internal priorities, including the weakening of the capacity of organized crime groups active in West Africa to traffic cocaine and heroin to and within the EU, the mitigation of the role of the Western Balkans as a key transit and storage zone for illicit commodities destined for the EU and logistical centre for organized crime groups, and the reduction of the capacity of organized crime groups to facilitate illegal immigration into the EU.[29]

The fourth, and final, category consists of strategy and programme documents regarding specific third countries or groups of third countries. These range from external AFSJ objectives as part of general EU regional strategy documents—such as the still valid external AFSJ objectives defined in the Commission's 2004 'European Neighbourhood Policy (ENP) Strategy Paper'[30]—over specific AFSJ external regional action plans—such as the 2010 action-oriented paper on combating organized crime (especially drug-trafficking) originating in West Africa[31]—to the formulation of country-specific AFSJ external strategy elements—such as the JHA cooperation objectives defined in the EU's 'ENP Ukraine country strategy paper 2007–2013'.[32]

Cooperation with third countries

Any AFSJ related cooperation between the EU and third countries going beyond diplomatic or informal exchanges requires formal agreements. One can distinguish between multi- and bilateral framework agreements concluded with third countries in which cooperation on AFSJ matters is provided for as one of several fields of cooperation, and agreements addressing specifically external AFSJ matters.

---

[28] Council of the EU, 'JHA external relations—trio programme', Council document 12004/11, 4 July 2011, 5–6.

[29] Council of the EU, 'Council conclusions on setting the EU's priorities for the fight against organised crime between 2011 and 2013', Council document 11050/11, 6 June 2011, 4–5.

[30] European Commission, 'European Neighbourhood Policy strategy paper', COM (2004)373, 12 May 2004, 16–17.

[31] Council document 5069/3/10, 25 March 2010.

[32] European Commission, 'Ukraine country strategy paper 2007–2013', 2007, 14.

As regards the first category, the framework agreements, since the Treaty of Amsterdam the EU has more or less systematically sought to introduce certain external AFSJ elements into the negotiation and conclusion of such framework agreements. This applies, in particular, to 'readmission clauses'—that is, clauses providing for the principle of readmission of nationals residing unlawfully in the territory of an EU member state—cooperation on readmission issues and often the later negotiation of a specific agreement on that matter. Since the 9/11 terrorist attacks the EU has also regularly sought to insert counter-terrorism cooperation clauses in framework agreements. These counter-terrorism clauses are based on a standardized model defined by the Council, but they vary in scope and detail depending on the specifics of EU relations with the respective countries, and demands put forward by them during the negotiations.

Apart from the insertion of clauses on specific AFSJ matters in framework agreements, the EU has also increasingly sought to use such agreements to create a framework for cooperation with partner countries on a wider range of issues in this domain. All Association Agreements (AAs) and Stabilization and Association Agreements (SAAs) concluded during the last decade contain clauses on cooperation in various JHA fields in line with internal AFSJ objectives. In the case of the 2005 AA with Algeria, for instance, detailed provisions on AFSJ related to institution-building, migration issues, fight against organized crime, drug-trafficking, terrorism and corruption as well as legal and judicial cooperation have been included.[33] But the politically and institutionally less far-reaching Partnership and Cooperation Agreements (PCAs) have also provided pathways for broader cooperation on AFSJ related issues. The 1997 PCA with the Russian Federation, for instance, has provided a basis for the development of the 'EU–Russia Common Space on Freedom, Security and Justice' set up under the 2003 EU–Russia Partnership and Cooperation Agreement, which, in spite of serious political and data-protection problems, has made possible, inter alia, cooperation progress on visa facilitation, drugs precursors, training of law enforcement agencies and border management cooperation.[34]

Of the second abovementioned category of agreements, those addressing specifically external AFSJ matters, the EU has since the entry into force of the Treaty of Amsterdam concluded 60, amongst which there 20 multilateral and 40 bilateral agreements.[35] The multilateral agreements consist mainly of the participation of the EU/member states in AFSJ-related international legal instruments—such as the 2007 Convention on Jurisdiction and the Recognition and Enforcement of Judgments in Civil and Commercial Matters[36] (which has replaced the 1988 Lugano Convention)—and the agreements concluded with Iceland, Norway, the Swiss Confederation and Liechtenstein concerning aspects

---

[33] Articles 82–91 of the Euro-Mediterranean Agreement establishing an association between the European Community and its member states and the People's Democratic Republic of Algeria, Official Journal of the European Union L265, 10 October 2005.

[34] European Commission, 'EU–Russia common spaces progress report 2010 of March 2011' (no pagination).

[35] European Commission Treaties Office Database, 'List of agreements in the fields of justice, freedom and security', accessed 17 September 2011.

[36] Council Decision 2009/430/EC (Official Journal of the European Union L 147, 10 June 2009).

of their association with the Schengen system. The majority of the bilateral agreements concern cooperation on readmission and visa facilitation, but there are also agreements on cooperation in criminal justice[37] and law enforcement,[38] as well as the association of third countries with the EU's Monitoring Centre for Drugs and Drug Addiction. A special sub-category includes agreements that Europol, Eurojust, Frontex and the European Asylum Support Office (EASO) can conclude with third-country authorities. While the number of these agreements is steadily increasing—Europol alone has already concluded 18 agreements with third countries and three with international organizations[39]—their scope is limited to the exchange of certain categories of information, support for operational cooperation involving national authorities, and training.

It is especially the range of agreements specifically concluded on AFSJ issues which show that the EU has become an actor in its own right in the AFSJ external dimension, and that it has as such also been recognized by third countries. Yet one also has to see the EU's persistent limitations in this respect; in line with the 'shared competence', principal member states remain free to conclude individual agreements with third countries in fields not wholly pre-empted by EU action—a freedom that is amply used according to national interests. A recent example is the 1 October 2008 agreement that Germany signed with the US on access to biometric data and the spontaneous sharing of data about known and suspected terrorists, which also provides for mutual assistance in preventing serious threats to public security, including terrorist entry into either country. There was no EU involvement in the agreements' negotiation, and only its preamble contains a vague reference to an expectation of other EU member states following the model of this agreement.[40] The continuation of separate bilateral treaty-making by member states does surely not add to the cohesiveness and credibility of the EU as an international actor in the domain.

Another limitation results from the fact that the EU has no 'operational capabilities' in the sense of deployable personnel (police, judicial or other) and technical means of its own to participate in joint operations (law enforcement, intelligence-sharing, border protection, migration management, et cetera), as all these capabilities remain at the level of the member states. This reduces both the potential scope of agreements and the attractiveness of concluding agreements with the EU from the perspective of third countries, which may still achieve more effective operational arrangements by concluding bilateral agreements with individual member states.

---

[37] Such as the aforementioned 2003 EU–US agreements on extradition and mutual legal assistance (both Official Journal of the European Union L181, 19 July 2003) and the EU–Japan agreement on mutual legal assistance in criminal matters (Official Journal of the European Union L39, 12 February 2010).

[38] Such as the 2010 EU–US 'Agreement on the processing and transfer of financial messaging data from the EU to the United States for the purposes of the Terrorist Finance Tracking Program', Official Journal of the European Union L195, 27 July 2010.

[39] Europol, 'International relations', < https://www.europol.europa.eu/content/page/ international-relations-31 > , accessed 2 October 2011.

[40] Deutscher Bundestag, 'Drucksache', 16/13123, 25 May 2009.

Capacity-building in third countries

Capacity-building can be considered as a separate form of AFSJ-related external action, as it is aimed not only at cooperation with third countries but at transforming their JHA systems in line with AFSJ objectives. Such capacity-building—which has become the financially most substantial form of external AFSJ action[41]—is based on the simple rationale that one can transform third countries into more effective partners (for addressing external challenges to the AFSJ) by building up their national capabilities in terms of organization, infrastructure, training and legal framework. External capacity-building measures have been developed in most AFSJ policy fields from asylum and immigration policy over border control and surveillance to police and judicial cooperation in criminal matters. The global context of many of the EU's internal security challenges has resulted in even geographically remote countries being targeted by capacity-building measures. The support provided by the EU to the Jakarta Centre for Law Enforcement regarding its training programmes for the fight against transnational crime is an example.[42] Yet most of the capacity-building is currently focused on the ENP and Western Balkan countries, as they constitute, in a sense, the EU's external 'glacis' when it comes to preventing crime and migration challenges from reaching and crossing EU external borders. Enhancing neighbouring countries' law enforcement and border management capabilities has so far clearly been the main objective of these capacity-building efforts, of which the external AFSJ approach to the Mediterranean is a primary example (Longo 2011, 367–388). Measures can address all major internal security issues from terrorism through organized crime to illegal immigration, using a wide variety of instruments from the transfer of technical expertise and training through advice on legislation and the restructuring of police, court and border management structures to the funding of equipment.

While the rationale of third-country capacity-building as one way of reducing external AFSJ challenges seems compelling enough, it has its problems on the implementation side. The potential and limits of the EU's possibilities to bring third countries to effectively cooperate on EU internal security objectives and standards depend crucially on the EU's political leverage. In the case of the Western Balkan countries, perspective EU membership clearly accounts for a greater leverage than, for instance, for ENP countries that do not have such an opportunity. The European Commission's progress reports on ENP partners[43] confirm that, in spite of capacity-building assistance, progress can be very limited if this leverage is low or non-existent. Examples are the persisting significant shortcomings of Azerbaijan as regards the fight against corruption and money-laundering,[44] the continuing deficits of national capabilities and

---

[41] External AFSJ capacity-building uses a range of different EU policy and geographical budget lines such as 2011 budget items 19 02 01, 19 06 03, 19 06 01, 19 08 010 01 and 19 08 01 03 (Official Journal of the European Union L 68, 15 March 2011). These provide an overall funding framework for 2011 of over €800 million, but only part of this is specifically used for AFSJ-related capacity-building.

[42] Under EuropeAid project 127452, 'Support to improved security by provision of capacity building to the Jakarta Centre for Law Enforcement Co-operation' (JCLEC).

[43] See the Commission's ENP individual country progress reports (European Commission, SEC(2011) 637–652, 25 May 2011).

[44] SEC(2011) 640, 25 May 2011, 4, 11.

legislation with regard to asylum and trafficking in human beings in the Ukraine,[45] the—in spite of major EU efforts—still 'totally unsatisfactory' reform of the judiciary in Tunisia[46] and the almost complete lack of progress regarding the implementation of an effective legislative framework for asylum and refugee policy in Morocco which the Commission reported, again, in 2011.[47]

Cooperation with and within international organizations

International organizations constitute in many cases very effective frameworks for pursuing external AFSJ objectives, this not only because they provide an established setting for multilateral cooperation but also because previously established multilateral conventions bind the EU member states. The primary fora for multilateral action by the EU in the fight against corruption, for instance, remain thus the UN, the Council of Europe and the Organization for Economic Co-operation and Development (OECD) (Mitsilegas 2011, 241–242). The internal EU controversies surrounding the implementation of UN Security Council Resolutions regarding the freezing of funds and financial resources of individuals and entities suspected of being involved in terrorist financing—which led to the European Court of Justice's (ECJ) landmark judgement on the (in)famous 'terrorist listing' in the *Kadi* and *Al Barakaat* cases[48]—have shown that the legal obligations defined in the context of international organizations can also raise fundamental questions about the extent to which the EU is a mere instrument of execution of these obligations or retains a certain degree of autonomy and the capacity to maintain its own benchmarks in a important field such as counter-terrorism (Eeckhout 2011b, 326–335, 338).

Since the entry into force of the Amsterdam Treaty there can be no question that the EU has increasingly asserted its position within international organizations as an actor on various AFSJ-related matters, in line with the growth of its internal powers. Major indicators of this increasing 'actorness' within international organizations are the Community's (now Union's) adhesion to the 2000 UN Convention against Transnational Organized Crime (Palermo Convention) and to its three protocols regarding the prevention of illicit manufacturing and trafficking of firearms, the prevention of the smuggling of migrants and the prevention of trafficking of persons, and to the 2003 UN Convention Against Corruption.[49] In the domain of international judicial cooperation in civil matters, the EU has been able to increase its presence significantly, which can be seen in its accession to the Hague Conference on International Private Law (in 2007) and its subsequent signing of the (Hague) Convention on Choice of Court Agreements (in 2009) and the 2007

---

[45] SEC(2011) 646, 25 May 2011, 15.

[46] SEC(2011) 652, 25 May 2011, 4.

[47] SEC(2011) 651, 25 May 2011, 15.

[48] Joined Cases C-402/05 P and C-415/05 P *Kadi and Al Barakaat* v *Council and Commission* [2008] ECR I–6351.

[49] Council Decisions 2001/748/EC (Official Journal of the European Union L 280, 24 October 2001), 2004/579/EC (Official Journal of the European Union L 261, 6 August 2004), 2006/616/EC, 2006/617/EC, 2006/618/EC, 2006/619/EC (all Official Journal of the European Union L 262, 22 September 2006) and 2008/801/EC (Official Journal of the European Union L 287, 29 October 2008).

(Hague) Convention on the International Recovery of Child Support and Other Forms of Family Maintenance (in 2011).[50]

Conclusions

For the EU as whole, the emergence of the external dimension of the AFSJ can be regarded as a positive development. It has allowed the EU, gradually and with an increasingly wide range of external instruments, to complement internal action on AFSJ objectives with external action. Because many of the challenges to which the AFSJ must respond have a major—and in some cases (such as illegal immigration) even a primarily—external EU dimension, the development of a corresponding dimension of external action constitutes a necessary part of the development of the AFSJ itself and of the effectiveness of its policies. The use of the combined political weight of the EU—comprising both the collective weight of the member states and the whole range of the EU's external action possibilities—has made it easier to secure cooperation of third countries on a range of AFSJ-relevant issues such as readmission, anti-money-laundering measures and the sharing of law enforcement data. The adoption of common positions on fundamental AFSJ issues also offers the EU and its member states a better chance to defend common interests—such as that in high standards of personal data protection in law enforcement cooperation—even against powerful external pressures like those of the US in the context of counter-terrorism cooperation (Bendiek 2011, 13–14).

The Treaty of Lisbon has clearly strengthened the EU's potential to further develop the external dimension of the AFSJ through the abolition of the 'pillar structure', the creation of a single legal personality, a unified procedure for the negotiation and conclusion of agreements and the extension of qualified majority voting. The 2009–2014 Stockholm Programme also places a greater emphasis on this dimension of the AFSJ than any of its predecessors. This, along with the fact that the external challenges to the AFSJ continue to figure prominently in EU threat assessments, should contribute to a growing expansion of the AFSJ external dimension until the end of the current programming period, and beyond.

Yet a number of factors will continue to impact negatively on the development potential of the external side of the AFSJ. The diversity of the fields covered—from asylum and immigration over civil and criminal justice to police cooperation—limits the potential for the external AFSJ dimension to develop into a single 'policy'. The resulting relative fragmentation makes it more difficult for AFSJ external objectives to be given the same political weight as those of other more established and homogeneous external EU policies (such as the CFSP, trade, development). This in turn contributes to the difficulties of an effective integration of AFSJ objectives with other external EU policies, which is also hampered by different strings of decision-making and the complex post-Lisbon institutional structure. If one adds to this the continuing limitations resulting from the EU's only 'shared' competences, it seems clear that progress in this domain will ultimately continue to depend crucially on the extent of the member states'

---

[50] Council Decisions 2006/719/EC (Official Journal of the European Union L 297, 26 October 2006), 2009/397/EC (Official Journal of the European Union L 133, 29 May 2009) and 2011/220/EU (Official Journal of the European Union L 93, 7 April 2011).

interest in common external action. As this interest is very much conditioned by the perception of international challenges and threats, it may well be that over the next few years the most important role for the EU institutions will be that of making the member states fully realize the nature and extent of the commonality of international challenges in the various AFSJ fields, and hence the need for corresponding common external action.

Notes on contributor

Jörg Monar is Professor and Director of European Political and Administrative Studies at the College of Europe (Bruges) and Professor of Contemporary European Studies at the Sussex European Institute, University of Sussex (Brighton).

References

Archik, Kristin (2011) 'U.S.–EU-cooperation against terrorism', CRS report for Congress 7–5700, Congressional Research Service, Washington.

Bendiek, Annegret (2011) *An den Grenzen des Rechtsstaates: EU–USA-Terrorismusbekämpfung* (Berlin: Stiftung Wissenschaft und Politik)

Cremona, Marise (2011) 'EU external action in the JHA domain: a legal perspective' in Marise Cremona, Jörg Monar and Sara Poli (eds) *The external dimension of the European Union's area of freedom, security and justice* (Brussels: PIE Peter Lang), 77–115

De Schoutheete, Philippe and Sami Andoura (2007) 'The legal personality of the European Union', *Studia Diplomatica*, 60:1, 1–9

Eeckhout, Piet (2011a) *EU external relations law*, 2nd edn (Oxford: Oxford University Press)

Eeckhout, Piet (2011b) 'Kadi and the EU as instrument or actor: which rule of law for counter-terrorism?' in Marise Cremona, Jörg Monar and Sara Poli (eds) *The external dimension of the European Union's area of freedom, security and justice* (Brussels: PIE Peter Lang), 323–339

European Council (2010) 'The Stockholm Programme', *Official Journal of the European Union*, C 115, 4 May

Europol (2011a) *EU organised crime assessment: OCTA 2011* (The Hague)

Europol (2011b) *EU TE–SAT 2011: terrorism situation and trend report* (The Hague)

Frontex (2011) *Frontex: annual risk analysis 2011* (Warsaw)

Longo, Francesca (2011) 'The Mediterranean dimension of the area of freedom, security and justice' in Marise Cremona, Jörg Monar and Sara Poli (eds) *The external dimension of the European Union's area of freedom, security and justice* (Brussels: PIE Peter Lang), 367–388

Martenczuk, Bernd (2008) 'Variable geometry and the external relations of the EU' in Bernd Martenczuk and Servaas van Thiel (eds) *Justice, liberty, security: new challenges for EU external relations* (Brussels: Brussels University Press), 493–523

Mitsilegas, Valsamis (2011) 'The European Union and the implementation of international norms in criminal matters' in Marise Cremona, Jörg Monar and Sara Poli (eds) *The external dimension of the European Union's area of freedom, security and justice* (Brussels: PIE Peter Lang), 239–272

Monar, Jörg (2004) 'The EU as an international actor in the domain of justice and home affairs', *European Foreign Affairs Review*, 9:1, 395–415

Monar, Jörg and Hans Nilsson (2009) 'Enhancing the EU's effectiveness in response to international criminality and terrorism: current deficits and elements of a realist post-2009 agenda' in Olaf Cramme (ed) *Rescuing the European project: EU legitimacy, governance and security* (London: Policy Network), 109–122

Peers, Steve (2011) *EU justice and home affairs law*, 3rd edn (Oxford: Oxford University Press)

Trauner, Florian and Imke Kruse (2008) 'EC visa facilitation and readmission agreement', Centre for European Policy Studies, Working Document 290, Brussels

UNHCR (2011) *Asylum levels and trends in industrialized countries* (Geneva)

Exporting EU integrated border management beyond EU borders: modernization and institutional transformation in exchange for more mobility?

Raül Hernández i Sagrera
Institut d'Estudis Internacionals Barcelona (IBEI)

Abstract *The external dimension of European Union (EU) border management cooperation has recently been developed, in particular through the promotion of integrated border management (IBM). The European Commission has been keen to foster IBM, an attempt to reach EU standards in the absence of an EU common border service. Integrated border management is regulated under the Treaty of Lisbon, and the Stockholm Programme calls for its further development. This article analyses and compares the policy instruments promoting IBM standards beyond EU borders, namely the European Agency for Operational Cooperation at the External Border of the Member States of the EU (FRONTEX) (with the signature of Working Arrangements with the border services of third countries) and the activity of the EU Border Assistance Mission to the Republic of Moldova and to Ukraine (EUBAM) at the Ukrainian–Moldovan border. Moreover, it provides an empirical account of IBM activity carried out in the Eastern Partnership and Russia, and explains the reasons underlying the lack of IBM promotion in the southern Mediterranean countries.*

Introduction

Research on European Union (EU) migration cooperation with neighbouring countries has been extensive (Balzacq 2008; Cremona 2008; Lavenex 2006; Sterkx 2008; Wolff et al 2009). Yet this research has focused on the study of EU readmission and visa policies in the region.[1] The literature also analyses the nascent EU labour migration policy towards third countries (Kunz et al 2011). Scholarly work has, however, devoted scant attention to the promotion of integrated border management (IBM) activity beyond EU borders, which has been particularly relevant in the countries that border the EU to the east: the Eastern Partnership countries and Russia. This article aims to shed light on this gap, providing empirical evidence of EU border management cooperation with third

---

The author is grateful to all the officials interviewed for the purpose of this article, as well as to the participants in the conference 'The Governance of Migration and Asylum in the European Union', University of Salford, 26–27 January 2012, for their comments on this article.

[1] See for instance the work of Trauner and Kruse (2008) and Hernández i Sagrera (2010) on the readmission-visa facilitation nexus.

countries, as well as linking this policy with other under-researched areas such as visa and labour migration policies.

European Union border management cooperation with third countries has been an integral part of the security-driven migration policy that the EU has conducted since the entry into force of the Treaty of Amsterdam, which paved the way for the development of an EU migration policy with regard to third countries. While the readmission policy of the EU has been clearly regulated in legally binding treaties, including agreements with third countries in the field,[2] the external dimension of the EU border management policy has been developed in a 'soft' fashion. Nevertheless, the lack of integration of the border services at the EU level has not prevented the EU from including in its agenda the Eastern Partnership[3] and Russia (hereinafter referred to as 'Eastern Europe') and the promotion of the concept of IBM, which is an attempt to reach EU standards on border management. The EU has channelled IBM promotion through two actors: the European Agency for Operational Cooperation at the External Border of the Member States of the EU (FRONTEX) and, in the particular case of Ukraine and Moldova, the EU Border Assistance Mission to the Republic of Moldova and to Ukraine (EUBAM).

This article thus pursues three aims. First, it analyses the content of IBM promotion in third countries in order to specify whether EU–Eastern-Europe border management cooperation is 'in accordance to EU best practice'; whether it follows an 'objective of alignment with EU standards and practices'; and whether there has been 'great attention to developing and advancing the Integrated Border Management processes' (EUBAM 2011a, 9). In the same vein, Udo Burkholder, head of EUBAM, expressed his opinion that the adoption by Ukraine and Moldova of an IBM strategy and concept was 'a significant step forward towards the approximation of EU standards in border management' (EUBAM 2011a, 2). Second, the article looks at how IBM promotion has been articulated, analysing and assessing the policy instruments developed by FRONTEX and EUBAM in the field. Those institutions have been specifically deployed in Eastern Europe and not to the southern Mediterranean countries. In this sense, the third aim seeks to explain the geographical difference in IBM promotion, referring to the offer of incentives that foster mobility such as the Schengen visa liberalization process or the launch of Mobility Partnerships.

Due to the recentness of EU border management cooperation with third countries, the article draws mainly on extensive fieldwork carried out at the FRONTEX and EUBAM headquarters in Warsaw and Odessa, respectively, as well as in the Border Services of the Eastern European countries. In addition, the analysis of primary sources on the IBM approach and implementation in third countries has been essential.

The article begins with a section that outlines the origins of EU border management cooperation, at both the internal and external levels, and the development of the IBM concept. The next section looks at the origins and legal basis

---

[2] On readmission policy, see Coleman (2009).

[3] The Eastern Partnership was launched in 2009 at a Summit in Prague as the first attempt to provide a multilateral framework for the countries neighbouring the EU to the east. See the Joint Declaration of the Eastern Partnership Summit in Warsaw (Council of the EU 2011a). Russia refused to take part in the initiative. The Eastern Partnership countries are Armenia, Azerbaijan, Belarus, Georgia, the Republic of Moldova, and Ukraine.

of the policy instruments that the EU has at its disposal for IBM promotion, namely FRONTEX Working Arrangements and EUBAM. The third section analyses and assesses IBM activity carried out in Eastern Europe so far. Finally, the main findings are summarized as regards the content of IBM promotion, the policy instruments used and the reasons underpinning its development in Eastern Europe and not in the southern Mediterranean countries.

Integrated border management within the EU border management policy

When dealing with the external dimension of the EU border management policy, the first element to be borne in mind is that EU border services are not integrated at the EU level. Consequently, 'member states continue to be competent in controlling their external borders' (Wolff 2010, 26). Furthermore, as a FRONTEX official stressed, 'Member States do not want to give up sovereignty (in the border management field), even though there is a need for more cooperation among Member States.'[4] Actually, there are huge differences among EU member states regarding the competences of border services. Surprisingly, most of the law enforcement authorities responsible for border control are actually police officers, except in Finland, Latvia, Lithuania, the Netherlands and Poland (Carrera 2010, 9).

Indeed, with the Schengen area allowing movement without internal border checks and encompassing 25 states,[5] the EU has gradually developed a policy oriented towards integrating the border guard services of the member states. Some argue that FRONTEX is the first step towards the establishment of an eventual European Border Guard Service. The Commission recommended the 'support of European Corps of Border Guards, which '[a]t the first stage could exercise real surveillance functions at the external borders' (European Commission 2002, 20). Furthermore, Commissioner for Home Affairs Cecilia Malmstöm 'identified the creation of a European border guard as one of the most important policy actions to be debated before the end of her mandate' (Carrera 2010, 1). In this sense, a FRONTEX official argued that a European Border Guard Service is in the making, steps in that direction including the launch of the Rapid Border Intervention Teams (RAPIT) (European Parliament and Council of the EU 2007).[6] RAPIT has been deployed so far at the Greek–Turkish border, one of the main entry points of irregular migration into the EU.

At the EU internal level, the legal basis regulating border control is the so-called Schengen Borders' Code (European Parliament and Council of the EU 2006). Paradoxically, this Code entered into force after the creation of the FRONTEX agency. The Border's Code stipulates that border management is a policy area that 'should help to combat illegal immigration and trafficking in human beings and to prevent any threat to the Member States' internal security, public policy, public health and international relations' (European Parliament and Council of the EU 2006, recital 6).

---

[4] Interview with a FRONTEX official, Brussels, May 2010.
[5] The 27 EU member states except for Bulgaria, Cyprus, Ireland, Romania and the United Kingdom and including three non-EU member states (Iceland, Norway and Switzerland).
[6] Interview with a FRONTEX official, Warsaw, November 2010.

This rhetoric reproduces the security-driven rationale that has characterized EU migration policy since the time of its inception. Border management is conceived as a means to reduce irregular migration flows. In that regard, Carrera points out that 'the current EU policy on irregular migration legitimise(s) the practice and promotion of a paradigm of control and surveillance, whose implementation ... opens a series of concerns regarding the principle of legality, transparency and accountability as well as the compliance with human rights and European Community Law on borders' (2007, 8). Yet the amended FRONTEX Regulation, which entered into force in November 2011, reinforces a fundamental rights-based approach including references to the Charter for Fundamental Rights and international refugee law (European Parliament and Council of the EU 2011, article 1).

In an attempt to give stimulus to the integration at EU level of EU border management, the European Commission presented a Communication on IBM in 2002. The Commission, aware of the reluctance of member states to move forwards in the integration of border surveillance practices, opted to coin this concept.[7] According to the Commission (2002), IBM allows 'practitioners of the checks at the external borders to come together around the same table to co-ordinate their operational action in the framework of an integrated strategy' (European Commission 2002, 5). In line with the Commission Communication on IBM, the Council Conclusions in 2006 defined IBM as a concept embedding border control (according to the Schengen Borders' Code), detection of cross-border crime, and interagency cooperation (Council of the EU 2006, 2).

As Wolff contends, IBM 'is linked to the development of the EU internal security strategy' (Wolff 2010, 26). In this regard, Carrera stresses that the '"border management" of the common Schengen regime external border must be "integrated" and must cover all border-related threats that the EU is supposed to be facing' (2007, 3), which is stressed in the European Security Strategy (Council of the EU 2003). Carrera believes that IBM 'legitimises and reinforces the practice of security as coercion in the EU external territorial border' (2007, 27). Besides, in line with the Schengen Borders' Code, the promotion of IBM and the 'strengthening of security' are intertwined (FRONTEX 2011, 8). Similarly, the Commission conveyed that '[t]he security of the external borders of the European Union is an essential subject for European citizens' (European Commission 2002, 4). In the same vein, the Stockholm Programme, which sets out the agenda for action in the Justice and Home Affairs domain for the period 2009–2014, defines IBM as an 'effective policy to combat illegal immigration' (Council of the EU 2009b, 108).

With the Treaty of Lisbon, the concept of IBM was introduced into the primary law of the EU. Therefore, the European Parliament and the Council of the EU may regulate legal provisions in the field. More specifically, the Treaty establishes that the EU should develop a policy aimed at '[t]he gradual introduction of an integrated management system for external borders' (Treaty of Lisbon 2009, article 77, 1.c). The Stockholm Programme calls for the further development of IBM by means of the reinforcement of FRONTEX and the European Asylum Support Office (EASO) (Council of the EU 2009b, 91).

In a nutshell, IBM promotion in third countries has consisted mainly of the launch of activities whose goal has been the modernization of not only the

---

[7] On the IBM concept, see Hobbing (2006).

EU border checks and procedures along the EU common border with Eastern Europe, but also the borders between Eastern European countries. This is the case in the promotion of IBM along the Moldovan–Ukrainian border. Yet the IBM concept has not been free from criticism. Bigo highlighted the increased use of technology in the proliferation of databases of the EU external border and the juxtaposition of border checkpoints. As a result, the EU is 'an island'.[8] In this sense, Carrera underlines that '[t]echnology ... is now presented as the "ultra-solution" to any imagined threat to the EU's internal security' (Carrera 2010, 7). The shortcomings of IBM have also been stressed by Monar: '[t]he "integrated" system clearly continues to suffer from major limitations: There are still substantial coordination and evaluation deficits as well as major constraints imposed by the absence of cross-border law enforcement powers pertaining to border guards' (Monar 2006, 80). Yet one EUBAM official argued, while acknowledging the lack of specificity of the IBM concept, that it contributes to a gradual process whereby the actors involved cooperate more on border management. As a result, the IBM concept is gradually being implemented.[9]

The FRONTEX working arrangements and EUBAM activity as policy instruments to promote IBM in third countries

European Union border management cooperation with third countries has so far been fruitful only with Eastern Europe, where it has been articulated through FRONTEX Working Arrangements and, in the case of Ukraine and Moldova, also in the framework of EUBAM. Despite the difference in the format of these two policy instruments, they are suitable for comparison because they carry out very similar IBM promotion activities. Prior to the deployment of EU cooperation tools in Eastern Europe, some EU member states with interests in the area, such as Poland, had developed bilateral relations between their own border guard services and their Eastern European counterparts, by means of setting up focal points.

FRONTEX has labelled itself 'the anchor stone' of IBM (FRONTEX 2011, 15). It has been the only agency that has undertaken activities aimed at promoting IBM in the whole of Russia and the Eastern Partnership. It is the EU agency in charge of coordinating operational cooperation along the EU external border.[10] FRONTEX is the 19th Agency of the EU and is regulated under Regulation 2004/2007, which laid the foundations for its creation, stipulating its functions and structure (Council of the EU 2004).

The Agency became operational in 2005 and has its headquarters in Warsaw (Council of the EU 2005). The idea to place FRONTEX in Poland stems from the perception that the activity of the Agency would be much more intense along the EU's external eastern border than along the southern border. Yet the activity of the Agency, in particular its joint operations, has mainly been focused on irregular

---

[8] Speech by Didier Bigo at the workshop 'Human Mobility and Governance in a Global Context', Fundació CIDOB, Barcelona, 22 September 2011. On the proliferation of databases and the technological development of the EU borders, see Geyer (2008) and Bigo and Jeandesboz (2009).

[9] Interview with the Head of the Analytical and Operational Support Unit, EUBAM, Odessa, April 2011.

[10] On the origins of FRONTEX, see also Jorry (2007) and Léonard (2009).

migration flows from the southern Mediterranean,[11] as well as from the African Atlantic coast into the Canary Islands. In Eastern Europe, FRONTEX has deployed, with others, a joint operation along the EU–Ukrainian border named JUPITER.

As EU member states hold executive powers in border management, the FRONTEX founding Regulation clearly states that '[t]he responsibility for the control and surveillance of the external borders lies with the member states' (Council of the EU 2004, article 1.2). In other words, the Agency acts only at the operational level coordinating EU member states border guard services. Among the functions that FRONTEX carries out, the elaboration of risk assessments,[12] capacity-building provision for border guards and supporting joint return operations stand out. These are launched in circumstances in which EU member states require further technical and operational assistance at the external border, in application of the principle of burden-sharing. In total, they account for 60 per cent of the Agency's total budget.[13] In addition, the Agency also conducts research on border control and surveillance.

In February 2010, the European Commission presented a proposal aimed at reforming FRONTEX, which led to the amended Regulation 1168/2011 in November 2011 (European Parliament and Council of the EU 2011). The new Regulation includes a series of reforms. On the one hand, a leading role of the Agency together with member states is the deployment of joint return operations, able to control the operational plan in case of need and to decide where EU member states' experts should be deployed. Also, the Regulation foresees rendering compulsory the equipment contribution from member states and the possibility for FRONTEX to have its own equipment. On the other hand, the Regulation envisages the possibility for FRONTEX to fund technical-assistance projects with third countries.

In the context of negotiations on the proposal, the possibility for FRONTEX to access personal data has been an issue of controversy, since it is not a law enforcement agency. In this regard, the European Data Protection Supervisor (EDPS) expressed his concern about the lack of clarity in the Proposal on the scope of activities where personal data could be processed (EDPS 2010, 9). Finally, the new Regulation foresees the obligatory introduction of a fundamental rights approach in the contents of capacity-building training and seminars (European Parliament and Council of the EU 2011, article 5).[14]

A measure that deserves special attention is the institutionalization of the so-called Common Core Curriculum for border guards, within the package on

---

[11] FRONTEX joint operations have been mainly deployed to the central Mediterranean (Malta and the Italian island of Lampedusa) and the eastern Mediterranean (Greek coast). See Carrera (2007) for a comprehensive analysis of FRONTEX joint operations in the Canary Islands.

[12] Risk analysis monitors the irregular migration routes into the EU. In 2009, there was a reduction of 24 per cent of irregular migrants apprehended at the EU external border, mainly due to the economic crisis. The major gateway of irregular migrants into the EU is at the Greek–Turkish border. Data provided by Richard Ares Baumgartner, FRONTEX official, at his presentation in the short course 'EU Immigration and Asylum Policies, Border Security: State of Play and Prospects of Russia–EU Cooperation on Migration', Moscow State Institute of International Relations, Moscow, 25–29 October 2010.

[13] Interview with a FRONTEX official, Brussels, May 2010.

[14] Ibid. See Carrera et al (2011) for an analysis of the impact of FRONTEX on the implementation of the EU Fundamental Rights Charter. In this regard, FRONTEX and the EU Fundamental Rights Agency signed a cooperation arrangement in 2010.

capacity-building measures. Launched in 2007, it consists of a standard code of the skills and knowledge of border guards, with the goal to create a 'European culture of border guards of the Member States' (Council of the EU 2010b, 2). In other words, the proposal is a sort of 'Erasmus' for border guards from the 27 EU member states. Moreover, common core curriculum for border guards has already been included in some of the Working Arrangements signed with Eastern European countries.

Finally, FRONTEX had shortcomings right from the moment of its inception. Bigo and Guild highlight that FRONTEX came into existence before the Schengen Borders' Code came into force (2009, 268). Consequently, the Agency started operating when no common EU norm pinning down the conditions under which individuals should cross the EU external border was in force. Furthermore, Neal (2009) has approached the origins of FRONTEX from the point of view of securitization, claiming it was not a securitization response to the 9/11 attacks.

The external dimension of FRONTEX has been articulated through the signature of Working Arrangements with the corresponding border guard services of third countries. The legal basis for these Arrangements is established in article 14 of the FRONTEX founding Regulation, which vaguely regulates their content and aims. More specifically, article 14 stipulates that the Arrangements 'shall facilitate the operational cooperation between member states and third countries' (Council of the EU 2004, article 14). Under the term 'operational cooperation', the Arrangements may encapsulate any kind of cooperation that might arise, with no references to priorities in the cooperation.

In principle, the fact that FRONTEX cooperation with third countries does not prevent EU member states from developing their own bilateral cooperation arrangements could lead to overlapping of FRONTEX and third country arrangements. As Wolff stresses, '[t]he multiplication of bilateral agreements between the EU, its member states and third countries to control immigration and co-operate on border management has opened a Pandora box full of legal and political uncertainties' (2010, 29). Illustrative of this is the active cooperation between the Polish and Ukrainian border guard services, although apparently there has been no overlap between their activities.[15]

According to Bigo and Guild, 'none of the Arrangements specifies the legal basis on which they were negotiated or agreed' (2009, 273). Actually, contrary to the EU Readmission or Visa Facilitation Agreements, the FRONTEX Working Arrangements are non-legally-binding tools, soft law instruments with a structure flexible enough to adapt to the interests of the signatories. As the Working Arrangements stipulate, they 'shall not be considered an international treaty' (FRONTEX and Border Guard Service of the Federal Security Service of the Russian Federation 2006).

This non-legally-binding character of the Working Arrangements has been defended by FRONTEX officials, as it gives room for manoeuvre[16] and allows an 'individual approach, mutually beneficial for both the EU and the third country, which has led to different speeds in implementation'.[17] Yet the soft law character poses problems from a perspective of legal certainty and enforcement of the

---

[15] Interview with the Deputy Chief of the Department of International Cooperation of the State Border Guard Service of Ukraine, Kiev, May 2011.
[16] Interview with a FRONTEX official, Warsaw, November 2010.
[17] Ibid.

commitments set out in the Working Arrangements. At this point, it is worth recalling that the EU has the legal personality to sign international agreements in an issue area such as border management with a third country in light of article 79(3) of the Treaty on the Functioning of the European Union (TFEU). Besides providing legal certainty and the guarantee of enforcement, the involvement of the European Parliament in the ratification process of an international agreement would increase legitimacy.

In the particular case of Ukraine and Moldova, the EU has also been promoting IBM through the EUBAM. Launched in December 2005, its mandate has subsequently been extended every two years until 2011. EUBAM's specificity lies in the fact that it is a Commission mission and not a Council mission, like EUBAM Rafah. According to Kurowaska and Tallis, the Commission put forward to the Council the arguments that it was not a military mission and that it had extensive experience in the region (2009, 50). It has its headquarters in the Ukrainian city of Odessa, on the shore of the Black Sea.[18] EUBAM activity has been mainly focused on assisting and advising on the reduction of irregular migration flows, combating cross-border crime such as trafficking in human beings and corruption, as well as providing know-how in the customs field. Like FRONTEX, the Mission also carries out joint operations at borders.

Moreover, EUBAM gives advice to the Ukrainian and Moldovan governments in the process of demarcation of their common border. A Joint Ukrainian–Moldovan Commission on Border Demarcation is in charge of the task, a difficult one because of the conflict in the breakaway region of Transnistria. Two-thirds of the common border between Ukraine and Moldova has been demarcated so far, and the demarcation of the central section of the border started in 2010. In this regard, EUBAM has been involved, alongside the EU Special Representative to Moldova, in the settlement of the Transnistrian conflict and the set-up of confidence-building measures between Chişinău and Tiraspol. As a result, the railway services between Chişinău and Odessa via Tiraspol were reintroduced in 2010.

The foundations of EUBAM are set in a Memorandum of Understanding signed by the European Commission and the governments of Ukraine and Moldova. The Memorandum states that the Mission 'will promote coordinated action and assist the Governments of the Republic of Moldova and of Ukraine in areas involving border, customs and fiscal matters' (European Commission, Government of the Republic of Moldova and Government of Ukraine 2005, 1). Like FRONTEX, the Mission has no executive powers and works closely with its four partners: the Ukraine State Border Guard Service and the Border Guard Service of the Republic of Moldova, and the customs services of the two countries. In 2010, EUBAM employed 200 people, was supported by 19 EU member states and was in charge of 1222 kilometres of common Moldovan–Ukrainian border (EUBAM 2011a, 2). Assessments of the Mission have been generally positive. An official from the Mission labelled it 'the most efficient international EU mission'.[19] Yet Kurowska and Tallis have called into question the alleged success of EUBAM. While acknowledging the

---

[18] The headquarters also serve as the EUBAM liaison office for Ukraine. The liaison office for Moldova is in Chişinău. EUBAM has a network of six field offices along the Moldovan–Ukrainian border.

[19] Interview with the EUBAM advisor on IBM, Odessa, April 2011.

progress made by the Mission in border monitoring, they stress that its contribution to solving the Transnistrian conflict has still to be shown.

Before moving to the next section, a note should be added about the EU Special Representative Border Support Team in Georgia (Council of the EU 2010a). The Team assists the Georgian Border Police with officials from six EU member states, again with the aim of implementing IBM standards. The border zones with South Ossetia and Abkhazia are excluded from its scope of action.

European Union IBM activity in Eastern Europe

An analysis of the EU border management agenda, looking at the provisions set out in the European Neighbourhood Policy (ENP) Action Plans in the case of the Eastern Partnership countries and, in the case of Russia, at the Road Map for the Common Space on Freedom, Security and Justice, reveals that the main measures to be implemented in the field are exchange of data regarding irregular migration flows and socialization measures in the form of capacity-building programmes. Within the Eastern Partnership, the EU and its partners launched a flagship initiative on IBM in October 2009. Furthermore, an IBM Panel has been launched in the framework of the Eastern Partnership in order to share experiences and track the development of the IBM promotion activity (European Commission 2011b, 20). Under this flagship initiative, EUBAM has provided support (EUBAM 2011b, 2) and the International Centre for Migration Policy Development (ICMPD) has delivered training activities (European Commission 2011a, 11).

As for FRONTEX, the Working Arrangements are relevant, as they are the only tool that covers the exchange of data regarding irregular migration flows. FRONTEX has signed Arrangements with Russia and all the Eastern Partnership countries except Azerbaijan.[20] An Arrangement was also signed with Belarus, the only Eastern European country that has no contractual relations with the EU. However, the Working Arrangement with the Belarusian Border Guard Service has, it seems, not materialized in any concrete measures.[21]

The FRONTEX Working Arrangement with the Russian Border Guard Service of the Federal Security Service was signed in June 2006 (FRONTEX and State Border Guard Service of Ukraine 2007). It was the first Working Arrangement signed by FRONTEX and apparently 'the most developed' of all the Arrangements signed by the Agency.[22] Among its activities, it has framed an EU–Russia joint operation along the border between the EU and the Russian exclave of Kaliningrad in 2009. In addition, FRONTEX and the Russian Federal Border Service agreed on implementing a Joint Cooperation Plan for the period 2007–2013. According to Bigo and Guild, most of the cooperation under the Working Arrangement has been on investing in technological equipment to meet IBM standards (2009, 275). The Arrangement has not foreseen the training of Russian border guards, most likely because Russia is against receiving training

---

[20] FRONTEX is currently negotiating a Working Arrangement with the Azerbaijan Border Guard Service.

[21] Interview with a FRONTEX official, Warsaw, November 2010.

[22] Ibid.

from the EU. According to a representative of the Federal Border Service of Russia, the implementation of the Working Arrangement has been rather positive.[23]

The Working Arrangement with Ukraine came into force in 2007. Unlike the Arrangement with Russia, it foresees the '[d]evelopment of activities in the field of training' (FRONTEX and State Border Guard Service of Ukraine 2007). A FRONTEX official highlighted that Poland played a vital role in setting the substantial content of operational cooperation with the State Border Guard Service of Ukraine.[24] A Ukrainian official expressed his opinion that it was quite fruitful.[25] The State Border Guard Service of Ukraine approved in January 2011 an Action Plan implementing the Working Arrangement signed with FRONTEX.

The Arrangements with the Moldovan Border Guard Service and the Border Police of Georgia were signed in 2008. Both of them also envisage training. The Arrangement with Moldova has led to enhanced cooperation on border management. There are currently 14 projects that are being implemented in Moldova within the framework of the Working Arrangement.[26] The promotion of IBM in Moldova has been fruitful due to the interest of Chişinău in strengthening its overall migration cooperation with the EU. Indeed, Moldova has been a laboratory for the launch of new EU initiatives such as the aforementioned common core curriculum and others such as Mobility Partnerships or the Common Visa Application centre. Moldova approved an Action Plan implementing the Working Arrangement for the period from 2009 to 2011.

The Working Arrangement with Georgia, on the other hand, has led to scarce results. First, it has to be taken into consideration that Georgia does not share borders with the EU, so that cooperation in border management is not as relevant for the EU.[27] Second, the permanent changes in the Ministry of the Interior in Georgia have slowed down the process of deployment of the Working Arrangement, as a FRONTEX official stated.[28] In addition, the Agency has not carried out a risk analysis in Georgia, most likely because it has no common border with the EU. As a result of the FRONTEX cooperation with Eastern European countries, these have participated as observers in FRONTEX joint operations. An example of FRONTEX cooperation with Eastern Europe is the deployment of the JUPITER Joint Operation, in which Russia, Ukraine and Moldova have been involved.

In terms of IBM promotion, EUBAM activity in Ukraine and Moldova has consisted of the training of border guards. EUBAM set up a capacity-building unit, aimed at coordinating the entire training project with partner services, in both the migration and customs sphere. Moreover, EUBAM offered seminars on

---

[23] Presentation of the Head of Strategic Planning Department of the Federal Border Service of Russia in the short course 'EU Immigration and Asylum Policies, Border Security: State of Play and Prospects of Russia–EU Cooperation on Migration', Moscow State Institute of International Relations, Moscow, 25–29 October 2010.

[24] Interview with a FRONTEX official, Warsaw, November 2010.

[25] Interview with a representative from the Permanent Mission of Ukraine to the EU, Brussels, April 2010.

[26] Interview with an official of the Border Guard Service of the Republic of Moldova, Chişinău, April 2011.

[27] Nonetheless, the European Neighbourhood and Partnership Instrument has funded a project enhancing border management between Georgia and Armenia (European Commission 2011b, 10).

[28] Interview with a FRONTEX official, Brussels, May 2010.

the Schengen *acquis* to the officials involved in the visa liberalization process, so that the legislation could be amended according to Schengen.

A note should be added on the territorial scope of the Mission. Although EUBAM's geographical scope was originally limited to the Moldovan–Ukrainian border, it has actually been extended to the whole of Ukrainian and Moldovan territory. Thus it has a say in all the border management initiatives that take place. As a Ukraine representative put it: 'The recommendations of EUBAM are very useful and not limited to the Moldovan–Ukrainian border, but to all over Ukraine.'[29] Taking into consideration that FRONTEX and EUBAM have not concluded a Memorandum of Understanding specifying the terms of their cooperation, there could be a risk of overlap in their activity. Instead, there is an analytical support unit that coordinates their common tasks.

In Ukraine, EUBAM has been crucial in the implementation of IBM and has, according to an officer from the International Organization for Migration (IOM), been the actor that has dealt with most of the border management cooperation.[30] In this role, EUBAM organized jointly with the border guard services of Ukraine and Moldova two international conferences on IBM in Kiev and Chişinău in 2010. The activity of EUBAM in Ukraine has been coined as positive for the training of border guards and the transfer of good practices and know-how.[31] Similarly, the 'great contribution to the development of IBM of the Mission, implementing funding from the Commission and providing consultation', has been underlined.[32]

The assessment of FRONTEX and EUBAM in Moldova has been uneven. On the one hand, a representative from the Ministry of Foreign Affairs and European Integration expressed his satisfaction with FRONTEX but regretted that Ukraine was not involved more in EUBAM; the high costs associated with the Mission; and that the Mission could be more efficient.[33] On the other hand, a member of the State Border Service highlighted that the Mission was '[t]imely, important and necessary'.[34]

When one compares the role of FRONTEX and EUBAM in IBM promotion in Eastern Europe, it seems that EUBAM's activity has been more far-reaching than that of FRONTEX in the particular cases of Ukraine and Moldova. Not only has the Mission extended its territorial scope to the whole of Ukraine and Moldova, but it has delivered training in areas such as customs, which is also a part of IBM (Council of the EU 2006, 3). Moreover, the Mission has supported the implementation of the Eastern Partnership flagship initiative on IBM, which is addressed to the whole of

---

[29] Interview with the Deputy Chief of the Department of International Cooperation, State Border Guard Service of Ukraine, Kiev, May 2011.

[30] Interview with an officer from the International Organisation for Migration office in Ukraine, Kiev, April 2011.

[31] Interview with the Deputy Head of the Permanent Mission of Ukraine to the EU, Brussels, May 2009.

[32] Interview with the Deputy Chief of the Department of International Cooperation, State Border Guard Service of Ukraine, Kiev, May 2011.

[33] Interview with the Deputy Head of the Unit of Political Cooperation with the EU, Ministry of Foreign Affairs and European Integration of the Republic of Moldova, Chişinău, April 2011.

[34] Interview with the Head of the General Director's office, Border Guard Service of the Republic of Moldova, Chişinău, April 2011.

the Eastern Partnerships. As a result, it could be argued that IBM promotion has served as a platform for EUBAM to extend its territorial scope well beyond the remits of the common Moldovan–Ukrainian border. This raises concerns over the legitimacy of the actual territorial scope of EUBAM activity.

In light of empirical analysis of the activities in the context of IBM carried out by FRONTEX in Russia and the Eastern Partnership and EUBAM in the cases of Ukraine and Moldova, a set of remarks can be made, both general and country-specific. As for the general remarks of IBM promotion in Eastern Europe, the content of IBM, which as this article has shown, is not specific enough and is non-legally binding. It has been inspired by the security-driven rationale underlying EU migration policy. In principle, its aim has been to 'maintain a high level of border security' (EUBAM 2011a, 16). The bulk of IBM has been about the modernization and provision of equipment as well as capacity-building training for border guards. In any case, IBM activity in Eastern Europe has proven to be a learning process, whereby information and best practices have been shared. In brief, IBM has consisted of the development of operational and technical cooperation in the border management field with third countries.

Regarding intraregional differences, the preceding analysis shows that IBM activities have had varying effects, depending on the structure of the relationship between the EU and the Eastern European country concerned. In other words, the flexible cooperation that the FRONTEX Working Arrangements enable has led to different results according to the symmetry or asymmetry of EU relations with each Eastern European country. Thus, the actual content of IBM promotion activities varies. For instance, the symmetry of EU–Russia relations has triggered a scenario in which FRONTEX has not carried out training based on the common core curriculum for border guards. On the contrary, Moldova has been a pioneer in receiving the first FRONTEX common core curriculum courses. This is not only due to the asymmetrical structure of power between the EU and Moldova, but also because of the country's willingness to approximate to EU standards. In brief, if the Eastern European country has more leverage vis-à-vis the EU, the IBM promotion activities are less far-reaching and the other way round. As a result, the non-legally-binding nature of the Working Arrangements could mean they have a differentiated content in comparison with the more standardized Readmission Agreement (RA) and Visa Facilitation Agreement (VFA).

European Union IBM promotion has also led to major institutional changes in countries like Ukraine and Moldova. It must be taken into account that Kiev and Chişinău have strived to implement the IBM concept. EUBAM noted that IBM has been recognized as 'the strategic basis for a national border management strategy, both in Ukraine and in the Republic of Moldova' (EUBAM 2011a, 16). Kiev and Chişinău endorsed the IBM concept and adopted Action Plans implementing it, though the Moldovan Action Plan is more systematized and far-reaching than the Ukrainian Action Plan (Government of Ukraine 2011; Government of the Republic of Moldova 2011). In Ukraine, the State Border Guard Service is in charge of developing IBM, whereas Moldova has launched a National IBM Council.

Consequently, the border guard services of Ukraine and Moldova have undergone a deep transformation in becoming autonomous bodies to be integrated within the Ministry of the Interior, which is in turn undergoing a deep transformation.[35] Both services have replaced their military staff with professional staff, although to differing extents. In the case of Moldova, some personnel in the Border Guard Service are conscripts.[36] Yet, the professionalization of the border services has not meant the loss of the military status of its personnel. In fact, holding military status is perfectly compatible with a fully professional body. In this sense, some EU member states have opted to retain the military status of their border guards.

The Ukraine State Border Guard Service is considered to be 'the most developed body in the context of the European integration of Ukraine, setting up controls according to EU standards. It is the leading agency in the context of the Visa Liberalisation Action Plan'.[37] Ukraine has more experience and a wider network of liaison offices abroad than Moldova, and has a stronger and better-equipped communications system. Furthermore, the border management legislation is more integrated at the EU level in Ukraine than in Moldova.[38]

If the ongoing EU–Eastern-Europe migration cooperation is seen from a wider perspective, including the Schengen Visa Liberalisation processes and the launch of EU Mobility Partnerships, IBM promotion constitutes a tool of conditionality. In other words, the structure of power or the willingness to approximate to EU initiatives does not suffice to explain IBM promotion in Eastern Europe. In the countries where the preceding empirical analysis shows that border management has been more intense, namely in Ukraine and Moldova, IBM has been a requirement in the set of benchmarks on the road towards a visa-free regime with the EU.

Indeed, the second block on Migration Management in the Visa Liberalisation Action Plans with Ukraine and Moldova asks for the adoption of an IBM strategy 'containing a timeframe and specific objectives for the further development of legislation, organization, infrastructure, equipment, as well as sufficient financial and human resources in the area of border management' (EU–Republic of Moldova Visa Dialogue 2010, 5; EU–Ukraine Visa Dialogue 2010, 5). Ukraine has launched a Visa Liberalisation Coordination Centre, whose structure includes a Working Group on IBM represented at the deputy minister level.

Likewise, the Joint Declarations on EU Mobility Partnerships with Moldova, Georgia and Armenia include provisions aimed at strengthening and providing assistance for the implementation of IBM (Council of the EU 2008, 9; 2009a, 5; 2011b, 6). This is striking when one considers that EU Mobility Partnerships were in principle conceived to foster mobility through the launch of circular migration schemes.

Conclusions

The external dimension of EU border management cooperation has recently been developed, in particular through the promotion of the concept of IBM, coined by the Commission in 2002 in an attempt to reach EU standards in the absence of an

---

[35] The Ministries of the Interior are shifting from former Soviet military into civilian structures.

[36] Interview with a EUBAM official, Odessa, April 2011.

[37] Interview with the Head of the Justice, Liberty and Security Division, Ukraine Ministry for Foreign Affairs, Kiev, June 2011.

[38] Interview with the EUBAM advisor on IBM, Odessa, April 2011.

EU common border service. Integrated border management promotion beyond the EU borders has been particularly intense in the countries neighbouring the EU to the east: Russia and the Eastern Partnership. This article has provided an empirical account of the IBM in the Eastern Partnership and Russia, in order to assess the extent and goals of EU border management cooperation with Eastern Europe.

First, regarding IBM, this article has stressed the soft law character of the activities carried out in Eastern Europe. The EU has the competence to sign international agreements in any given field and IBM was incorporated into primary law with the Treaty of Lisbon. In the absence of a common border service at the EU level, IBM, whose further development has been foreseen in the Stockholm Programme, has consisted mainly of the modernization and technologization of the border equipment in Eastern Europe, as well as the provision of capacity-building programmes. Generally speaking, IBM has been a key part of the security-driven EU migration policy towards third countries.

Second, this article has analysed and provided empirical evidence of the activity of the two policy instruments that have promoted IBM standards in Eastern Europe: FRONTEX Working Arrangements and EUBAM. It concludes that EUBAM, despite formally dealing only with the Moldovan–Ukrainian border, has managed to promote IBM standards in the whole of the territories of Ukraine and Moldova and even support the implementation of the IBM Eastern Partnership flagship initiative. Unlike FRONTEX, EUBAM also provides assistance and advice in the customs field, and has been labelled the most relevant agent of IBM promotion in Ukraine and Moldova.

Third, the external dimension of the EU border management policy has implications from an intraregional and interregional perspective. On the former, this analysis has shown that, according to the structure of power between the EU and each Eastern European country, the content of IBM activity has been shaped in one or another direction. For instance, the Russian Border Guard Service has not received any capacity-building training, whereas Moldova has been the first country to adopt EU Common Core Curriculum standards among its border guards. Indeed, Russia's relations vis-à-vis the EU have been framed in terms of symmetry, with outcomes in which Moscow has managed to shape EU policy, such as in the visa facilitation regime. On the contrary, the Republic of Moldova is an example of a country that willingly adopts EU initiatives in the migration field.

Concerning the interregional dimension, this article claims that the offer of incentives is the factor that explains the fruitful EU border management cooperation with Eastern Europe and the lack of development with the southern Mediterranean countries in the field. In other words, the structure of power does not suffice to explain the scope of activity of IBM in Eastern Europe. The development of an IBM strategy is conceived as conditional for progress in other migration policies such as the visa liberalization process or the deployment of Mobility Partnerships. In Ukraine and Moldova, IBM is part of a set of benchmarks to be implemented before the abolition of the visa regime. This has led to significant transformations at the institutional level, such as the changes in the border guard services from military to professional autonomous bodies within the framework of the Ministries of the Interior.

Finally, the current EU border management cooperation with Eastern Europe raises considerations about the exportability of IBM standards and may explain why FRONTEX has failed to foster IBM standards with the countries of the southern Mediterranean. As FRONTEX officials interviewed for the purpose of this article have recognized, the Agency lacks incentives to negotiate Working Arrangements with Morocco, Tunisia, Libya or Egypt because of lack of leverage. The post-Arab-Spring context has been good for the EU in terms of offering prospects for mobility (Visa Facilitation and Mobility Partnerships) to these countries. So far the EU has not specified the conditions under which those new policies fostering mobility will take place. Further research on the external dimension of the EU border management policy will need to look at relationships with the southern Mediterranean countries and whether IBM promotion there can follow the path of Eastern Europe.

Notes on contributor

Raül Hernández i Sagrera is Research Fellow at the Institut Barcelona d'Estudis Internacionals (IBEI) and PhD candidate in International Relations at the Universitat Autònoma de Barcelona. Hernández i Sagrera was a visiting fellow at the Centre for European Policy Studies (CEPS) in Brussels (spring 2009 and 2010) and at the International Centre for Policy Studies in Kyiv (spring 2011).

References

Balzacq, Thierry (2008) 'The external dimension of EU Justice and Home Affairs; tools, processes, outcomes', CEPS Working Document no 303, Centre for European Policy Studies, Brussels

Bigo, Didier and Elspeth Guild (2009) 'The transformation of European border controls' in B Ryan and V Mitsilegas (eds) *Extraterritorial immigration control: legal challenges* (Leiden: Martinus Nijhoff)

Bigo, Didier and Julien Jeandesboz (2009) 'Border security, technology and the Stockholm Programme', INEX Policy Brief no 3

Carrera, Sergio (2007) 'The EU border management strategy: FRONTEX and the challenges of irregular immigration in the Canary Islands', CEPS Working Document no 261, Centre for European Policy Studies, Brussels

Carrera, Sergio (2010) 'Towards a common European border service?', CEPS Working Document no 331, Centre for European Policy Studies, Brussels

Carrera, Sergio, Elspeth Guild, Leonhard den Hertog and Joanna Parkin (2011) 'Implementation of the EU Charter of Fundamental Rights and its impact on EU home affairs agencies. Frontex, Europol and the European Asylum Support Office', Study of the Directorate General for Internal Policies, European Parliament, Brussels

Coleman, Nicole (2009) *European readmission policy: third country interests and refugee rights* (Leiden: Martinus Nijhoff)

Council of the EU (2003) *A secure Europe in a better world: European security strategy*, 10881/03

Council of the EU (2004) *Regulation 2007/2004 of 26 October 2004 establishing a European Agency for the Management of Operational Cooperation at the External Borders of the Member States of the European Union*, OJ L 349/1

Council of the EU (2005) *Decision 2005/358 of 26 April 2005, designating a seat of the European Agency for the Management of Operational Cooperation at the External Borders of the Member States of the European Union*, OJ L 114

Council of the EU (2006) *Council Conclusions on integrated border management*, 2768th Justice and Home Affairs Council meeting, 4–5 December

Council of the EU (2008) *Joint Declaration on a Mobility Partnership between the European Union and Moldova*, 9460/08 Add1, 21

Council of the EU (2009a) *Joint Declaration on a Mobility Partnership between the European Union and Georgia*, 16396/09

Council of the EU (2009b) *The Stockholm Programme: an open and secure Europe serving the citizen*, 17024/09

Council of the EU (2010a) *Council Decision 2010/109/CFSP of 22 February 2010 extending the mandate of the European Union Special Representative for the South Caucasus*, OJ L 46/16

Council of the EU (2010b) *Council Conclusions on 29 measures for reinforcing the protection of the external borders and combating illegal immigration*, 6435/3/10

Council of the EU (2011a) *Joint Declaration of the Eastern Partnership Summit* (Warsaw, 29–30 September), 14983/11, Presse 341

Council of the EU (2011b) *Joint Declaration on a declaration between the European Union and Armenia*, 14963/11 Add1

Cremona, M (2008) 'EU external action in the JHA domain: a legal perspective', EUI Working Paper LAW no 2008/24, European University Institute, San Domenico di Fiesole, Florence

EDPS (2010) 'Opinion on the proposal for a regulation of the European Parliament and of the Council amending Council Regulation (EC) No 2007/2004 establishing a European Agency for the Management of Operational Cooperation at the External Borders of the Member States of the European Union (FRONTEX)', <http://www.edps.europa.eu/EDPSWEB/webdav/site/mySite/shared/Documents/Consultation/Opinions/2010/10-05-17_FRONTEX_EN.pdf>, accessed 20 October 2011

EUBAM (2011a) *Annual Report 1 December 2009—30 November 2010* (Odessa: EUBAM)

EUBAM (2011b) 'Phase 8 Action Plan—detailed description of activities', <http://www.eubam.org/files/P8AP_ENG.pdf>, accessed 25 October 2011

EU–Republic of Moldova Visa Dialogue (2010) 'Action Plan on visa liberalisation', Mission of the Republic of Moldova to the EU, <http://www.eumission.mfa.md/img/docs/action-plan-visa-liberalisation.pdf>, accessed 3 February 2011

European Commission (2002) 'Communication: towards integrated management of the external borders of the member states of the European Union', 233 final

European Commission (2011a) 'Joint Staff Working Paper—implementation of the European Neighbourhood Policy in 2010—Country Report Eastern Partnership', SEC 641 final

European Commission (2011b) 'Communication on cooperation in the area of justice and home affairs in the Eastern Partnership', COM 564 final

European Commission, Government of the Republic of Moldova and Government of Ukraine (2005) 'Memorandum of Understanding between the European Commission, the government of the Republic of Moldova and the government of Ukraine on the European Commission Border Assistance Mission to the Republic of Moldova and to Ukraine', <http://www.eubam.org/files/memorandum_of_understanding_en.pdf>, accessed 26 October 2011

European Parliament and Council of the EU (2006) *Regulation 562/2006 of 15 March 2006 establishing a Community Code on the rules governing the movement of persons across borders (Schengen Borders Code)*, OJ L 105

European Parliament and Council of the EU (2007) *Regulation 863/2007 of 11 July 2007 establishing a mechanism for the creation of Rapid Border Intervention Teams*, OJ L 199

European Parliament and Council of the EU (2011) *Regulation (EU) no 1168/2011 of 26 October 2011 amending Council Regulation (EC) 2007/2004 establishing a European Agency for the Management of Operation Cooperation at the External Borders of the Member States of the European Union*, OJ L204/1

EU–Ukraine Visa Dialogue (2010) *Action Plan on visa liberalisation*, 17883/10

FRONTEX (2011) 'Programme of work 2011', <http://www.frontex.europa.eu/gfx/frontex/files/programme_of_work/2011/fx_pow_2011.pdf>, accessed 27 October 2011

FRONTEX) and Border Guard Service of the Federal Security Service of the Russian Federation (2006) *Terms of Reference on the establishment of operational co-operation between the European Agency for the Management of Operational Co-operation at the External Borders of the European Union (FRONTEX) and the Border Guard Service of the Federal Security Service of the Russian Federation*

FRONTEX and State Border Guard Service of Ukraine (2007) *Working Arrangement on the establishment of operational cooperation between the European Agency for the Management of*

Operational Co-operation at the External Borders of the European Union and the Administration of the State Border Guard Service of Ukraine

Geyer, Florian (2008) 'Taking stock: databases and systems of information exchange in the area of freedom, security and justice', CHALLENGE Research Papers no 9

Government of the Republic of Moldova (2011) 'Decision on approval of the Action Plan on implementing the National Strategy for Integrated Border Management for the period of years 2011–2013', <http://www.eubam.org/en/knowledge/bmp/ibm_concept>, accessed 25 October 2011

Government of Ukraine (2011) *Action Plan on realization of the Concept of Integrated Border Management, approved by the Resolution of the Cabinet of Ministers of Ukraine of 5th January 2011, no 2-r*

Hernández i Sagrera, Raül (2010) 'The EU–Russia readmission-visa facilitation nexus: an exportable model for Eastern Europe?', *European Security*, 19:4, 569–584

Hobbing, Peter (2006) 'Integrated border management at the EU level' in Sergio Carrera and Thierry Balzacq (eds) *Security versus freedom? A challenge for Europe's future* (Farnham, United Kingdom: Ashgate), 155–182

Jorry, Hélène (2007) 'Construction of a European institutional model for Managing Operational Cooperation at the EU's External Borders: is the FRONTEX Agency a decisive step forward?', CHALLENGE Research Papers no 6

Kunz, Rachel, Sandra Lavenex and Marion Lavenex (eds) (2011) *Multilayered migration governance: unveiling the promise* (London: Routledge)

Kurowska, Xymena and Benjamin Tallis (2009) 'EU Border Assistance Mission: beyond border monitoring?', *European Foreign Affairs Review*, 14, 47–64

Lavenex, S (2006) 'Shifting up and out: the foreign policy of European immigration control', *West European Politics*, 29:2, 329–335

Léonard, Sarah (2009) 'The creation of FRONTEX and the politics of institutionalisation in the European Union External Borders Policy', *Journal of Contemporary European Research*, 5:3, 371–388

Monar, Jörg (2006) 'The external shield of the area of freedom, security and justice: progress and deficits of the integrated border management of external EU borders' in Jaap de Zwaan and Flora Goudappel (eds) *Freedom, security and justice in the European Union: implementation of the Hague Programme* (The Hague: Asser Press), 73–88

Neal, Andreas (2009) 'Securitization and risk at the EU border: the origins of FRONTEX', *Journal of Common Market Studies*, 47:2, 333–356

Sterkx, S (2008) 'The external dimension of EU asylum and migration policy: expanding fortress Europe?' in J Orbie (ed) *Europe's global role: external policies of the European Union* (Aldershot, United Kingdom: Ashgate), 117–138

Trauner, Florian and Imre Kruse (2008) 'EC visa facilitation and readmission agreements: a new standards EU foreign policy tool?', *European Journal of Migration and Law*, 10:4, 411–438

Treaty of Lisbon (2009) 'Consolidated versions of the Treaty on European Union and the Treaty on the Functioning of the European Union', OJ C 115/73

Wolff, Sarah (2010) 'EU integrated border management beyond Lisbon: contrasting policies and practic' in Ricard Zapata-Barrero (ed) *Shaping the normative contours of the European Union: a migration–border framework* (Barcelona: CIDOB), 23–36

Wolff, S, N Wichmann and G Wichmann (eds) (2009) *The external dimension of justice and home affairs: a different security agenda for the European Union?* (London: Routledge)

Index